Sheryl
Lokomowitz

SHERYL

Fri.

88-89

D, E, F   Pages 91-92

A CONVERSATIONAL
SPANISH
REVIEW GRAMMAR

RUDOLPH J. MONDELLI
PROFESSOR AND CHAIRMAN OF THE
DEPARTMENT OF FOREIGN LANGUAGES
PACE COLLEGE

ITALO L. PONTEROTTO
PROFESSOR AND CHAIRMAN OF THE
DEPARTMENT OF MODERN LANGUAGES
IONA COLLEGE

THE RONALD PRESS COMPANY · NEW YORK

Library of Congress Catalog Card Number: 61–7738

PREFACE

This book is designed for students with an elementary knowledge of Spanish who wish to improve their audio-lingual skills and, at the same time, review the fundamentals of grammar. It combines natural dialogues and oral exercises with a thorough and systematic discussion of the structure of the language. It takes the student from the known to the unknown, introducing him to the use of verbal forms, idiomatic expressions, and grammar principles prior to the presentation of the reasons for the grammatical constructions. By memorizing and pronouncing the practical and meaningful sentences and phrases in this book, the student will have sufficient expressions at his disposal for immediate and fluent use.

The text has fifteen lessons, an appendix of verb forms, and Spanish-English, English-Spanish vocabularies. Each lesson is divided into four parts. The first part, *Conversación,* presents natural and idiomatic Spanish dialogues, with expressions and vocabulary of a practical nature and topics of cultural interest. The conversations and their idiomatic English translations have been put on the same page so that the meaning of the Spanish sentences will be immediately clear to the students. The second part, *Frases Importantes,* notes the pertinent expressions in the accompanying conversation and includes in addition phrases related to the situation. Either of these sections can serve as a start for further discussion and reading.

The third part, *Puntos Gramaticales,* gives a concise analysis of the structure of Spanish. The examples that illustrate the rules explained in each lesson come from the dialogue, thus insuring integration of conversation and grammar in the text. The grammar rules, consecutively numbered for easy reference, progress from the simple

iii

to the complex; hence the most elementary structural principles are thoroughly reviewed and merge with the more advanced intermediate principles.

The fourth part, *Ejercicios,* useful for both oral and written drill, affords the student the opportunity to repeat, reword, and expand the particular expressions he has learned from the lesson's dialogue. Through practice on these numerous and varied exercises he can further increase his audio-lingual proficiency.

The appendix of the verb forms, also consecutively numbered, covers regular and irregular verbs, radical-changing and orthographic-changing verbs, and verbs requiring a preposition. The two vocabularies include the meanings of all words and phrases within this text.

In the preparation of this work, the authors are indebted to Dr. María Teresa Babín of New York University, and to Professors Ernest V. Speranza and Rito M. Maldonado of Manhattan College for reading the manuscript and offering valuable suggestions for the contents of the lessons.

RUDOLPH J. MONDELLI
ITALO L. PONTEROTTO

February, 1961

CONTENTS

v

Rudolph J. Mondelli, Ph.D. Fordham University, is Professor and Chairman of the Department of Foreign Languages at Pace College. Dr. Mondelli previously taught at Fordham University, St. John's University, Iona College, and St. Peter's College.

Italo L. Ponterotto, Ph.D. New York University, is Professor of Modern Languages and Chairman of the Department of Modern Languages at Iona College. Dr. Ponterotto has been a high school teacher and has taught conversational Spanish at New York University's School of Education.

A CONVERSATIONAL
SPANISH
REVIEW GRAMMAR

Lección Primera

EN EL HOTEL

I. Conversación

[*Léase en voz alta varias veces y apréndase de memoria.*]

—Buenos días, Pedro.

Good morning, Peter.

—Muy buenos, señor García. ¿Cómo está Ud.?

Good morning, Mr. García. How are you?

—Bastante bien, gracias. Busco al señor Smith.

All right, thank you. I'm looking for Mr. Smith.

—El cuarto del señor Smith está en el segundo piso, la última puerta a la derecha.

Mr. Smith's room is on the second floor, the last door on the right.

—Muchas gracias. ¿Está en su cuarto ahora?

Thank you very much. Is he in his room now?

—Creo que sí. ¿Desea Ud. llamarle por teléfono?

I think so. Do you wish to call him on the phone?

—Sí, lo llamo ahora mismo. Hola, Juan, ¿qué tal?

Yes, I'll call him right now. Hello, John, how are you?

—José, ¡qué sorpresa! ¿Dónde estás?

Joseph, what a surprise! Where are you?

—Aquí, abajo, en el salón de entrada del hotel.

Here, downstairs, in the lobby of the hotel.

—¿Por qué no subes arriba? Estoy en el cuarto número veinte y nueve.

Why don't you come upstairs? I'm in room twenty-nine.

—Sí, por supuesto. Pero primero quiero comprar un paquete de cigarrillos y unas revistas.

Yes, of course. But first I want to buy a pack of cigarettes and some magazines.

3

—Muy bien, pero no te tardes.   Very well, but don't delay.
—No, subo en seguida.   No, I'll come right up.

II. Frases Importantes

[*Apréndanse de memoria.*]

a la derecha; a la izquierda	to the right; to the left
ahora mismo	right now, this very minute
arriba; abajo	up, upstairs; downstairs
bastante bien	all right, pretty well
buenos días	good morning
¿cómo está Ud.?	how are you?
creo que sí	I think so
en seguida	right away, immediately
llamar por teléfono (**telefonear**)	to telephone
muchas gracias	many thanks, thank you very much
muy buenos	good morning (*used only as an answer*)
no te tardes	don't be late, don't delay
¿qué tal?	how are you? how are things?
subir	to go up, to climb
tardarse	to be late, to delay

III. Puntos Gramaticales

1. **El género de los nombres y artículos definidos** (Gender of nouns and definite articles)

el profesor	*the professor*	**la revista**	*the magazine*
el libro	*the book*	**la cosa**	*the thing*

All Spanish nouns are either masculine or feminine. The definite article (**el, la**) indicates the gender of the noun. **El** is used with masculine nouns and **la** with feminine nouns.

BUT:

When a feminine noun begins with accented **a** or **ha** the article used is **el**, not **la**: **el agua**, *the water;* **el hacha**, *the axe;* **el hambre**, *the hunger;* **el alma**, *the soul.* The plural is regular: **las aguas, las almas, las hachas.**

2. **El plural de los nombres y de los artículos definidos** (Plural of nouns and definite articles)

el cuarto	the room	los cuartos	the rooms
el profesor	the professor	los profesores	the professors
la puerta	the door	las puertas	the doors
la flor	the flower	las flores	the flowers

The plural of most nouns is formed by adding –s to those that end in a vowel and –es to those that end in a consonant. The plural of **el** is **los** and of **la** is **las**.

3. **El artículo indefinido** (Indefinite article)

(a)

un hombre	a man	una mujer	a woman
un pasillo	a corridor	una ventana	a window

The indefinite article **un** is used with masculine nouns and **una** with feminine nouns.

un cigarrillo	a cigarette	unos cigarrillos	some cigarettes
una pared	a wall	unas paredes	some walls

The plural of **un** is **unos** and of **una**, **unas**.

(b)

el hermano y la hermana	the brother and sister
un padre y una hija	a father and daughter

The definite and indefinite articles are repeated, in Spanish, before each noun in a series.

4. **Posesión** (Possession)

el libro de la muchacha	the girl's book
la revista de José	Joseph's magazine

In Spanish, possession is expressed by **de** + the noun or possessor.

5. **Contracciones** (Contractions)

El hombre va al cuarto.	The man goes to the room.
las páginas del libro	the pages of the book

The prepositions **a** (*at, to*) and **de** (*from, of*) combine with the definite article **el** to become **al** and **del** respectively.

6. Los usos del artículo definido (Uses of the definite article)

La justicia y la fortaleza son virtudes cardinales.	*Justice and fortitude are cardinal virtues.*
Las máquinas son útiles.	*Machines are useful.*
El señor Rojas vive en Madrid.	*Mr. Rojas lives in Madrid.*
La señora Jones no habla español.	*Mrs. Jones doesn't speak Spanish.*
El general Rivera comprende los problemas militares.	*General Rivera understands military problems.*

BUT:

Buenas noches, señor Rojas, ¿cómo está Ud.?	*Good evening, Mr. Rojas, how are you?*

In Spanish, unlike English, the definite article is used before abstract nouns, before nouns used in a generic sense, and before nouns indicating titles, except **don** and **doña**. When titles are used in direct address the article is not used.

7. Las conjugaciones regulares (Regular conjugations)

Regular verbs in Spanish are divided into three conjugations according to the ending of the infinitive. Verbs ending in –ar belong to the first conjugation; verbs ending in –er, to the second; and verbs ending in –ir, to the third.

8. El presente de indicativo (Present indicative)

(a)

	hablar	*to speak*
yo	hablo	*I speak*
tú	hablas	*you speak*
él, ella, Ud.	habla	*he, she speaks, you speak*
nosotros	hablamos	*we speak*
vosotros	habláis	*you speak*
ellos, ellas, Uds.	hablan	*they, you speak*

	comprender	*to understand*
yo	comprendo	*I understand*
tú	comprendes	*you understand*
él, ella, Ud.	comprende	*he, she understands, you understand*
nosotros	comprendemos	*we understand*
vosotros	comprendéis	*you understand*
ellos, ellas, Uds.	comprenden	*they, you understand*

	vivir	*to live*
yo	vivo	*I live*
tú	vives	*you live*
él, ella, Ud.	vive	*he, she lives, you live*
nosotros	vivimos	*we live*
vosotros	vivís	*you live*
ellos, ellas, Uds.	viven	*they, you live*

The present indicative of regular verbs is formed by dropping the ending (–ar, –er, –ir) of the infinitive and adding –o, –as, –a, –amos, –áis, –an, for –ar verbs; –o, –es, –e, –emos, –éis, –en, for –er verbs; –o, –es, –e, –imos, –ís, –en, for –ir verbs.

(b) **Juan habla con María.**   *John speaks to Mary.*
Ellos comprenden la lección.   *They understand the lesson.*
Nosotros vivimos en Nueva *We live in New York.*
York.

The present indicative is used to indicate present time. Remember that in English present time may be expressed in three ways. **Juan habla,** for example, can be translated by *John speaks, John is speaking, John does speak.*

NOTE: In Spanish there are two forms for expressing you: **tú,** and its plural, **vosotros,** are the familiar forms used in speaking to members of one's family, close friends, children, and animals. **Usted,** and its plural, **Ustedes,** are the polite forms of address used when speaking to strangers, older people, and superiors. In Hispanic America the **vosotros** and its corresponding verb form are not used. **Ustedes** and the third person plural of the verb are used instead.

9. Negación e interrogación (Negation and interrogation)

Ellos no comprenden la pregunta. *They do not understand the question.*

¿No vive Ud. arriba?   *Don't you live upstairs?*
¿Hablas tú español?   *Do you speak Spanish?*

A sentence is made negative in Spanish by placing no (*not*) before the verb and interrogative by inverting the subject and the verb.

10. *Estúdiese, en el apéndice, el presente de indicativo de los verbos irregulares* **estar** *e* **ir.**

IV. Ejercicios

A. *Contéstense las preguntas siguientes usando oraciones completas en español:*

1. ¿Con quién habla Pedro?
2. ¿Cómo está el señor García?
3. ¿Cómo está Ud.?
4. ¿A quién busca el señor García?
5. ¿Dónde está el señor Smith?
6. ¿Dónde está el señor García?
7. ¿A quién llama el señor García por teléfono?
8. ¿Cuál es el número del cuarto del señor Smith?
9. ¿Qué desea comprar el señor García?
10. ¿En qué piso está su cuarto?

B. *Escríbase una pregunta en español con cada una de las «frases importantes» que siguen:*

1. en seguida
2. abajo
3. a la izquierda
4. subir
5. llamar por teléfono

C. *Escríbase una oración completa en español con cada una de las «frases importantes» que siguen:*

1. arriba
2. a la derecha
3. ahora mismo
4. muchas gracias
5. bastante bien

D. *Complétense las oraciones siguientes con la forma correspondiente del presente de los verbos entre paréntesis:*

1. (hablar)   El muchacho _____ mucho.
2. (comprender) Yo no _____ la lección.
3. (creer)   Juan y María _____ que Antonio está aquí.
4. (subir)   ¿Por qué no _____ tú arriba?
5. (buscar)   Nosotros _____ un buen hotel.
6. (comprar)   ¿_____ Uds. muchas revistas?
7. (ir)   Yo _____ a casa y él _____ al hotel.
8. (estar)   Ellos no _____ en el centro.

9. (vivir)   ¿Dónde _____ Ud. ahora?
10. (desear)   ¿Qué _____ los señores?

E. *Complétense las oraciones siguientes:*

1. (to the)   El señor García habla _____ muchacho.
2. (of the)   Ve las páginas _____ libro.
3. (Mr. Smith)   _____ está en su cuarto.
4. (justice)   Los hombres desean _____.
5. (to the)   Ellos van _____ escuela.
6. (to Mrs. García) Él habla _____.
7. (Professor Torres) _____ no está en la clase.
8. (the)   _____ flores son hermosas.
9. (a)   El muchacho compra _____ revista.
10. (a)   Ellos desean _____ paquete de cigarrillos.

F. *Cámbiense las oraciones siguientes al plural:*

1. El profesor busca un periódico.
2. La casa queda cerca de la tienda.
3. ¿Compras tú un paquete de cigarrillos?
4. No escribe a la mujer.
5. ¿Responde el muchacho a la pregunta?
6. Yo estudio la lección de español.
7. ¿Adónde va el hombre?
8. ¿Comprende Ud. el ejercicio?
9. ¿Dónde vive el amigo de Carlos?
10. La niña canta una canción popular.

G. *Tradúzcase al español:*

1. The boy goes up to the second floor.
2. Mr. Rojas lives in Madrid.
3. The girls are in the room.
4. They understand the lesson.
5. The professor's book is not here.
6. Good morning, Mr. Rivera, how are you?
7. All right, thank you.
8. Is General Blanco in the hotel?
9. I think so. Do you wish to phone him?
10. No, I'm going home right away.

H. *Dictado tomado de la conversación* «**En el hotel**», pp. 3–4.

Lección Segunda

UNA VISITA

I. Conversación

[Léase en voz alta varias veces y apréndase de memoria.]

(Entrando en el ascensor)

(Entering the elevator)

—El cuarto del señor Smith está en el segundo piso, ¿verdad?

Mr. Smith's room is on the second floor, isn't it?

—Sí señor, es el número veintinueve.

Yes sir, it's number twenty-nine.

—Muchas gracias.

Thank you very much.

—A sus órdenes, señor.

At your service, sir.

(El señor García llama a la puerta)

(Mr. García knocks on the door)

—Entra, hombre, entra.

Come in, come in.

—¡Juan, qué gusto verte otra vez después de tantos años!

What a pleasure to see you again, John, after so many years!

—Hace más de tres años que no nos vemos.

We haven't seen each other for more than three years.

—Sí, «cómo pasa la vida tan callando», dice el poeta.

Yes, "how life passes so silently," says the poet.

—Ah, eres el filósofo de siempre. Pero tienes razón. Nunca hay tiempo para ver a los amigos.

Ha, you're still the same old philosopher. But you're right. There is never any time to see one's friends.

—¡Qué barbaridad es esta vida moderna!

How foolish this modern life is!

—Pues, ¿qué haces aquí en Madrid?

Well, what are you doing here in Madrid?

—Estoy visitando la sucursal que mi casa tiene aquí. Tengo que permanecer un par de semanas y después salgo para Barcelona.

I'm visiting the branch that my firm has here. I have to stay a couple of weeks and then I leave for Barcelona.

—Tu casa debe de ser muy grande.

Your company must be very large.

—Sí, tenemos diez y seis sucursales y más de quince mil empleados.

Yes, we have sixteen branches and more than fifteen thousand employees.

—¡ No me digas! ¿Qué produce tu firma?

You don't say! What type of business is your firm in?

—Productos medicinales: píldoras de vitaminas, pasta dentífrica, penicilina y muchos más.

Medicinal products: vitamin pills, tooth paste, penicillin, and many more.

—Bueno, bueno, y ¿qué es de tu familia? ¿Cómo están los niños y la señora? ¿Cuántos hijos tienes ya?

Fine, fine. And what about your family? How are the children and your wife? How many children do you have now?

—¡Hombre! ¡Cuántas preguntas! ¿Por qué no vamos abajo a tomar un café? ¿Quieres? Allí podemos charlar mejor.

Boy! All the questions! Why don't we go downstairs to have a cup of coffee? Do you want to? It is better to chat there.

—Con mucho gusto.

With pleasure.

II. Frases Importantes

[*Apréndanse de memoria.*]

«cómo pasa la vida, cómo viene la muerte tan callando»

"how life passes by, how death comes so silently"

(*from a poem by Jorge Manrique*)

deber (de) + *inf*.
dos veces

ought, must, probably
twice, two times

hay   there is, there are
la última vez   the last time
llamar a la puerta   to knock on the door
muchas veces   many times
¡no me digas!   you don't say!
otra vez   again
¿qué es de tu familia?   what about your family?
¡qué placer! ¡qué gusto!   what a pleasure!
tener que + *inf*.   to have to, must
tengo que permanecer   I have to remain
tener razón; no tener razón   to be right; to be wrong
un par de semanas   a couple of weeks
¿verdad?   isn't it? right?

III. Puntos Gramaticales

11. Los números cardinales (Cardinal numbers)

0	cero	31	treinta y uno, etc.
1	uno, un, una	40	cuarenta
2	dos	50	cincuenta
3	tres	60	sesenta
4	cuatro	70	setenta
5	cinco	80	ochenta
6	seis	90	noventa
7	siete	100	ciento, cien
8	ocho	101	ciento uno
9	nueve	110	ciento diez
10	diez	115	ciento quince
11	once	200	doscientos(as)
12	doce	300	trescientos(as)
13	trece	400	cuatrocientos(as)
14	catorce	500	quinientos(as)
15	quince	600	seiscientos(as)
16	diez y seis (dieciséis)	700	setecientos(as)
17	diez y siete (diecisiete)	800	ochocientos(as)
18	diez y ocho (dieciocho)	900	novecientos(as)
19	diez y nueve (diecinueve)	1,000	mil
20	veinte	2,000	dos mil
21	veinte y uno (veintiuno), etc.	1,000,000	un millón
30	treinta	2,000,000	dos millones

(a)   cien años   *a hundred years*
         cien lecciones   *a hundred lessons*
         cien mil píldoras   *a hundred thousand pills*
         mil libros   *a thousand books*
         un millón de libros   *a million books*

Ciento is shortened to **cien** when used immediately before a noun or a larger number. **Un** is not used with **ciento** (**cien**) or **mil**; it is used with **millón**.

(b)   un empleado   *one employee*
         una página   *one page*
         veintiún libros   *twenty-one books*
         veintiuna lecciones   *twenty-one lessons*
         trescientas muchachas   *three hundred girls*
         dos millones de habitantes   *two million inhabitants*

Cardinal numbers are invariable except for **uno**, multiples of a hundred, and **millón**.

(c)   quinientos setenta y cuatro   *five hundred seventy-four*
         setecientos ochenta y nueve   *seven hundred eighty-nine*
         novecientos treinta y siete   *nine hundred thirty-seven*

         BUT:

         en el año mil cuatrocientos   *in the year fourteen hun-*
            noventa y dos   *dred ninety-two (1492)*
         mil novecientos empleados   *nineteen hundred em-*
                                       ployees

In Spanish one counts in hundreds only up to nine hundred. For higher numbers the word **mil** (*one thousand*) is used. **Y** is used to connect multiples of ten, up to ninety, with numbers less than ten.

12. Los usos de ser y estar (Uses of **ser** and **estar**)

(a)   **Estar**

     1.   El señor García **está** en su   *Mr. García is in his room.*
        cuarto.
        El museo del **Prado** está en   *The Prado museum is in*
        Madrid.   *Madrid.*

      Estar is used to express location.

2. El vaso está sucio.   *The glass is dirty.*
La casa está llena de gente.   *The house is full of people.*
El café está frío.   *The coffee is cold.*
La mujer está muerta.   *The woman is dead.*

Estar is used to express an accidental condition (a condition that is not an inherent or characteristic quality) of a person or thing.

3. ¿Qué estás haciendo?   *What are you doing?*
Estoy abriendo este paquete.   *I'm opening this package.*

Estar is used to express the progressive form of the present.

4. Está viejo.   *He has aged* (meaning that he appears older than expected).

María está muy hermosa   *Mary looks* (is unusually)
con ese sombrerito.   *pretty with that hat.*

Estar is sometimes used with adjectives to indicate something unusual or not expected.

NOTE: **Estar** is also used with a past participle to express the passive voice. See p. 120, section 64 (c).

(b) Ser

1. La casa es pequeña.   *The house is small.*
El señor Moreno es joven.   *Mr. Moreno is young.*
El niño es bueno.   *The child is good.*
El perro es leal.   *The dog is loyal.*
El Aconcagua es la montaña   *Aconcagua is the highest*
más alta de América.   *mountain in America.*

Ser is used to express a characteristic or inherent condition of a person, place, or thing.

2. Juan es de Venezuela.   *John is from Venezuela.*
La mesa es de madera.   *The table is made of wood.*
Este sombrero es mío.   *This hat is mine.*

Ser is used to express origin, material, or ownership.

3. Él es professor.   *He is a professor.*
Madrid es la capital de   *Madrid is the capital of*
España.   *Spain.*
Soy yo.   *It is I.*

Ser is used to introduce a predicate noun or pronoun.

4. Es la una.   *It is one o'clock.*
    Son las dos.   *It is two o'clock.*

Ser is used to express time.

NOTE: **Ser** is also used with the past participle to express the passive voice. See p. 120, section 64(a).

13. Los adjetivos (Adjectives)

(a)
el libro viejo	*the old book*
la casa vieja	*the old house*
el auto verde	*the green car*
la corbata verde	*the green tie*
el libro fácil	*the easy book*
la lección fácil	*the easy lesson*

In Spanish, adjectives agree in gender and number with the noun they modify. Adjectives ending in –o in the masculine singular change –o to –a for the feminine. Adjectives ending in –e or in a consonant usually remain unchanged in the feminine.

(b)
el traje inglés	*the English suit*
la moda inglesa	*the English fashion*
el niño holgazán	*the lazy child*
la muchacha holgazana	*the lazy girl*
el muchacho preguntón	*the inquisitive boy*
la niña preguntona	*the inquisitive child*
el hombre hablador	*the talkative man*
la mujer habladora	*the talkative woman*

However, all adjectives of nationality, even those ending in a consonant, and adjectives ending in –án, –ón (and some in –or), form their feminine singular by adding –a.

(c)
el autor rico	*the rich author*
los autores ricos	*the rich authors*
la falta grave	*the grave fault*
las faltas graves	*the grave faults*
el encargo difícil	*the difficult errand*
los encargos difíciles	*the difficult errands*
la obra útil	*the useful work*
las obras útiles	*the useful works*

The plural of an adjective, like that of a noun, is formed by adding –s to those ending in a vowel and –es to those ending in a consonant.

14. **Hacer con expresiones temporales** (**Hacer** with time expressions)

¿Cuánto tiempo hace que estudia Ud.?	*How long have you been studying?*
Hace dos horas que estudio.	*I have been studying for two hours.*
Hace siete años que vive en Madrid.	*He has been living in Madrid for seven years.*

To express an action which has begun in the past and which is still going on in the present, the present tense of **hacer** and of another verb is used usually in this order: **hace** + expression of time + **que** + present tense of the verb.

The same thought can also be expressed as follows:

¿Desde cuándo estudia Ud.?	*How long have you been studying?*
Estudio desde hace dos horas.	*I have been study for two hours.*
Vive en Madrid desde hace siete años.	*He has been living in Madrid for seven years.*

15. *Estúdiese, en el apéndice, el presente de indicativo de los verbos irregulares* **ser, tener, hacer.**

IV. Ejercicios

A. *Contéstense las preguntas siguientes usando oraciones completas en español:*

1. ¿Quién llama a la puerta?
2. ¿Qué responde el señor Smith?
3. ¿Cuánto tiempo hace que no se ven?
4. ¿Dónde se encontraron la última vez?
5. ¿Por qué es la vida moderna una barbaridad?
6. ¿Por qué está en Madrid el señor Smith?
7. ¿Dónde hay sucursales de la casa del señor Smith?
8. ¿Qué produce la casa?
9. ¿Cuántos empleados tiene la casa?
10. ¿Quién toma píldoras de vitaminas?

B. *Escríbase una pregunta en español con cada una des las «frases importantes» que siguen:*

1. llamar a la puerta
2. no tener razón
3. muchas veces
4. ¿verdad?
5. hay

C. *Escríbase una oración completa en español con cada una de las «frases importantes» que siguen:*

1. deber de estudiar
2. ¡qué placer!
3. tener que ir
4. otra vez
5. ¡qué barbaridad!
6. con mucho gusto
7. ¡cuántas preguntas!
8. un par de semanas

D. *Léanse en voz alta:*

1. 9, 14, 15, 33, 60, 84, 70, 59, 98
2. 125, 506, 718, 776, 867, 346, 615
3. 220, 934, 570, 100, 1000, 5000, 500,000, 1,000,000
4. 1440, 1555, 1492, 1040, 1811, 1571, 1962

E. *Complétense las oraciones siguientes con la forma correcta del presente del verbo entre paréntesis:*

1. (estar) El señor García _____ visitando la sucursal.
2. (ir) Los amigos _____ abajo a tomar un café.
3. (ser) Su casa no _____ muy grande.
4. (tener) Yo _____ que permanecer aquí.
5. (hacer) ¿Qué _____ Juan y sus niños?
6. (llamar) Nosotros no _____ a la puerta.
7. (ser) Tú _____ el filósofo de siempre.
8. (tener) Carlos nunca _____ razón.
9. (estar) Hace dos años que ellos _____ en España.
10. (subir) ¿Por qué no _____ tú arriba?

F. *Ecríbase el plural de las oraciones siguientes:*

1. la puerta grande
2. el número cardinal
3. el tiempo pasado
4. la sucursal extranjera
5. el producto medicinal
6. la pasta dentífrica
7. la familia numerosa
8. otra vez
9. una lección fácil
10. la charla divertida

11. la penicilina milagrosa
12. una nación poderosa
13. una pregunta difícil
14. el vestido verde
15. el muchacho holgazán
16. la mujer habladora

G. *Complétense las oraciones siguientes con el presente de* **ser** *o* **estar:**

1. España _____ en Europa.
2. El muchacho _____ bueno.
3. La casa _____ llena de gente.
4. La corbata _____ de lana.
5. El señor Gómez _____ profesor de lenguas.
6. Los libros _____ del profesor.
7. Buenos Aires _____ la capital de la Argentina.
8. Buenos días, ¿cómo _____ Ud.?
9. El cuarto _____ limpio.
10. María _____ muy guapa hoy.

H. *Tradúzcase al español:*

1. You are wrong. There are only two books here.
2. How long have you been in Madrid?
3. I have been living here for three years.
4. John is a philosopher, isn't he?
5. What time is it? It is one o'clock.
6. Why don't you knock on the door?
7. There are four million inhabitants in the city of Buenos Aires.
8. The company has one hundred employees in the Madrid branch.
9. You don't say! Your firm must be big.
10. I have to visit the city many times.

I. *Dictado tomado de la conversación* «**Una visita**», pp. 10–11.

Lección Tercera

EN EL CAFÉ

I. Conversación

[Léase en voz alta varias veces y apréndase de memoria.]

—Aquí hay una mesa desocupada. Sentémonos.

Here is an empty table. Let's sit down.

—¡Cuántas mesas! Y casi todas están ocupadas.

Look at all the tables! And they are almost all occupied.

—Y es lo mismo todos los días.

And it's the same every day.

—Al parecer las discusiones son acaloradas. ¿De qué hablan?

Apparently the discussions are quite heated. What do they talk about?

—De todo, de las últimas noticias del día, de los acontecimientos políticos, de la próxima corrida, de filosofía, de mujeres . . . pero por la mayor parte critican el gobierno, el entretenimiento favorito de los españoles.

Everything: the latest news, political events, the next bull-fight, philosophy, women . . . but in the main they criticize the government, the favorite pastime of the Spaniards.

—¡De veras! ¿Y duran mucho estas conversaciones?

You don't say! Do these conversations last long?

—Horas y horas. La tertulia en el café es una institución nacional.

Hours on end. The gathering in the café is a national institution.

—Es lástima que esta costumbre no exista en mi país.

It's a pity that this custom doesn't exist in my country.

—Pues, bien, dime algo de tu viaje. ¿Cuándo llegaste?

Well, then, tell me something about your trip. When did you arrive?

—Ayer, a eso de las diez. Apenas aterrizó el avión, corrí a la oficina de telégrafos y envié un radiograma a mi señora para asegurarle que todo estaba en regla.

Yesterday, around ten o'clock. As soon as the plane landed, I ran to the telegraph office and sent a radiogram to my wife to reassure her that everything was all right.

—Claro, las mujeres se preocupan mucho de los peligros de un viaje.

Naturally, women worry a great deal about the dangers of a trip.

—Después de esperar un siglo en la oficina de la aduana tomé un taxi que me llevó al hotel.

After waiting a very long time in the customs office I took a taxi which brought me to the hotel.

—Y me llamaste por teléfono.

And then you called me on the phone.

—No, primero descansé un poquito.

No, first I rested a bit.

—¡Ah, echaste una siesta, eh! Me da gusto saber que ya aprendes nuestro modo de vivir.

Ha, you took a nap, eh! I'm pleased to know that you are already learning our way of life.

—Pues, es fácil aprender las cosas agradables.

Well, it's easy to learn pleasant things.

II. Frases Importantes

[*Apréndanse de memoria.*]

a eso de	at about
al parecer	apparently
apenas	as soon as
dar gusto	to please (*lit.*, to give pleasure)
¡de veras!	really! you don't say!
echar una siesta	to take a nap
en regla	in order, all right
es lástima	it's a pity

esperar un siglo	to wait a long, long time (*lit.,* a century)
horas y horas	hours on end
la corrida de toros (la corrida, los toros)	the bullfight
lo mismo	the same thing, the same
me da gusto	I'm glad, it pleases me
modo de vivir	way of life, manner of living
por la mayor parte	in the main, for the most part
sentémonos	let's sit down
sentarse	to sit down
todos los días	every day

III. Puntos Gramaticales

16. **El pretérito indefinido de verbos regulares** (Preterite of regular verbs)

(a)

−ar

hablé	*I spoke, did speak*
hablaste	*you spoke, did speak*
habló	*he, she, you spoke, did speak*
hablamos	*we spoke, did speak*
hablasteis	*you spoke, did speak*
hablaron	*they, you spoke, did speak*

−er	**−ir**
comprendí	viví
comprendiste	viviste
comprendió	vivió
comprendimos	vivimos
comprendisteis	vivisteis
comprendieron	vivieron

The preterite of regular verbs is formed by adding −é, −aste, −ó, −amos, −asteis, −aron to the stem of −ar verbs and −í, −iste, −ió, −imos, −isteis, −ieron to the stem of −er and −ir verbs.

(b) The preterite of irregular verbs studied thus far:

estar: estuve, estuviste, estuvo, estuvimos, estuvisteis, estuvieron

hacer: hice, hiciste, hizo, hicimos, hicisteis, hicieron

ir and ser: **fuí, fuiste, fué, fuimos, fuisteis, fueron**
tener: **tuve, tuviste, tuvo, tuvimos, tuvisteis, tuvieron**

(c) | | |
|---|---|
| **Abrió la puerta.** | *He opened the door.* |
| **Compramos un coche nuevo.** | *We bought a new automobile.* |
| **Tomaron café.** | *They had coffee.* |
| **¿Vino el profesor ayer?** | *Did the professor come yesterday?* |
| **No, no tuvo tiempo.** | *No, he didn't have time.* |

The preterite tense is used to express a definite action completed in the past, an action with a beginning and an end expressed or implied.

17. Los pronombres personales; objeto directo y objeto indirecto (Personal pronouns; direct and indirect object)

(a)

DIRECT OBJECT

SINGULAR	PLURAL
me *me*	**nos** *us*
te *you* (fam.)	**os** *you* (fam.)
le *you* (m.), *him*	**les** *you, them*
lo *him, it* (m.)	**los** *you* (m.), *them* (m.)
la *her, you* (f.), *it* (f.)	**las** *you* (f.), *them* (f.)

INDIRECT OBJECT

SINGULAR	PLURAL
me *to me*	**nos** *to us*
te *to you* (fam.)	**os** *to you* (fam.)
le *to him, to her, to you, to it*	**les** *to you, to them*

(b) | | |
|---|---|
| **Me envió una tarjeta postal.** | *He sent me a postal card.* |
| **Lo dejé en casa.** | *I left it at home.* |
| **Juan quiere verte inmediatamente.** | *John wants to see you immediately.* |
| **Estoy aprendiéndola.** | *I am learning it* (f.). |
| **Escríbales hoy.** | *Write to them today.* |

Both the direct and indirect object pronouns are usually placed immediately before a conjugated verb. However, with infinitives, present participles, and affirmative commands they are placed after the verb and are attached to it.

(c) Me la explican. — *They explain it* (f.) *to me.*
Nos las envió. — *He sent them* (f.) *to us.*
Quiere mostrártelo. — *He wants to show it* (m.) *to you.*
¿Quiere Ud dárselo? — *Do you want to give it* (m.) *to him?*
Está escribiéndosela. — *He is writing it* (f.) *to them.*
Dámelas. — *Give them* (f.) *to me.*

When both direct and indirect objects are used in the same sentence, the indirect precedes the direct. When both begin with the letter **l**, the indirect **le** or **les** is changed to **se**.

(d) Quiere mostrárselo a él. — *He wants to show it to him.*
Está escribiéndosela a ellos. — *She is writing it to them.*
Me conoce a mí y (te conoce) a ti. — *He knows me and you.*

To avoid ambiguity or for emphasis, **a él, a Ud.,** etc., is added to the sentence.

18. **El género de los nombres, continuado** (Gender of nouns, continued)

(a) la bondad — *the kindness*
la ciudad — *the city*
la costumbre — *the custom*
la serie — *the series*
la actitud — *the attitude*
la virtud — *the virtue*
la revolución — *the revolution*

Nouns ending in **–dad, –umbre,** unaccented **–ie, –tud,** and **–ción** are feminine. **El pie** (*the foot*), **el hincapié** (*the emphasis*), **el balompié** (*soccer*) end in accented **–ie** and are masculine.

(b)
el clima	*the climate*	**el telegrama**	*the telegram*
el dogma	*the dogma*	**el drama**	*the drama*
el idioma	*the language*	**el síntoma**	*the symptom*
el sistema	*the system*	**el mapa**	*the map*
el problema	*the problem*	**el poeta**	*the poet*
el poema	*the poem*	**el planeta**	*the planet*

Some nouns, usually of Greek origin, ending in **–a** are masculine.

(c)

el actor	*the actor*	el monarca	*the monarch*
el padre	*the father*	el joven	*the young man*
el cura	*the priest*	el príncipe	*the prince*
el cardenal	*the cardinal*	el rey	*the king*
el policía	*the policeman*	el conde	*the count*
el autor	*the author*	el monje	*the monk*
el compatriota	*the compatriot*	el farsante	*the fraud, the*
el huésped	*the guest, host*		*pretender*

Nouns denoting male beings or occupations are masculine, regardless of ending.

(d)

el arte	la arte *	*the art*
el mar	la mar	*the sea*
el sartén	la sartén	*the frying pan*

Some nouns are occasionally used in either gender.

(e)

el orden dórico	*the Doric order*
la orden religiosa	*the religious order*
el corte	*the cut*
la corte	*the court*
el pez	*the fish*
la pez	*the tar*
el moral	*the mulberry tree*
la moral	*the moral*
el frente	*the front*
la frente	*the forehead*

The meaning of some nouns differs according to the gender.

19. **El adjetivo posesivo** (Possessive adjective)

(a) The possessive adjective has the following forms:

SINGULAR	PLURAL	
mi	mis	*my*
tu	tus	*your* (fam.)
su	sus	*his, her, your, its*
nuestro −a	nuestros −as	*our*
vuestro −a	vuestros −as	*your* (fam.)
su	sus	*their*

* The masculine form is usually used in the singular (**el arte dramático,** *dramatic art*) and the feminine form is usually used in the plural (**las bellas artes,** *the fine arts*).

(b) **Mi libro está allí.** / *My book is there.*

Nuestra ciudad tiene un millón de habitantes. / *Our city has one million inhabitants.*

Estas costumbres no existen en su país. / *These customs do not exist in his country.*

Dime algo de tu viaje. / *Tell me something about your trip.*

Envió un radiograma a sus hijos. / *She sent a radiogram to her children.*

The possessive adjective agrees in gender and number with the noun it modifies (the thing possessed), and not with the possessor.

(c) **su hermano y su hermana** / *his brother and sister*

mi libro y mi cuaderno / *my book and notebook*

The possessive adjective must be repeated before each noun in a series.

(d) **Recibió el telegrama de Ud (Uds., él, ella, ellos –as).** / *He received your (his, her, their) telegram.*

Ví a las amigas de Ud (Uds., él, ella, ellos –as). / *I saw your (his, her, their) friends.*

Since **su** and **sus** have several possible meanings, ambiguity may be avoided by substituting the definite article for **su** (**sus**) before the noun, and the phrase **de Ud., de él, de ella,** etc., after the noun.

(e) **El alumno levanta la mano.** / *The student raises his hand.*

Me pongo el sombrero. / *I put on my hat.*

The definite article is frequently used in place of the possessive adjective before nouns denoting parts of the body or articles of clothing when the possessor is clearly understood.

(f)

mío, –a, **–os, –as**	*my, mine*	**nuestro, –a,** **–os, –as**	*our, ours*
tuyo, –a, **–os, –as**	*your, yours*	**vuestro, –a,** **–os, –as**	*your, yours*
suyo, –a, **–os, –as**	*his, her, hers, its, your, yours*	**suyo, –a,** **–os, –as**	*their, theirs*

Querido amigo mío, ¿como estás?	My dear friend, how are you?
¡Dios mío!	Good Lord!
Fué a visitar a una amiga suya.	She went to visit a friend of hers.

The stressed or long forms of possessive adjectives are used in direct address, in exclamations, and to translate the English phrases of mine, of yours, etc.

20. *Estúdiese en el apéndice el presente de indicativo y el pretérito de los verbos irregulares* venir, querer, dar.

IV. Ejercicios

A. *Contéstense las preguntas siguientes usando oraciones completas en español:*

1. ¿Adónde van los dos amigos?
2. ¿Dónde se sientan?
3. ¿Hay muchas o pocas mesas en el café?
4. ¿Cómo son las discusiones?
5. ¿De qué hablan los hombres en el café?
6. ¿Cuánto duran las conversaciones?
7. ¿Por qué no existe esta costumbre en los Estados Unidos?
8. ¿Qué hizo el señor Smith apenas aterrizó el aeroplano?
9. ¿Cómo llegó al hotel?
10. ¿Cuándo llamó por teléfono a su amigo?

B. *Escríbase una pregunta en español con cada una de las «frases importantes» que siguen:*

1. en regla
2. echar una siesta
3. todos los días
4. ¡de veras!
5. la corrida de toros

C. *Ecríbase una oración completa en español con cada una de las «frases importantes» que siguen:*

1. horas y horas
2. a eso de
3. esperar un siglo
4. es lástima
5. dar gusto
6. modo de vivir
7. al parecer
8. por la mayor parte

D. *Complétense las oraciones siguientes con la forma exacta del
pretérito de los verbos entre paréntesis:*

1. (comprar)   El señor Rivera _____ muchas revistas.
2. (mirar)   ¿Y vosotros los _____ bien?
3. (aprender) Nosotros los norteamericanos nunca _____ el
               arte de vivir sin ansias.
4. (venir)   Ud. no _____ a la tertulia anoche.
5. (tomar)   Ellos _____ un taxi para ir al hotel.
6. (ir)   Tú _____ a la casa de mi amigo.
7. (vivir)   Mis amigos _____ en este hotel.
8. (aterrizar) El avión _____ a eso de las diez.
9. (tener)   Yo _____ que mandar un telegrama.
10. (hacer)   ¿Qué _____ Uds. ayer?
11. (correr)   Ella _____ a la oficina de telégrafos.
12. (charlar) Los amigos _____ en el café.

E. *Cámbiese cada nombre por el pronombre correspondiente:*

1. Vieron el avión.
2. Compré las revistas.
3. Mandó el telegrama a la señora.
4. Escribió la carta a su padre.
5. No quiere enviarme el libro.
6. Pidieron el café al camarero.
7. Está hablando a su amigo.
8. Me envió una carta ayer.
9. Ella no sabe traducir la carta al español.
10. Dime la dirección.

F. *Tradúzcanse al español las palabras entre paréntesis:*

1. (my)   El tiene _mis_ libros.
2. (his)   _Sus_ padres están en Nueva York.
3. (our)   _Nuestras_ discusiones siempre son interesantes.
4. (their)   _Su_ coche es nuevo y cómodo.
5. (your)   Lo tiene Ud. en _el_ bolsillo.
6. (the poet)   _El poeta_ tiene que ser un hombre de finas
                sensibilidades.
7. (their hands) Los alumnos inteligentes siempre levantan
                las manos

8. (they like)   _Se gustan_ el libro que Ud. les envió.
9. (I didn't like) _No me gusta_ éstas discusiones.
10. (he liked)   _Se gustó_ nuestro modo de vivir.
11. (the custom)   El joven me explicó _la costumbre_
12. (a language)   El español es _lengua_ muy agradable.
13. (fish)   _El pescado_ no pueden vivir sin agua.
14. (order)   _El orden_ en una casa es necesario.
15. (dramatic art) Lope de Vega es uno de los maestros de
                    arte dramático

G. *Tradúzcanse las oraciones siguientes al español:*

1. Apparently all the tables are occupied.
2. The men in the café talk about the latest news.
3. The conversation lasts hours on end.
4. My friends never have time to discuss politics.
5. I wrote the letter but I didn't send it to him.
6. I'm glad that you took a nap.
7. We had to take a taxi to the hotel.
8. Isn't it a pity that that custom doesn't exist in our country?
9. As soon as she arrived, she sent a telegram to her mother to reassure her that everything was all right.
10. Did you have to wait a very long time in the customs office?

H. *Dictado tomado de la conversación:* «**En el café**», pp. 19–20.

Lección Cuarta

CHARLANDO EN EL CAFÉ

I. Conversación

[*Léase en voz alta varias veces y apréndase de memoria.*]

—Ah, al fin llegó el camarero.

—¿Qué desean, señores?

—Un café con leche y un vermut.

—¿Quieren dulces también?

—No, nada más.

—Muy bien. A sus órdenes.

—Pues, estabas para darme noticias de tu familia. ¿Cómo están María y los chicos?

—Muy bien, gracias. Dolores, mi hija mayor, acaba de graduarse y en septiembre va a matricularse en la universidad.

—¿De veras? Parece mentira. No hace mucho que la llevaba de paseo conmigo cuando era una niñita.

—¿Recuerdas cuánto se divertía al dar de comer a las palomas en el parque?

Ha! The waiter finally got here.

What do you wish, gentlemen?

One coffee with milk and a glass of vermouth.

Do you want some pastries too?

No, nothing else.

Very well. At your service.

Well, you were about to give me some news of your family. How are Mary and the children?

Very well, thank you. Dolores, my oldest daughter, has just graduated and in September she is going to enroll in the University.

Really? It doesn't seem possible. Not long ago I used to take her walking with me when she was a little girl.

Do you remember how she used to enjoy feeding the pigeons in the park?

—¡Vaya si me acuerdo! | Of course I remember!

—¡Qué linda era, y qué charladora! | How pretty she was and what a talker!

—Esa es una peculiaridad de todas las mujeres. | That is a characteristic of all women.

—Le gusta mucho el español y me dijo que quiere visitar a España y también estudiar la literatura española aquí. ¿Qué te parece? | She likes Spanish very much and she told me that she wants to visit Spain and also study Spanish literature here. What do you think?

—Feliz idea. Hay cursos de verano para estudiantes extranjeros aquí en la Universidad de Madrid y también en Santander. | A good idea. There are summer courses for foreign students here in the University of Madrid and also in Santander.

—Bueno. Puede venir durante las vacaciones. ¿Dónde puede alojarse? | Good. She can come during her vacation. Where can she live?

—Con nosotros, por supuesto, si quiere estudiar en Madrid, o en una casa de huéspedes en Santander. | With us, of course, if she wishes to study in Madrid, or in a boarding house in Santander.

—¿Me costará mucho? | Will it cost me much?

—Creo que no. Los derechos de matrícula no son muy altos, ni el hospedaje. | I don't think so. The tuition fees are not very high, nor are the room and board.

—No te olvides de la ropa. | Don't forget about the clothes.

—Ah, sí. ¡Eso sí que es costoso cuando se trata de mujeres! | Ah, yes. That surely is expensive when you're dealing with women.

II. Frases Importantes

[Apréndanse de memoria.]

abonar los derechos de matrícula | to pay the tuition fees

acabar de + *inf.* | to have just + *past part.*

acordarse de | to remember

al dar	on giving, upon giving
al fin (finalmente)	finally
alojarse	to live, to lodge, to take up lodgings
alto	high, expensive (*in price*)
caro; costoso	dear, expensive
colegio	college, secondary school *
creo que no	I don't think so, I think not
cursos de verano	summer courses, summer school
charlar	to chat, to discuss (*informally*)
dar de comer	to feed (*lit.*, to give something to eat)
dar noticias	to give news, to inform, to tell about
de paseo	strolling
dulces	pastry, sweets, candy
el hospedaje	the lodging, the board
eso sí que es	that certainly is
estar para	to be about to
hija mayor (menor)	oldest (youngest) daughter
ir de paseo	to go for a walk
las vacaciones (*used in the plural*)	the vacation, vacation time, holidays
los derechos de matrícula	the tuition fees
nada más	nothing else, nothing more, no more
no hace mucho	not long ago
parece mentira	it doesn't seem possible, it can't be true (*lit.*, it seems a lie)
por supuesto	of course, naturally
¿qué desean?	what do you wish? what would you like to order?

* **Colegio** is not the equivalent of the American college. In Spain the system of education is different. There, the student studies 5 years in the **escuela elemental** (elementary school), 3 years in the **escuela media** (secondary school), then 5 years in the **colegio** (which is a private boarding school) or in the **instituto** (which is public) prior to attending the **Universidad** either in the **Facultad** (*School*) **de Medicina, de Leyes** (*Law*), **de Ingeniería** (*Engineering*), **de Economía** (*Economics*), etc.

¿qué te parece?   what do you think? what do you think of the idea? (*lit.*, how does it seem to you?)

recordar   to remember

III. Puntos Gramaticales

21. El pretérito imperfecto (Imperfect)

(a)

–ar	–er	–ir
habl*aba*	comprend*ía*	viv*ía*
habl*abas*	comprend*ías*	viv*ías*
habl*aba*	comprend*ía*	viv*ía*
habl*ábamos*	comprend*íamos*	viv*íamos*
habl*abais*	comprend*íais*	viv*íais*
habl*aban*	comprend*ían*	viv*ían*

To form the imperfect tense *of nearly all verbs,* add the endings –aba, –abas, –aba, –ábamos, –abais, –aban to the stem of –ar verbs and –ía, –ías, –ía, –íamos, –íais, –ían to the stem of –er and –ir verbs.

The imperfect tense may be translated in the following ways:

hablaba *I was speaking, I used to speak, I spoke*
comprendía *I was understanding, I used to understand, I understood*
vivía *I was living, I used to live, I lived*

(b) There are only three irregular verbs in the imperfect tense: ir, ser and ver.

ir: iba, ibas, iba, íbamos, ibais, iban
ser: era, eras, era, éramos, erais, eran
ver: veía, veías, veía, veíamos, veíais, veían

22. Los usos del pretérito imperfecto (Uses of the imperfect)

(a)
María era hermosa.	*Mary was beautiful.*
Llovía.	*It was raining.*
Estábamos sentados.	*We were seated.*
Los niños saltaban y corrían.	*The children jumped and ran.*

The imperfect is used to describe a situation, a thing, a person, or an action in the past.

(b) **A menudo se volvía.**

He turned often. (or) He kept turning often.

Iba a Misa todos los días.

She used to go to Mass every day

Compraban el periódico por la mañana.

They used to buy the paper in the morning.

The imperfect is used to express a repeated or customary past action.

(c) **¿Cuánto tiempo hacía que estudiaba Ud. el español cuando su padre fué a México?**

How long had you been studying Spanish when your father went to Mexico?

Hacía dos meses que estudiaba el español cuando mi padre fué a México.

I had been studying Spanish for two months when my father went to Mexico.

Hacía un año que estaba en España cuando murió su amiga.

She had been in Spain for a year when her friend died.

When an action or state begun in the remote past is interrupted in the more immediate past, the imperfect of **hacer** and of another verb is used usually in this order: **hacía** + expression of time + **que** + imperfect tense.

The same thought may be expressed as follows:

¿Desde cuándo estudiaba Ud. el español cuando su padre fué a México?

How long had you been studying Spanish when your father went to Mexico?

Estudiaba el español desde hacía dos meses cuando mi padre fué a México.

I had been studying Spanish for two months when my father went to Mexico.

Estaba en España desde hacía un año cuando murió su amiga.

She had been in Spain for a year when her friend died.

23. **Los usos del pretérito indefinido y del pretérito imperfecto** (Uses of the preterite and imperfect)

(a) **Los niños saltaban y corrían.**

The children were jumping and running.

Hablaba con su amigo.

He was talking to his friend.

El paquete llegó ayer.	*The package arrived yesterday.*
Juan recibió la nota de sobresaliente.	*John received the grade of A*
El catedrático dió una conferencia.	*The professor gave a lecture.*

In general, the imperfect describes a situation or a scene and the preterite tells what happened.

(b) Llovía cuando salimos de la biblioteca.	*It was raining when we left the library.*
Estudiábamos cuando entró el decano.	*We were studying when the dean entered.*

The imperfect is used to describe the situation or to set the scene for the preterite which expresses the action.

(c) No quería ver a sus amigos, porque tenía que estudiar.	*He didn't want to see his friends, because he had to study.*
Cuando vió a Isabela tan agitada quiso calmarla.	*When he saw Isabella so excited he tried to calm her.*
No sabían la lección.	*They didn't know the lesson.*
Cuando supo que su hijo no resultó aprobado, el padre se enfureció.	*When he learned (found out) that his son didn't pass, the father became furious.*
Conocía ya al rector.	*She already knew the principal.*
Conocí a los señores Ribera en casa de mi tía.	*I met Mr. and Mrs. Ribera at my aunt's house.*
No podía aprender a tocar la guitarra.	*He wasn't able (i.e., didn't have the ability) to learn how to play the guitar.*
No pudo ver al rector ayer, porque estaba ocupado.	*He wasn't able to see (i.e., didn't succeed in seeing) the principal yesterday, because he was busy.*

Verbs like **querer, saber, conocer,** and **poder** are usually used, in the past, in the imperfect because they describe a state of mind. Sometimes, these verbs are used in the preterite, especially when the beginning of an action is stated or implied. When so used, their meaning varies from that of the imperfect.

(d) Compare the following two paragraphs:

Don Francisco era amable con todos, ayudaba a los menesterosos y vivía en santa paz y armonía con todos.

The author is describing and is not interested either in the duration or in the end of the actions expressed.

Don Francisco fué amable con todos, ayudó a los menesterosos, y vivió en santa paz y armonía con todos hasta que pasó a mejor vida.

The author is describing the same actions as in the preceding paragraph, but with the implication that each action lasted only a definite length of time.

(e)

El alumno estudiaba todas las noches después de la cena.	*The pupil used to study every night after dinner.*
Antonio estudió con ahinco cada año y siempre recibió buenas notas.	*Anthony studied earnestly every year and always received good marks.*
La madre siempre besaba a sus hijos cuando salían de casa.	*The mother always kissed her children when they went out.*
Su madre lo besó repetidamente.	*His mother kissed him repeatedly.*

The imperfect is used to describe repeated or customary actions in the past. The preterite may also express repeated actions in the past; but when so used, each action is considered as a completed entity.

(f) The diagrams below may help to illustrate the differences between the imperfect and the preterite tenses:

Los niños saltaban.
El alumno estudiaba todas las noches.

$$\left.\begin{array}{c} \text{————————} \\ \text{— —— —— —} \end{array}\right\} \text{IMPERFECT}$$

Antonio estudió cada año y siempre recibió buenas notas.
El año pasado Antonio estudió mucho.

$$\left.\begin{array}{c} \text{|-|-|-|-|-|} \\ \text{|————————|} \end{array}\right\} \text{PRETERITE}$$

24. Los verbos reflexivos (Reflexive verbs)

(a)

	levantarse	to get up *
yo	me levanto	I get up
tu	te levantas	you get up
él, ella, Ud.	se levanta	he, she gets up, you get up
nosotros	nos levantamos	we get up
vosotros	os levantáis	you get up
ellos, ellas, Uds.	se levantan	they (m. & f.), you get up

A verb is reflexive when the subject performs and receives the action of the verb. The pronouns **me, te, se, nos, os, se** must be used with reflexive verbs.

(b) Juan se levantó, se afeitó, se bañó y después de vestirse, se dirigió a la oficina.

John got up, shaved himself, bathed, and after dressing, went to the office.

Lávate las manos, Pepe.

Wash your hands, Joe.

Al fin, hallándose solo y sin dinero, decidió escribir a su tío, el conde.

Finally, finding himself alone and without money, he decided to write to his uncle, the count.

The reflexive pronouns take the same position in a sentence as other personal pronouns; that is, they are usually placed immediately before a conjugated verb. In compound tenses they precede **haber.** However with an infinitive, an affirmative command or a gerund, they follow and are attached to the verb.

(c) Al encontrarse, los dos amigos se saludaron.

Upon meeting each other, the two friends greeted each other.

Nosotros nos veíamos todos los veranos.

We used to see one another every summer.

The reflexive pronoun may also express a reciprocal action. In this case it is equivalent to the English *each other* or *one another.*

(d) Los muchachos levantaron la mano.

The boys raised their hands.

Las muchachas se levantaron.

The girls got up.

---

* Other common reflexive verbs are: **atreverse,** *to dare;* **callarse,** *to keep quiet;* **despedirse,** *to take leave of;* **detenerse,** *to stop;* **encontrarse** *to meet;* **hacerse,** *to become;* **meterse,** *to place oneself;* **pararse,** *to stop;* **quedarse,** *to remain* **quejarse,** *to complain;* **tratarse** (**de**), *to be a matter of;* **sentarse** *to sit down;* **volverse,** *to turn around.*

La criada lavó la ropa.	*The servant washed the clothes.*
Luisito nunca quiere lavarse.	*Louis never wants to wash himself.*
El barbero lo afeitó con mucho cuidado.	*The barber shaved him very carefully.*
Se afeitó de prisa.	*He shaved himself hurriedly.*

Verbs may be both transitive (one that requires a direct object to complete its meaning) or reflexive.

(e) The following transitive verbs when used reflexively change their meaning:

dormir	*to sleep*	dormirse	*to fall asleep*
estar	*to be*	estarse	*to remain, to stay*
hacer	*to make, to do*	hacerse	*to become*
ir	*to go*	irse	*to go away*
levantar	*to raise, to lift*	levantarse	*to get up*
poner	*to put, to place*	ponerse	*to put on, to wear*
sentar	*to seat*	sentarse	*to sit down*
venir	*to come*	venirse	*to come along*
volver	*to return*	volverse	*to turn around*

25. El verbo gustar (Verb gustar)

Le gusta el libro.	*He likes the book.*
Me gustan las flores.	*I like flowers.*
Nos gustaba ir a caballo por la mañana.	*We liked to go horseback riding in the morning.*
Les gustó el drama.	*They liked the play.*

The verb gustar (*to like*) is usually used in the third person. The construction of gustar in a Spanish sentence is the reverse of English. The subject becomes the indirect object and vice versa; e.g., *I like flowers = The flowers are pleasing to me* = Me gustan las flores.

26. *Estúdiese en el apéndice el presente de indicativo, el pretérito y el imperfecto de los verbos irregulares* ver, saber, poder.

IV. Ejercicios

A. *Contéstense las preguntas siguientes usando oraciones completas en español:*

1. ¿Qué pidieron los dos amigos al camarero?
2. ¿Cómo está la familia del señor Smith?

3. ¿Quién acaba de graduarse?
4. ¿En qué Universidad se va a matricular Dolores?
5. ¿En qué escuela se matriculó Ud.?
6. ¿Qué se divertía hacer Dolores cuando era niña?
7. ¿Qué asignatura le gusta a Dolores?
8. ¿Qué asignatura le gusta a Ud. más?
9. ¿Qué país quiere visitar Dolores?
10. ¿Qué país le gustaría visitar a Ud.? ¿Por qué?
11. ¿Dónde hay cursos de verano para estudiantes extranjeros?
12. ¿Dónde puede vivir un estudiante extranjero?
13. ¿Qué es una casa de huéspedes?
14. ¿Hay cafés al estilo español en los Estados Unidos?
15. ¿Cree Ud. que los derechos de matrícula en su escuela son bajos?

B. *Escríbase una pregunta en español con cada una de las «frases importantes» que siguen:*

1. abonar los derechos de matrícula
2. costoso
3. acordarse de
4. cursos de verano
5. al fin

6. dar noticias
7. las vacaciones
8. parece mentira
9. charlar

C. *Escríbase una oración completa en español con cada una de las «frases importantes» que siguen:*

1. acabar de
2. alojarse
3. estar para
4. por supuesto
5. el hospedaje

6. al dar
7. dar de comer
8. ir de paseo
9. no hace mucho
10. hija mayor

D. *Complétense las oraciones siguientes con la forma exacta del imperfecto de los verbos entre paréntesis y tradúzcanse al inglés:*

1. (saltar)   Los chicos corrían y _____ por las calles del pueblo.
2. (bañarse)   Ellos _____ todas las mañanas.
3. (gustar)   A mí _____ ir de paseo.
4. (afeitar)   El barbero _____ al hombre con lentitud.

5. (acabar)   María _____ de limpiar el cuarto cuando su marido entró.
6. (acercarse)   Los días de los exámenes _____ y yo no sabía nada.
7. (atreverse)   Juan no _____ a decirlo a su padre.
8. (parecer)   A él le _____ una cosa absurda.
9. (saber)   El señor Rojas no _____ que hacer.
10. (llamarse)   ¿Cómo _____ ese profesor?
11. (vivir)   Mientras nosotros _____ allí vimos muchos dramas.
12. (querer)   Los padres _____ ver como vivía su hijo en la ciudad.
13. (ser)   Don Francisco _____ amable con todos.
14. (ir)   Dolores _____ de paseo todas las mañanas.
15. (ver)   Los dos amigos se _____ todos los veranos.

E. *Complétense las oraciones siguientes con el pretérito o el imperfecto del verbo entre paréntesis:*

1. Mientras yo (was studying) ella (entered).
2. (He knew) desde muchos años a los Ribera.
3. (They met) al señor Ribera en una tertulia.
4. Yo lo (bought) en una librería.
5. La vieja (went) a Misa todos los días.
6. La madre (kissed) a su hijo el día que salió de su pueblo natío.
7. (It was raining) cuando nosotros (entered) en el café.
8. El decano (wanted) hablar con los estudiantes antes de las vacaciones.
9. Cuando (he was) niño, (he liked) visitar a su tío en la finca.
10. (I didn't like) la comida ayer.

F. *Tradúzcase al español:*

1. "What do you wish, gentlemen?" said the waiter.
2. When did the foreign students enroll in the University?
3. What did you think of the meal? Did you like it?
4. He put on his hat and went out.
5. While we were studying he was enjoying himself.
6. He paid the tuition fees last week.
7. Professor Guerra gave an interesting lecture yesterday.

8. We were about to telephone them when they arrived.
9. Of course I remember your daughter's birthday.
10. He arrived yesterday and took up lodging in a boarding house immediately.

G. *Dictado tomado de la conversación* «Charlando en el café», pp. 29–30.

Lección Quinta

DE COMPRAS

1. Conversación

[*Léase en voz alta varias veces y apréndase de memoria.*]

—José, ¿puedes indicarme dónde están las tiendas? Tengo que hacer compras.

Joseph, can you show me where the stores are? I have to do some shopping.

—¡Cómo no! Hay unas tiendas elegantes no muy lejos de aquí. Vamos.

Why not! There are some elegant shops not very far from here. Let's go.

—¿Qué quieres comprar?

What do you want to buy?

—Unas camisas y un regalo para un amigo mío.

Some shirts and a gift for a friend of mine.

—Mira, allí está la tienda de ropa. ¿Entramos?

Look, there is the clothing store. Shall we go in?

—Primero quiero echar un vistazo al escaparate.

First I want to take a look at the show window.

—Parece que tienen un buen surtido. ¡Entremos!

It looks as if they have a large stock. Let's go in!

—Buenos días, señores, ¿en qué puedo servirles?

Good morning, gentlemen, may I be of service?

—¿Puede mostrarme una camisa?

Can you show me a shirt?

—Con mucho gusto. ¿Qué número?

With pleasure. What size?

—Treinta y ocho.

Thirty-eight.

41

—Aquí las tiene Ud. Éstas son de algodón fino y éstas de rayón con mangas cortas o largas.

Here you are. These are made of fine cotton and these of rayon with short or long sleeves.

—¿Cuánto cuestan?

How much are they?

—Solamente ciento setenta y cinco pesetas porque este mes tenemos rebaja.

Only one hundred seventy five pesetas because this month we have a sale.

—Me quedo con esta blanca.

I'll take this white one.

—Tenemos unas corbatas bonitas. Ésta hace juego con la camisa.

We have some pretty ties. This one matches the shirt.

—No me gusta, los colores son demasiado vivos. Parece pintada por un surrealista.

I don't like it, the colors are too bright. It looks as if it were painted by a surrealist.

—Las tenemos de todos colores.

We have them of all colors.

—Ahí está el problema; cada una tiene todos los colores.

That's the trouble; each one has all the colors.

—¿Necesitan algo más . . . pañuelos, calcetines, ropa interior?

Do you need anything else . . . handkerchiefs, socks, underwear?

—No, gracias, pero querría comprar un regalo para un amigo mío.

No, thanks, but I should like to buy a present for a friend of mine.

—Tenemos unos guantes de cuero de última moda.

We have some leather gloves in the latest style.

—¿Cuánto valen?

How much are they?

—Seiscientas pesetas.

Six hundred pesetas.

—Son muy caros.

They're very expensive.

—No, señor, son hechos a mano. A ese precio son una verdadera ganga.

No, sir, they are made by hand. At that price they are a real bargain.

—Está bien. Aquí tiene Ud. el dinero.

All right. Here is the money.

—Aquí están la vuelta y el paquete. Muchas gracias, señor.

Here are the change and the package. Thank you very much, sir.

—¿Dónde puedo comprar un

Where can I buy a roll of film?

rollo de películas? Quiero sacar unas fotografías.	I want to take some pictures.
—Hay una tienda de materiales y aparatos fotográficos calle abajo.	There is a camera supply store down the street.
—¿Revelan películas allí?	Do they develop film there?
—Sí, y lo hacen dentro de unos días. Si Ud. las deja el lunes, por ejemplo, se las devuelven el jueves.	Yes, and they do it within a few days. If you leave them there on Monday, for example, they return them on Thursday.
—Gracias, adiós.	Thank you, goodby.
—Adiós.	Goodby.

II. Frases Importantes

[*Apréndanse de memoria.*]

aquí las tiene	here they are
calle abajo	down the street
¡cómo no!	why not! of course!
¿cuánto cuesta? ¿cuánto vale?	how much is it? how much does it cost?
de compras	shopping
de última moda	in the latest style
dentro de	within
echar un vistazo a	to glance at
¿en qué puedo servirles?	can I be of service?
está bien	all right
hacer compras	to go shopping
hacer juego con	to match, to go well with
hecho a mano	hand made
la tienda de ropa	the clothing store
me quedo con ésta	I'll take this one
número treinta y ocho	size 38 (38 *centimeters = size 15; refers to collar*)
por ejemplo	for example
quedarse con	to take, to keep
sacar fotografías	to take pictures
tener rebaja	to have a sale

III. Puntos Gramaticales

27. **Posición de los adjetivos** (Position of adjectives)
In Spanish there is greater freedom and variety in the sentence position of the adjective than in English.

(a)			
la corbata	*the tie*
unos calcetines	*some socks*
diez libros	*ten books*
esa camisa	*that shirt*
mi hijo	*my son*
cualquier cosa	*anything*
¿cuál papel?	*which paper?*

Limiting adjectives (those that restrict the noun, such as articles, numerals, demonstratives, possessives, relatives, interrogatives, and negatives) generally precede the noun.

(b)			
la corbata amarilla	*the yellow tie*
la mujer preguntona	*the inquisitive woman*
la ópera italiana	*the Italian opera*
el niño inteligente	*the intelligent child*

Descriptive adjectives, or those that distinguish the noun by describing some characteristic of it, generally follow the noun.

(c)			
las altas montañas	*the high mountains*
el verde prado	*the green meadow*
la blanca nieve	*the white snow*

A descriptive adjective that expresses an inherent characteristic of the noun is placed before the noun.

(d)			
una pobre muchacha	*a poor* (unfortunate) *girl*
una muchacha pobre	*a poor* (poverty-stricken) *girl*
un nuevo coche	*a new* (different) *car*
un coche nuevo	*a new* (brand-new) *car*
un gran hombre	*a great man*
un hombre grande	*a big man*
el mismo profesor	*the same professor*
el profesor mismo	*the professor himself*
cierta persona	*a certain person*
una cosa cierta	*a sure thing*

The meaning of some adjectives changes when their position changes.

28. Los números (Ordinal numbers)

(a)
primero, –a	*first*	sexto, –a	*sixth*
segundo, –a	*second*	séptimo, –a	*seventh*
tercero, –a	*third*	octavo, –a	*eighth*
cuarto, –a	*fourth*	noveno, –a	*ninth*
quinto, –a	*fifth*	décimo, –a	*tenth*

el tomo cuarto	*the fourth volume*
la quinta lección	*the fifth lesson*
los primeros capítulos	*the first chapters*

Ordinal numbers are adjectives and agree in gender and number with the nouns they modify.

(b)
la lección quince	*the fifteenth lesson* (lesson fifteen)
la calle veintidós	*twenty second street*
Alfonso trece	*Alphonse the Thirteenth*
el Papa Pío once	*Pope Pius the Eleventh*

Ordinal numbers are generally used only through **décimo.** To express ordinal numbers above *tenth,* the cardinal numbers are used. With titles of royalty and popes the definite article is not used before the numeral.

(c)
el primer cuento	*the first story*
el tercer viaje	*the third trip*
el libro tercero	*the third book*
But:	
la primera visita	*the first visit*
la tercera palabra	*the third word*

Primero and **tercero** drop **–o** before masculine singular nouns.

29. Los meses del año (Months of the year)

(a)
enero	*January*	julio	*July*
febrero	*February*	agosto	*August*
marzo	*March*	septiembre	*September*
abril	*April*	octubre	*October*
mayo	*May*	noviembre	*November*
junio	*June*	diciembre	*December*

In Spanish, all months of the year are masculine; the article is not used and usually the months are not capitalized.

(b) **El cuatro de julio es la fiesta nacional de los Estados Unidos.**	*The fourth of July is the national holiday of the United States.*
El dos de mayo es la fiesta nacional de España.	*The second of May is the national holiday of Spain.*
En España el año escolar empieza el primero de octubre.	*In Spain the school year begins October first.*
¿A cuántos estamos? Estamos a quince de noviembre.	*What is the date?* (What day of the month is it?) *It is the fifteenth of November.*
¿Cuándo empiezan los exámenes? El once de junio.	*When do the examinations begin? The eleventh of June.*

In Spanish, cardinal numbers are used instead of ordinals to indicate dates, except for the first of the month, which is **primero.** The definite article **el** is used before the numeral and **de** before the name of the month.

30. **Los días de la semana y las estaciones del año** (The days of the week and the seasons of the year)

domingo	*Sunday*	**jueves**	Thursday	**el invierno**	*winter*
lunes	*Monday*	**viernes**	*Friday*	**la primavera**	*spring*
martes	*Tuesday*	**sábado**	*Saturday*	**el verano**	*summer*
miércoles	*Wednesday*			**el otoño**	*autumn*

El viernes fuimos al teatro.	*On Friday we went to the theatre.*
Todos los domingos vamos a la iglesia.	*We go to church every Sunday.*
Durante el verano vamos a la playa todos los sábados.	*We go to the beach every Saturday during the summer.*

The names of the days of the week are masculine and are not capitalized. To express *on* the definite article is used with the day of the week. All the seasons of the year are masculine except *spring*.

31. **La omisión del artículo indefinido** (Omission of the indefinite article)

(a) **Mi amigo es español.**	*My friend is Spanish.*
Yo soy nortamericano.	*I am an American.*
Él es ingeniero.	*He is an engineer.*

BUT:

| El doctor Torres es un buen profesor. | Dr. Torres is a good professor. |

The indefinite article is not used before predicate nouns that express nationality or profession. When the noun is modified the article must be used.

(b) | ¿Quiere Ud. otro vaso de vino? | Do you want another glass of wine? |
| Hay más de mil estudiantes en esta escuela. | There are more than a thousand students in this school. |
| Mi padre nunca compró tal libro. | My father never bought such a book. |

The indefinite article is omitted before the following words: **otro** (*another*), **tal** (*such a*), **cierto** (*certain*), **¡que!** (*what a!*), **cien** (*a hundred*), **mil** (*a thousand*), **medio, –a** (*a, one half*), **semejante** (*such a*).

32. *Estúdiese en el apéndice el pretérito y el imperfecto de* **estar, ir, ser, tener, hacer.**

IV. Ejercicios

A. *Contéstense las preguntas siguientes usando oraciones completas en español:*

1. ¿Qué tiene que hacer el señor Smith?
2. ¿Dónde están las tiendas?
3. ¿Qué quiere comprar el señor Smith?
4. ¿Qué quiere hacer primero?
5. ¿Qué les dice el dependiente al entrar ellos?
6. ¿Qué número lleva (wears) el señor Smith?
7. ¿Cuánto cuesta la camisa?
8. ¿Qué número lleva Ud.?
9. ¿Qué es una rebaja?
10. ¿Por qué no le gustan las corbatas al señor Smith?
11. ¿Le gustan a Ud. los colores vivos?
12. ¿De qué color es la corbata que Ud. lleva?
13. ¿Cuánto cuestan los guantes?
14. ¿Cuándo lleva Ud. guantes?
15. ¿Por qué quiere Ud. comprar unos rollos de películas?

B. *Escríbase una pregunta en español con cada una de las «frases importantes» que siguen:*

1. la tienda de ropa
2. hecho a mano
3. hacer compras

4. echar un vistazo a
5. tener rebaja

C. *Escríbase una oración completa en español con cada una de las «frases importantes» que siguen:*

1. hacer juego con
2. calle abajo
3. de compras
4. sacar fotografías
5. dentro de

6. de última moda
7. quedarse con
8. está bien
9. por ejemplo

D. *Complétense las oraciones siguientes con el pretérito de los verbos entre paréntesis:*

1. (estar)   El señor Torres _____ enfermo.
2. (ir)   Los amigos _____ a la tienda de ropa.
3. (ser)   El café _____ muy bueno.
4. (tener)   Él _____ que comprar un regalo.
5. (hacer)   Ellos _____ compras en el centro.
6. (comprar)   Yo _____ un par de calcetines.
7. (gustar)   No le _____ las corbatas.
8. (entrar)   Tú no _____ en la tienda, ¿verdad?
9. (comprender)   Nosotros no _____ nada.
10. (escribir)   Carlos _____ a sus padres.

E. *Complétense las oraciones siguientes con el imperfecto de los verbos entre paréntesis:*

1. (ir)   Todos los domingos ellos _____ a esa iglesia.
2. (ser)   El doctor Torres _____ un buen profesor.
3. (estar)   La tienda _____ calle abajo.
4. (hacer)   Lo encontré mientras _____ compras.
5. (tener)   Aquella tienda no _____ un buen surtido.
6. (echar)   La señora siempre _____ un vistazo al escaparate.
7. (dejar)   Mi amigo nunca _____ de visitarme.
8. (ver)   Yo lo _____ todos los días en el café.

9. (abrir)   Mientras él _____ la puerta yo salía.
10. (comer)   Nosotros _____ a las ocho.

F. *Complétense las oraciones siguientes:*

1. (the poor man)   *pobre hombre* estaba enfermo.
2. (a certain professor) Fué escrito por _____. *la nieva blanca*
3. (the white snow)   *la blanca* cubre todo con su manta fría.
4. (a brand new tie)   Compró *una corbata nueva*
5. (the white gloves)   Dió *guantes blancos* a su hija.
6. (anything)   *cualquier cosa* es mejor que esto.
7. (the third book)   Éste es *tercer libro* que leo este verano.
8. (the first lessons) *las primeras lecciones* son muy difíciles.
9. (Felipe the Second) *Felipe segundo* fué un buen administrador.
10. (Pope John the   Vimos al *papa* que bendecía (a) la
    Twenty-third)   gente. *Pope Juan veintetres*
11. (on the third of   Las vacaciones se acaban _____.
    January)
12. (on Sunday)   *El domingo* vamos a la corrida.
13. (on Saturdays)   Vamos de compras *los sabados*
14. (which shirt)   *Que comisa* quiere Ud.?
15. (the pretty girl)   Ayer vi *chica bonita*
16. (Spanish cities)   Sacó fotografías de las *cuidades españoles*
17. (a big man)   Nuestro padre es *un hombre grande*
18. (a sure thing)   Nuestra victoria es *una cosa cierta*
19. (forty third)   Vive en la calle *cuarenta y tres*

G. *Tradúzcase al español:*

1. We don't have to go shopping today. *las tiendas de ropa no están*
2. The clothing stores are not far from here. *lejos de aqui*
3. Do you want to take a look at the photographic equipment? *quiere tocar un mirro al equipo de photografia*
4. While I was buying some gloves he was looking at the socks. *mientras yo compraba algunos guantes, el miraba al calcetones*
5. We didn't like the color of his tie. *No nos gustaba la color de la corbata*
6. Of course I'm going with you. Let's go.
7. We arrived on the thirteenth of October, 1928. *llegamos en el diez y tres de octubre*
8. The professor himself could not write this exercise.
9. Can you show me the camera shop? *Puede usted enseñarme la tienda d fotografia?*
10. I left the roll of film on Tuesday and they developed it right
    away.

H. *Prepárese una composición oral de dos minutos usando uno de los temas siguientes:*

1. De compras
2. Los regalos para mi familia

I. *Dictado tomado de la conversación* «De compras», pp. 41–43

Lección Sexta

EL METRO

I. Conversación

[Léase en voz alta varias veces y apréndase de memoria.]

(Descolgando el receptor)

(Picking up the receiver)

—Diga . . . ah, Juan, buenos días. ¡Tempranito te levantaste, eh!

Hello . . . ah, John, good morning. You got up rather early, didn't you?

—Hombre, si ya son las diez y media. Me levanté a las siete como siempre.

Why, it's already ten thirty. I got up at seven as usual.

—Los domingos yo me levanto tarde. Pues, ¿qué quieres hacer hoy?

I get up late on Sundays. Well, what do you want to do today?

—No sé, querría ver algo interesante.

I don't know, I'd like to see something interesting.

—Yo voy a la corrida. ¿Te gustaría acompañarme?

I'm going to the bullfight. Would you like to go with me?

—Encantado. He oído hablar tanto de la corrida que tengo mucha gana de verla.

Gladly. I've heard so much about bullfighting that I'm very eager to see it.

—Muy bien. Tomaremos el metro.

Fine. We'll take the subway.

—¿A qué hora nos encontramos?

At what time shall we meet?

—Sería bueno citarnos para las cuatro porque la corrida empieza a las cinco en punto.

It would be good to meet at four because the bullfight begins at five sharp.

51

—De acuerdo. Hasta las cuatro.   Agreed. See you at four.

—Hasta luego.   See you later.

. . .   . . .

—Hola, Juan, ¿hace mucho que me esperas?   Hello, John, have you been waiting long?

—No, sólo unos cinco minutos.   No, only about five minutes.

—Vamos. ¿Dónde está la estación del metro?   Let's go. Where is the subway station?

—Por aquí, a la izquierda.   This way, to the left.

—¿Tenemos que comprar fichas?   Do we have to buy tokens?

—No, aquí venden billetes y se entregan al revisor.   No, here they sell tickets which are handed to the conductor.

—¿Tardará mucho en llegar el tren?   Will the train be long in arriving?

—Un poquito. Los días de fiesta no pasan tan a menudo.   A bit. They don't come by so often on holidays.

—Hay mucha gente en el andén.   There are a lot of people on the platform.

—No tanta como en Nueva York, y allí los trenes están siempre llenos hasta los topes.   Not as many as in New York, and the trains are always jampacked.

—Nueva York tiene muchos más habitantes.   Well, New York has many more inhabitants.

—Y este bendito tren que no viene.   And this darn train doesn't get here.

—Vendrá, vendrá. ¡No seas tan impaciente! Mira, aquí está. Entra.   It'll come, it'll come. Don't be so impatient! Look, here it is. Get in.

—Al menos aquí uno entra por su propia voluntad. En Nueva York se entra a fuerza de empujones y codazos.   At least here one enters of his own free will. In New York one gets in by dint of shoves and elbows.

—Los madrileños son muy corteses.   The Madrilenians are very courteous.

—En este metro también hay anuncios. Mira, aquél dice «Coca Cola refresca mejor».   In this subway they also have ads. Look, that one says, "Coca Cola refreshes better."

—Esa bebida se vende por todo el mundo.

That drink is sold all over the world.

—Sí, es una de nuestras contribuciones culturales a los países del mundo.

Yes, it's one of our cultural contributions to the other countries of the world.

—Ah, ah, siendo español yo no me habría atrevido a decir eso de tu país.

Ha, ha, being a Spaniard I should not have dared to say that about your country.

—¿Cuándo bajamos?

When do we get off?

—La próxima parada es la nuestra.

The next stop is ours.

II. Frases Importantes

[*Apréndanse de memoria.*]

a codazos	by blows with the elbow
a empujones	by pushing
a fuerza de	by dint of, by force of
a lo menos, al menos	at least
bendito	blessed (*ironically for* cursed, darn)
citarse	to make an appointment
descolgar el receptor	to pick up the phone (*lit.,* to unhook the receiver)
echar ficha en la ranura	to put a token in the slot
el billete de abono	the commutation ticket
el billete de ida y vuelta	the round trip ticket
el billete sencillo	the one-way ticket
encantado	gladly, with pleasure (*lit.,* enchanted)
estar lleno hasta los topes	to be jam-packed
hasta las cuatro	see you at four (o'clock)
por aquí	this way, through here
por la mañana	in the morning
tener gana(s) de	to wish, to desire to
tener mucha(s) gana(s) de	to wish very much to
tardar en	to be long in, to delay in

III. Puntos Gramaticales

33. El futuro (Future)

–ar

hablaré	*I shall speak*
hablarás	*you (fam.) will speak*
hablará	*he, she, you will speak*
hablaremos	*we shall speak*
hablaréis	*you (fam.) will speak*
hablarán	*they, you will speak*

–er	**–ir**
comprenderé	viviré
comprenderás	vivirás
comprenderá	vivirá
comprenderemos	viviremos
comprenderéis	viviréis
comprenderán	vivirán

The future of all regular verbs is formed by adding **–é, –ás, –á, –emos, –éis, –án** to the infinitive.

34. Los usos del futuro (Uses of the future)

(a) **La semana que viene compraremos un billete de abono.**
   Next week we shall buy a commutation ticket.

   Iremos a la playa durante las vacaciones.
   We shall go to the beach during the vacation.

   ¿Irá Ud. a España el verano que viene?
   Will you go to Spain next summer?

The future is generally used whenever futurity is expressed or clearly implied.

(b) **¿Dónde estará Tomás? Estará en su cuarto.**
   Where can Thomas be? He is probably in his room.

   ¿Qué hora será? Serán las tres.
   What time can it be? It is probably three o'clock.

Unlike English, the future in Spanish also expresses probability in the present.

35. El potencial o condicional (Conditional)

–ar

hablar*ía*	*I should speak*
hablar*ías*	*you* (fam.) *would speak*
hablar*ía*	*he, she, you would speak*
hablar*íamos*	*we should speak*
hablar*íais*	*you* (fam.) *would speak*
hablar*ían*	*they, you would speak*

–er	**–ir**
comprender*ía*	vivir*ía*
comprender*ías*	vivir*ías*
comprender*ía*	vivir*ía*
comprender*íamos*	vivir*íamos*
comprender*íais*	vivir*íais*
comprender*ían*	vivir*ían*

The conditional tense of all regular verbs is formed by adding –*ía*, –*ías*, –*ía*, –*íamos*, –*íais*, –*ían* to the infinitive.

36. Los usos del condicional (Uses of the conditional)

(a) **Dijo que vendría por la ma-**   *He said he would come in the*
    ñana.   *morning.*

    Escribió que querría vender   *She wrote that she would like*
    su casa.   *to sell her house.*

    María dijo que compraría un   *Mary said that she would buy*
    billete de ida y vuelta.   *a round trip ticket.*

The conditional tense is used generally as in English; that is, it depends on the past time whether stated or implied. It expresses future time in relation to the past, just as the future tense expresses future time in relation to the present.

(b) **¿Qué hora sería? Serían las**   *I wonder what time it was. It*
    dos.   *was probably two o'clock.*

    ¿Cuántos años tendría? Ten-   *How old could he have been?*
    dría diez años.   *He was probably ten years*
        old.

The conditional is used to express probability in the past.

NOTE:

(1) *Would,* in the sense of an habitual action, is translated by the imperfect and not by the conditional.

Venía a verme todos los días.	He would (used to) come to see me every day.

(2) *Should*, in the sense of *ought to*, is rendered by **deber**.

Deberíamos estudiar.	We ought to (should) study.

37. Verbos irregulares en el futuro y el condicional (Irregular verbs in the future and the conditional)

	FUTURE	CONDITIONAL
caber (*to fit*)	**cabré**, etc.	**cabría**, etc.
decir (*to say, to tell*)	**diré**	**diría**
haber (*to have*)	**habré**	**habría**
hacer (*to make, to do*)	**haré**	**haría**
poder (*to be able, can*)	**podré**	**podría**
poner (*to put, to place*)	**pondré**	**pondría**
querer (*to wish, to want*)	**querré**	**querría**
salir (*to leave, to go out*)	**saldré**	**saldría**
tener (*to have*)	**tendré**	**tendría**
valer (*to be worth*)	**valdré**	**valdría**
venir (*to come*)	**vendré**	**vendría**

The same verbs are irregular in both the future and the conditional. In both cases, the irregularity is in the stem. The endings are the same for all verbs, regular or irregular, in the future and the conditional.

38. La hora (Time of day)

¿Qué hora es?	What time is it?
Es la una.	It is one o'clock.
Son las dos.	It is two o'clock.
Era la una y media.	It was half past one.
Eran las tres y media.	It was half past three.
Son las diez y cuarto.	It is a quarter after ten.
Son las once menos cuarto.	It is a quarter to eleven.
Eran las seis y veinte.	It was twenty after six.
Son las ocho menos diez.	It is ten minutes to eight.
¿A que hora llegó?	At what time did he arrive?
A las cuatro en punto.	At four o'clock sharp.
A la medianoche.	At midnight.
Al mediodía.	At noon.
A las nueve de la mañana.	At nine A.M.
A las cinco de la tarde	At five P.M.

A las once de la noche.	At eleven P.M.
El tren sale a la una y cinco.	The train leaves at five minutes after one.
A la madrugada	At dawn
Al anochecer	At nightfall, at dusk

The third person of the verb **ser** is used to indicate the time of day, except in the expression ¿**Qué hora tienes?** (*What time do you have?*). Time in the past is rendered by the imperfect of **ser**. The cardinal number indicating the hour is always preceded by **la** or **las**.

39. Los adjetivos demostrativos (Demonstrative adjectives)

(a) The demonstrative adjective has the following forms:

SINGULAR			PLURAL		
M.	F.		M.	F.	
este	esta	*this*	estos	estas	*these*
ese	esa	*that*	esos	esas	*those*
aquel	aquella	*that*	aquellos	aquellas	*those*

(b)

Este sombrero pertenece a esa señora.	*This hat belongs to that lady.*
Aquella ciudad tiene más de un millón de habitantes.	*That city has more than a million inhabitants.*
Esos anuncios son muy interesantes.	*Those ads are very interesting.*

The demonstrative adjective agrees in gender and in number with the noun it modifies. **Este** and all its variants refer to what is near the speaker. **Ese** and its variants refer to what is near the person addressed. **Aquel** and its variants refer to what is away from both the speaker and the person addressed.

40. Los pronombres demostrativos (Demonstrative pronouns)

(a) The demonstrative pronoun has the following forms:

SINGULAR			PLURAL		
M.	F.		M.	F.	
éste	ésta	*this (one)*	éstos	éstas	*these*
ése	ésa	*that (one)*	ésos	ésas	*those*
aquél	aquélla	*that (one)*	aquéllos	aquéllas	*those*

In addition to the above forms there are three neuter pronouns:

esto	*this*
eso	*that*
aquello	*that*

(b) **Aquel ómnibus allí le llevará**   *That bus over there will take*
      a Ud. al centro; éste va a   *you downtown; this one*
      las afueras.   *goes to the suburbs.*

   Tendremos que limpiar estos   *We shall have to clean these*
   cuartos y aquéllos antes de   *rooms and those before four*
   las cuatro.   *o'clock.*

The demonstrative pronoun agrees in gender and in number with the noun it replaces. The written accent mark on the demonstrative pronouns distinguishes them from the adjectives. **Esto, eso, aquello** do not have an accent.

(c) **Todo eso es una tontería.**   *All that is nonsense.*
      Esto es difícil.   *This* (problem, situation) *is*
                                        difficult.

The neuter demonstrative pronouns **esto, eso, aquello** do not refer to any definite objects but to an abstract idea, a group of facts, or a situation.

(d) **Juan y Antonio se despidieron.**   *John and Anthony said goodby*
      Aquél tomó un taxi y éste   *to each other. The former*
      el tranvía.   *took a taxi and the latter the*
                                            trolley.

The demonstrative pronouns (**éste** and its variants and **aquél** and its variants) sometimes can be rendered into English by *the former* and *the latter*. (**Aquél,** etc. = the former and **éste,** etc. = *the latter*).

41. *Estúdiese en el apéndice el presente de indicativo, el pretérito, el imperfecto de los verbos irregulares* decir, poner, salir.

IV. Ejercicios

A. *Contéstense las preguntas siguientes usando oraciones completas en español:*

1. ¿A qué hora se levantó Juan?
2. ¿A qué hora se levanta José los domingos?

3. ¿A qué hora se levanta Ud. de costumbre?
4. ¿Adónde irán los dos amigos?
5. ¿Por qué tiene Juan ganas de ver una corrida?
6. ¿En qué medio de transporte irán?
7. ¿A qué hora empieza la corrida?
8. ¿Cuánto tiempo hace que Juan espera?
9. ¿Dónde está la estación del metro?
10. ¿Por qué no tendrán que comprar fichas los dos amigos?
11. ¿Tardará mucho en llegar el tren?
12. ¿Cómo están los vagones del tren en Nueva York?
13. ¿Cómo se entra en el metro de Nueva York?
14. ¿Le gustaría a Ud. viajar en el metro de Nueva York?
15. ¿Cree Ud. que la Coca Cola es una contribución cultural?

B. *Escríbase una pregunta en español con cada una de las «frases importantes» que siguen:*

1. echar ficha en la ranura
2. el billete de ida y vuelta
3. por aquí
4. por la mañana
5. tener ganas de

C. *Escríbase una oración completa en español con cada una de las «frases importantes» que siguen:*

1. al menos
2. citarse
3. encantado
4. el billete sencillo
5. descolgar el receptor
6. tardar en
7. a fuerza de
8. a codazos
9. estar lleno hasta los topes
10. hasta las cuatro

D. *Complétense las oraciones siguientes con la forma correspondiente del futuro o del condicional de los verbos entre paréntesis:*

1. (decir) Mañana Antonio me dirá lo que ocurrió.
2. (comprar) Dijo que compraría los libros sin falta.
3. (gustar) ¿Te gustaría ver una corrida de toros?
4. (valer) La opinión de este señor no valdrá mucho.
5. (querer) Escribió que querría pasar las vacaciones con nosotros.
6. (venir) Cree que su amigo vendría a la conferencia.
7. (levantarse) Yo me levantaré temprano mañana.

8. (hablar)   ¿De qué _hablaron_ ellos en la tertulia?
9. (comprender)   Tú no _comprenderás_ nada si no escuchas con
                   cuidado.
10. (esperar)   Sus amigos dijeron que no _esperaran_ más.
11. (ser)   Mi amigo pensó que _sería_ bueno citarnos
                   para las cuatro.
12. (salir)   Antonio y María _saldremos_ para España el
                   otoño que viene.
13. (ir)   Nosotros _iremos_ a la playa durante las vaca-
                   ciones.
14. (ponerse)   Creyeron que Juan _se pondría_ el gabán.
15. (tener)   La boda _tendrá_ lugar en junio.

E. *Cámbiense al plural los sujetos y los verbos de las oraciones
   siguientes:*

1. Puso las maletas en el cuarto.
2. Le dije que lo llamaría por teléfono.
3. ¿A qué hora saliste?
4. ¿Compró Ud. el billete de abono?
5. Siempre decía la misma cosa.
6. Hoy no vengo con Uds.
7. Él no quería asistir a la corrida.
8. Dijo que no querría verles.
9. Saldré a las ocho y cuarto.
10. ¿Dónde estará la niña?
11. ¿Por qué no te pones los guantes?

F. *Complétense las oraciones siguientes en español:*

1. A mí me gusta (this) libro, no (that one).
2. (That) hombre en el rincón parece un extranjero.
3. (Those) cigarrillos que Ud. fuma son caros.
4. En (this) periódico hay dos artículos interesantes.
5. (These) trenes nunca llegan a la hora anunciada.
6. Dos tranvías pasan por aquí el número 28 y el número 16: (the
   latter) le llevará a la plaza de toros y (the former) al centro.
7. La corrida empieza (at five o'clock sharp).
8. ¿A qué hora termina la clase? (At 10:00 A.M.)
9. ¿Dónde estarán mis libros? (They are probably) en tu cuarto.

10. (That) me parece mentira.
11. (Those) revistas son mías; (these) son suyas.
12. Me levanté esta mañana (at 8:30).

G. *Tradúzcase al español:*

1. The subway station is on the left and the hotel on the right.
2. My daughter will call you on the phone tomorrow at nine o'clock sharp.
3. We shall meet at a quarter after eleven. Agreed.
4. The bus is always jam-packed. Isn't it?
5. My friend was very eager to see the bullfight but he had to leave.
6. When shall we get off? In a few minutes.
7. There aren't so many people on the platform because it's a holiday.
8. The dean said that those classes would not begin on the third of October.
9. Is this stop or the next one ours?
10. At least we won't have to enter the car by dint of shoves and elbows.
11. They will enroll at the University of Madrid in the fall.
12. He got up at dawn, shaved, and after dressing himself took a stroll in the park.

H. *Prepárese una composición oral de dos minutos empleando uno de los temas siguientes:*

1. Viajando por una gran ciudad
2. Una visita a un viejo amigo
3. Tertulias en el café

I. *Dictado tomado de la conversación «El metro», pp. 51–53.*

Lección Séptima

LA CORRIDA DE TOROS

I. Conversación

[*Léase en voz alta varias veces y apréndase de memoria.*]

—Allí está la taquilla. Tendremos que hacer cola.

There is the ticket booth. We'll have to get in line.

—¡Qué gentío, qué animación! Al parecer este deporte es muy popular.

What a crowd, what excitement! Apparently this sport is very popular.

—Te equivocas si lo llamas un deporte.

You're mistaken if you call it a sport.

—Pues, ¿no es un deporte?

Well, isn't it a sport?

—Sí, pero también es algo más. Es una fiesta, la fiesta nacional; es un drama, una tragedia que siempre termina con la muerte de uno o ambos protagonistas.

Yes, but it's also something more. It's a celebration, the national fiesta; it's a drama, a tragedy that always ends with the death of one or both protagonists.

—¿Hay dos protagonistas?

There are two protagonists?

—Sí, el matador y el toro, y éste debe mostrar su ferocidad y aquél su valentía, su sangre fría, y su destreza.

Yes, the matador and the bull, and the former has to show his bravery, his coolness, his skill and the latter its ferocity.

—No me esperaba todo eso.

I didn't expect all of that.

—Se puede también llamar un baile, «un ballet bajo la sombra de la muerte», como dijo un escritor norteamericano.

It can also be called a dance, "a ballet under the shadow of death," as an American writer said.

62

—Nunca te he visto tan entusiasmado.

I've never seen you so enthusiastic.

—Tú también te entusiasmarás cuando hayas visto este espectáculo lleno de tradición y emoción.

You too will become enthusiastic when you have seen this spectacle which is full of tradition and emotion.

—No voy a ver nada si esta bendita fila no acaba.

I'm not going to see anything if this darn line doesn't end.

—No te apures, hay tiempo.

Don't worry, there's time.

—Ah, por fin. Dos billetes a la sombra, por favor. Ya tenemos los billetes. Toma el tuyo. Vamos.

Ha, finally. Two tickets in the shade, please. Here I have the tickets. Take yours. Let's go.

—¿Dónde están nuestros asientos?

Where are our seats?

—Por allí abajo. Éste es el mío y ése el tuyo. Siéntate.

Down there. This one is mine and that one is yours. Sit down.

—¿Qué ocurrirá primero?

What will happen first?

—Primero salen a la plaza dos alguaciles a caballo para pedir la llave del toril al presidente de la fiesta. Después sigue el paseo de los toreros en tres filas al son de un paso doble.

First the two bailiffs come out on horseback to ask the president of the fiesta for the key to the bull-pen. Then follows the parade of the bullfighters in three rows, to the sound of a two-step.

—Ha sonado un clarín. ¿Qué quiere decir eso?

A trumpet has sounded. What does that mean?

—Que ahora sale el toro. ¿Ves cómo el torero se acerca con la capa para darle pases?

That the bull is going to come out. Do you see how the matador is approaching the bull with the cape in order to "make passes" at him?

—¿Quién es aquel señor a caballo?

Who is that man on horseback?

—El picador. Va a clavar la pica en el cuello del animal.

The picador. He is going to sink the pike into the animal's neck.

—Mira cómo embiste. ¡Qué toro bravo!

Look how he charges. What a ferocious bull!

—Ahora viene el banderillero con las banderillas en alto para ponerlas, corriendo, en la cruz del toro.

Now comes the banderillero with the banderillas on high to put them, while running, into the withers of the bull.

—¿Y, ahora?

And now?

—Ahora la parte más importante. Mira, allí viene el matador con el estoque y la muleta para dar pases y mostrar todo su destreza y coraje.

And now the most important part. Look, there come the matador with a sword and the muleta to "make passes" and to show all his skill and courage.

—¡Qué calma, qué gracia! ¡De veras que parece un bailarín!

How calm, how graceful! He really does look like a dancer!

—Ha dejado la muleta y está para matar al toro.

He has let go of the muleta and is about to kill the bull.

—¡Olé! ¡Bravo! De veras que es una escena muy emocionante.

Olé! Bravo! It's really a very moving scene.

—No te dije yo que te entusiasmarías con los toros?

Didn't I tell you that you would get enthusiastic about bullfighting?

II. Frases Importantes

[*Apréndanse de memoria.*]

a caballo	on horseback
al son de	to the sound of, to the music of
asistir a	to attend, to be present at
darle pases (al toro)	to direct the charge of the bull by the use of a cape or muleta
el billete al sol	the ticket in the sun
el billete a la sombra	the ticket in the shade
hacer cola (fila)	to form a line, to get in line
la sangre fría	coolness under fire, courage
no te apures (apurarse)	don't worry (to worry)
por allí abajo	down there
por fin	finally, at last
por favor	please
¡qué toro bravo!	what a ferocious bull!
tener lugar	to take place

III. Puntos Gramaticales

42. **Los tiempos compuestos del indicativo** (Compound tenses of the indicative)

(a) **El pretérito perfecto** (Present perfect)

–ar

he hablado	*I have spoken*
has hablado	*you have spoken*
ha hablado	*he, she has spoken, you have spoken*
hemos hablado	*we have spoken*
habéis hablado	*you have spoken*
han hablado	*they, you have spoken*

–er	**–ir**
he comprendido	he vivido
has comprendido	has vivido
ha comprendido	ha vivido
hemos comprendido	hemos vivido
habéis comprendido	habéis vivido
han comprendido	han vivido

(b) **El pretérito pluscuamperfecto** (Pluperfect)

–ar

había hablado	*I had spoken*
habías hablado	*you had spoken*
había hablado	*he, she, you had spoken*
habíamos hablado	*we had spoken*
habíais hablado	*you had spoken*
habían hablado	*they, you had spoken*

–er	**–ir**
había comprendido	había vivido
habías comprendido	habías vivido
había comprendido	había vivido
habíamos comprendido	habíamos vivido
habíais comprendido	habíais vivido
habían comprendido	habían vivido

(c) **El pretérito anterior** (Preterite perfect)

-ar

hube hablado	*I had spoken*
hubiste hablado	*you had spoken*
hubo hablado	*he, she, you had spoken*
hubimos hablado	*we had spoken*
hubisteis hablado	*you had spoken*
hubieron hablado	*they, you had spoken*

-er | **-ir**

hube comprendido	hube vivido
hubiste comprendido	hubiste vivido
hubo comprendido	hubo vivido
etc.	etc.

(d) **El futuro perfecto** (Future perfect)

-ar

habré hablado	*I shall have spoken*
habrás hablado	*you will have spoken*
habrá hablado	*he, she, you will have spoken*
habremos hablado	*we shall have spoken*
habréis hablado	*you will have spoken*
habrán hablado	*they, you will have spoken*

-er | **-ir**

habré comprendido	habré vivido
habrás comprendido	habrás vivido
habrá comprendido	habrá vivido
etc.	etc.

(e) **El potencial perfecto** (Conditional perfect)

-ar

habría hablado	*I should have spoken*
habrías hablado	*you would have spoken*
habría hablado	*he, she, you would have spoken*
habríamos hablado	*we should have spoken*
habríais hablado	*you would have spoken*
habrían hablado	*they, you would have spoken*

-er | **-ir**

habría comprendido	habría vivido
habrías comprendido	habrías vivido

habría comprendido   habría vivido
etc.   etc.

The compound tenses are formed by using the appropriate form of the auxiliary verb **haber** plus the past participle of the verb concerned. The present perfect is formed by the present indicative of **haber** plus the past participle of the main verb; the pluperfect by the imperfect of **haber** plus the past participle of the main verb; the preterite perfect by the preterite of **haber** plus the past participle of the main verb; the future perfect by the future of **haber** plus the past participle of the main verb; the conditional perfect by the conditional of **haber** plus the past participle of the main verb.

43. El participio pasivo (Past participle)

(a) hablar: habl*ado*
    comprender: comprend*ido*
    vivir: viv*ido*

The past participle is formed by adding –**ado** to the stem of the infinitive of an –**ar** verb and –**ido** to the stem of the infinitive of an –**er** or an –**ir** verb.

(b) The following verbs have irregular past participles:

abrir: abierto
cubrir: cubierto
decir: dicho
escribir: escrito
hacer: hecho
morir: muerto
poner: puesto
resolver: resuelto
romper: roto
ver: visto
volver: vuelto

(c) las muchachas cansadas   *the tired girls*
    María fué castigada por su   *Mary was punished by her*
    padre.   *father.*
    Las ventanas están abiertas.   *The windows are open.*
    Nunca te he visto tan entu-   *I've never seen you so enthu-*
    siasmado.   *siastic.*

The past participle may be used as an adjective; with the verb **ser** in the passive voice; with the verb **estar** to express a state or condition; and with the verb **haber** to form the compound tenses.

NOTE: When used in compound tenses, the past participle is invariable.

44. Los usos de los tiempos compuestos (Uses of the compound tenses)

(a) Esta temporada Machito ha tenido mucho éxito en la plaza de Sevilla.

This season Machito has had great success in the Seville bull ring.

En este siglo hemos hecho mucho progreso en la tecnología.

In this century we've made great progress in technology.

No he estudiado mucho para este examen. Creo que voy a fracasar.

I haven't studied much for this exam. I think I'm going to fail.

Nunca han asistido a una corrida.

They have never attended a bullfight.

The present perfect tense expresses an action or a state (a) completed within a span of time which has not yet ended; (b) one that indicates a certain immediacy and effect upon the present; (c) one without any reference to any particular time.

(b) Fuí a su casa pero él había salido.

I went to his house but he had left.

Sabía que habíamos asistido a la corrida.

He knew that we had attended the bullfight.

The pluperfect expresses a state or an action completed before another past action.

(c) Apenas hubo salido cuando nosotros entramos.

Scarcely had he left when we entered.

Luego que hubimos comido salimos del restaurante.

As soon as we had dined, we left the restaurant.

The preterite perfect is used as the pluperfect but only after such expressions of time as **apenas** (*scarcely*), **cuando** (*when*), **así que, luego que** (*as soon as*), etc.

(d) **No se apure Ud.; en pocos minutos lo habremos arreglado todo.**

Don't worry; in a few minutes we will have arranged everything.

Lo habré leído para el martes.

I shall have read it by Tuesday.

The future perfect expresses an action or state which will be completed sometime in the future.

(e) **No te decía yo que habríamos arreglado todo en pocos minutos?**

Didn't I tell you that we would have arranged everything in a few minutes?

The conditional perfect expresses an action or state completed sometime in the future in relation to a past time. This parallels the future perfect which expresses a completed action in the future as viewed from the present time.

45. El pronombre posesivo (Possessive pronoun)

(a) The possessive pronoun has the following forms:

SINGULAR		PLURAL		
el mío	la mía	los míos	las mías	*mine*
el tuyo	la tuya	los tuyos	las tuyas	*yours* (fam.)
el suyo	la suya	los suyos	las suyas	*his, hers, its, yours*
el nuestro	la nuestra	los nuestros	las nuestras	*ours*
el vuestro	la vuestra	los vuestros	las vuestras	*yours* (fam.)
el suyo	la suya	los suyos	las suyas	*theirs, yours*

(b) **El tiene sus libros y yo tengo los míos.**

He has his books and I have mine.

Su casa está en el centro; la nuestra está en las afueras.

Her house is downtown; ours is in the suburbs.

The possessive pronoun agrees in gender and number with the noun it replaces or the thing possessed.

(c) **¿Dónde están sus libros? El suyo está aquí y el de ella está en la mesa.**

Where are their books? His is here and hers is on the table.

He visto su casa y la de ellos.

I saw his house and theirs.

When ambiguity may arise as to the meaning of **el suyo, la suya, los suyos** and **las suyas,** these forms may be replaced by

el de él, el de ella, el de Ud., etc., la de él, la de ella, la de Ud.,
etc., los de él, los de ella, los de Ud., etc., las de él, las de ella,
las de Ud., etc., according to the nouns to which they refer.

(d) Yo sé defender lo mío.   I know how to defend what is
                                     mine.

The possessive pronoun has also a neuter form: lo mío, lo tuyo,
lo suyo, lo nuestro, lo vuestro, lo suyo. The neuter pronoun
does not refer to any particular noun but rather to a group of
things, e.g. lo mío may mean the following: what is mine, my
possession, my people, etc.

NOTE: The possessive pronoun drops the definite article after
the verb ser when no distinction in ownership is emphasized:

Es suyo.   It is his.
Son nuestros.   They are ours.
BUT:
Ése es el mío.   That one is mine (specifically
                                     the one that belongs to me).

46. *Estúdiese en el apéndice el presente de indicativo, el pretérito,
el imperfecto, el futuro, el condicional y los tiempos compuestos
de los verbos irregulares* caer, creer, leer.

IV. Ejercicios

A. *Contéstense las preguntas siguientes usando oraciones completas en español:*

1. ¿Dónde se venden los billetes para la corrida?
2. ¿Por qué tendrán que hacer cola los dos amigos?
3. ¿Es la corrida solamente un deporte? ¿Por qué?
4. ¿Ha asistido Ud. a alguna corrida?
5. ¿Le gustaría a Ud. asistir a una corrida?
6. ¿Cree Ud. que la corrida es demasiado sangrienta (bloody)?
7. ¿Quiénes son los dos protagonistas de la corrida?
8. ¿Qué dijo un escritor norteamericano acerca de la corrida?
9. ¿Dónde tiene lugar la corrida?
10. ¿Dónde están los asientos de los dos amigos?
11. ¿Cómo empieza la corrida?
12. ¿Qué hace el picador?
13. ¿Qué hace el banderillero?

14. ¿Quién mata al toro?
15. ¿Qué cualidades debe tener un buen matador?
16. ¿Cuál es más emocionante, una corrida o un partido de fútbol?

B. *Escríbase una pregunta en español con cada una de las «frases importantes» que siguen:*

1. el billete al sol
2. tener lugar
3. asistir a
4. por favor
5. por allí abajo

C. *Escríbase una oración completa en español con cada una de las «frases importantes» que siguen:*

1. al son de
2. el billete a la sombra
3. sangre fría
4. por fin
5. apurarse
6. a caballo
7. hacer fila
8. darle pases

D. *Hágase una oración, en español, con el presente y el futuro de cada uno de los verbos siguientes:*

1. decir
2. caer
3. levantarse
4. poner
5. creer
6. irse
7. salir
8. leer
9. gustar

E. *Complétense las oraciones siguientes traduciendo los verbos entre paréntesis al español:*

1. (Have you seen) a nuestro amigo Antonio? *¿Ha visto*
2. Yo fuí a su casa pero él (had left). *había salido*
3. Dentro de dos días esta temporada (will have ended). *habrá terminado*
4. Apenas (he had eaten) se levantó y se fué. *hubo comido*
5. Me dijo que él (would have arranged) todo. *habría arreglado*
6. (I have written) a mis padres. *He escrito*
7. Nosotros (had done) todo el trabajo. *habían hecho*
8. Ana en su lugar, no lo (would have said). *habría dicho*
9. Antonio y su padre (had not returned) cuando llegamos. *no habían vuelto*
10. ¿Quién (has opened) aquellas ventanas? *ha abierto*
11. Luego que Pedro (had entered) empezó a hablar. *hubo entrado*
12. Dentro de dos horas la corrida (will have ended). *habrá terminado*
13. ¿Quién no (has read) esa novela? *ha leído*
14. Dolores (has believed) que lo hiciste. *ha creído*

F. *Complétense las oraciones siguientes traduciendo las formas inglesas al español:*

1. (My) libros están aquí. ¿Dónde están (yours)?
2. (His) padres se quedaron en Sevilla pero (mine) llegaron ayer.
3. (Her) amigas tomaron el metro; (ours) tomaron el ómnibus.
4. (My dear friend), ¿cómo estás?
5. (Our) casa está en el centro; (theirs) está en las afueras.
6. Algunos (friends of mine) me visitaron la semana pasada.
7. Este asiento es (his) y ése es (hers).
8. He leído (my) periódico y Carlos ha leído (his).
9. El matador tiene confianza en (his men).
10. La corrida es popular en los países hispanoamericanos pero no en (ours).

G. *Tradúzcase al español:*

1. What a crowd! What excitement!
2. Have you ever seen a bullfight?
3. The matador has shown coolness and courage.
4. He has not spoken to me for two weeks.
5. A bullfight is a very moving spectacle.
6. The bull charges out of the bull-pen with ferocity.
7. If we don't get in soon, the show will have already begun.
8. This seat is mine and that one is yours.
9. Didn't I tell you that you would have enjoyed it?
10. Let's go in. Our seats are down there.
11. We thought that we would have to stand in line.
12. You're mistaken; the trumpet has not yet sounded.
13. Why have the bailiffs asked the president for the key to the bull-pen?

H. *Prepárese una composición oral de tres minutos empleando uno de los temas siguientes:*

1. En el hotel
2. La corrida de toros

I. *Dictado tomado de la conversación «La corrida de toros», pp. 62–64.*

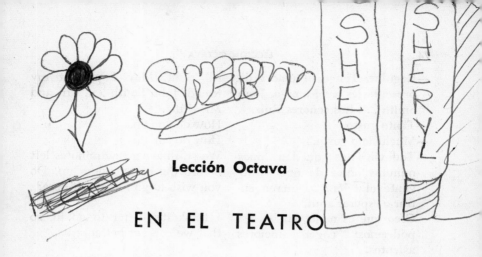

Lección Octava

EN EL TEATRO

1. Conversación

[*Léase en voz alta varias veces y apréndase de memoria.*]

—Buenas noches, Juan.

Good evening, John.

—Buenas noches. ¿Has comprado las entradas?

Good evening. Have you bought the tickets?

—No, porque el señor Ruiz nos ha invitado y ha ofrecido comprarlas.

No, because Mr. Ruiz has invited us and has offered to buy them.

—¿Ah, sí? A mí no me gusta molestar a nadie.

Ha, really? I don't like to impose upon anyone.

—No es ninguna molestia. Al contrario tendrá mucho gusto en hacerlo.

It's no imposition at all. On the contrary he'll be very pleased to do it.

—Pues, está bien. ¿Dónde lo encontramos?

Well, all right. Where do we meet him?

—En frente del teatro. Espero que lleve a su señora porque ella está al corriente de todos los sucesos teatrales.

In front of the theatre. I hope he takes his wife because she is well informed on all the events of the theatre.

(Más tarde delante del teatro)

(Later in front of the theatre)

—Buenas noches, señores. ¿Cómo están?

Good evening, Mr. and Mrs. Ruiz. How are you?

—Bien, gracias, y Ud.?

Fine, thank you, and you?

—Regular. Tengo el placer de presentarles a mi amigo, Juan Smith . . . Los señores Ruiz.

—Tanto gusto.

—Muchísimo gusto.

—Todavía nos quedan unos minutos antes de que se levante el telón. ¿Quieren entrar o esperar aquí?

—Creo que es mejor entrar, así podremos coger mejores asientos.

—Y podremos charlar un poquito.

(Entran y el acomodador los lleva a las butacas.)

—¿Qué vamos a ver esta noche?

—Se estrena una comedia de un joven autor que ha tenido mucho éxito en los últimos años.

—Espero que resulte divertida. Será el primer drama en español que habré visto. En un teatro de Nueva York yo ví «Bodas de Sangre» y por la televisión «Canción de Cuna» y «La Casa de Bernarda Alba», pero traducidos al inglés.

—¡No me diga! ¿Qué le parecieron?

—Me gustaron mucho. Pero me gustan más los dramas del Siglo de Oro. He leído unas

All right. May I present my friend, John Smith . . . Mr. and Mrs. Ruiz.

How do you do.

How do you do.

We still have a few minutes left before the curtain goes up. Do you wish to go in or wait here?

I think it's better to go in, so that we can get better seats.

And we can chat a bit.

(They enter and the usher takes them to the orchestra seats.)

What are we going to see tonight?

The opening of a new comedy by a young author who has had great success in the last few years.

I hope it will be amusing. It will be the first Spanish play that I shall have seen. I saw *Blood Wedding* in a New York theatre and *Cradle Song* and *The House of Bernarda Alba* on television, but translated into English.

You don't say! How did you like them?

I liked them very much. But I like the plays of the Golden Age more. I have read works by

cuantas obras de Lope de Vega, Calderón, y Tirso de Molina.

—Ah, claro. Las obras de esos dramaturgos son un espejo que reflejan la vida y el espíritu de aquella época.

—Es necesario comprender los temas centrales de aquellos autores para comprender el alma española de entonces.

—Sí, la idea del honor, la religión católica con sus temas teológicos del libre albedrío, la gracia, etc.

—Y la idea del monarca que representa la justicia, la cual es igual para el noble así como para el campesino.

—Se apagan las luces.

—Sí, el primer acto está para empezar. ¡Ojalá que sea interesante!

Lope de Vega, Calderón, and Tirso de Molina.

Oh, of course. The works of those dramatists are a mirror that reflect the life and spirit of that age.

It is necessary for one to understand the central themes of those authors to understand the Spanish soul of that time.

Yes, the concept of honor, the Catholic religion with its theological themes of free will, grace, etc.

And the idea of the king who represents justice which is equal for the nobleman as well as for the peasant.

They're dimming the lights.

Yes, the first act is about to begin. Oh, I do hope it will be interesting!

II. Frases Importantes

[*Apréndanse de memoria.*]

apagar la luz	to put out the light
así como	as well as
buenas noches	good evening, good night
coger asientos	to get seats
delante de	in front of
el día de estreno	opening day, opening night (*of a play*)
el estreno	the first showing, the debut, the opening performance
estrenarse	to show for the first time
en frente de	in front of

nte de	to be informed about, to be up on
(unos minutos)	we have (a few minutes) left (*lit.*, a few minutes are left to us)
¡ojalá (que)!	I wish (that)! Oh would that! (*from the Arabic "May Allah grant"*)
presentar (a una persona)	to introduce, to present (someone)
se levanta el telón	the curtain rises
subir (levantar) el telón	to raise the curtain
tanto gusto; mucho gusto; muchísimo gusto; encantado	how do you do (*in acknowledgment of an introduction*)
tengo el placer de presentarles	may I present (I have the pleasure to present)

III. Puntos Gramaticales

47. Los modos (Moods)

There are five moods in Spanish: the infinitive, the indicative, the conditional, the subjunctive and the imperative. The infinitive denotes the meaning of the verb in the abstract, without expressing time, number or person; the indicative expresses the fact of the verb as real or objective; the conditional indicates it as not real but possible; the imperative expresses it as a command; and the subjunctive expresses it as a desire, a supposition, a probabilty, an expectation or a fact with some emotional connotation.

48. El presente del subjuntivo (Present subjunctive)

(a)

PRESENT INDICATIVE	PRESENT SUBJUNCTIVE		
hablø	hable	(*that*)	*I may speak*
	hables	"	*you may speak*
	hable	"	*he, she, you may speak*
	hablemos	"	*we may speak*
	habléis	"	*you may speak*
	hablen	"	*they, you may speak*

comprend**ø**	comprend**a**	comprend**amos**
	comprend**as**	comprend**áis**
	comprend**a**	comprend**an**
viv**ø**	viv**a**	viv**amos**
	viv**as**	viv**áis**
	viv**a**	viv**an**
teng**ø**	teng**a**	teng**amos**
	teng**as**	teng**áis**
	teng**a**	teng**an**
dig**ø**	dig**a**	dig**amos**
	dig**as**	dig**áis**
	dig**a**	dig**an**

The present subjunctive of all regular and most irregular verbs is formed by adding to the stem of the first person singular of the present indicative the endings –e, –es, –e, –emos, –éis, –en for –ar verbs and –a, –as, –a, –amos, –áis, –an for –er and –ir verbs.

(b) These six verbs do not follow the above rule:

dar: dé, des, dé, demos, deis, den
estar: esté estés, esté, estemos, estéis, estén
haber: haya, hayas, haya, hayamos, hayáis, hayan
ir: vaya vayas, vaya, vayamos, vayáis, vayan
saber: sepa, sepas, sepa, sepamos, sepáis, sepan
ser: sea, seas, sea, seamos, seáis, sean

49. El uso del subjuntivo en cláusulas substantivas (Use of the subjunctive in noun clauses) *

(a) Quiero que él venga con nosotros.	I want him to come with us.
El director desea que los actores se preparen.	The director wishes that the actors get ready.
El capitán manda que todos salgan.	The captain orders all to come out.

*A noun clause is one which is the object or subject of the verb. In the sentence, Quiero que él venga con nosotros, Quiero (I wish) is the independent clause, él venga con nosotros (him to come with us) is a noun clause dependent upon and the object of quiero. Note that verbs of volition are found in the independent clause; the subjunctive is found in the noun clause.

El doctor Olmedo nos acon-   *Dr. Olmedo advises us to take*
seja que tomemos vita-   *vitamins.*
minas.

Le pido que me ayude.   *I beg you to help me.*

The subjunctive is used in noun clauses after verbs of volition.
Some common verbs of volition are: **desear** (*to wish*), **querer**
(*to want*), **mandar** (*to order*), **avisar** (*to notify, warn*), **advertir**
(*to notify, warn*), **permitir** (*to permit*), **dejar** (*to let*), **prohibir**
(*to prohibit*), **evitar** (*to avoid*), **impedir** (*to oppose, block*),
pedir (*to ask for*), **rogar** (*to request*), **preferir** (*to prefer*),
aconsejar (*to advise*).

(b) **Temo que no me diga todo.**   *I'm afraid that he isn't telling*
    me everything.

Esperan que la comedia sea   *They hope the comedy is amus-*
divertida.   *ing.*

Se alegra de que estén listos   *She is happy that they are*
para salir.   *ready to leave.*

The subjunctive is used in noun clauses after verbs of emotion:
sentir (*to be sorry*), **temer** (*to fear*), **alegrarse de** (*to be glad*),
gustar (*to like*), **enojarse** (*to be annoyed*), **esperar** (*to hope*),
sorprender (*to surprise*), **molestar** (*to bother*).

(c) **Dudo que estén en casa.**   *I doubt that they are home.*

No cree que el drama tenga   *He doesn't believe that the play*
mucho éxito.   *will be very successful.*

Niega que la pieza sea ori-   *She denies that the play is*
ginal.   *original.*

The subjunctive is used in noun clauses after verbs of doubt
or denial.

NOTE:

(1) When the subject of the verb in the dependent clause is
the same as that of the independent clause the infinitive,
not the subjunctive is used:

Quiero ir con él.   *I want to go with him.*

Dudan poder ayudarnos.   *They doubt that they can*
    help us.

Siento no poder encontrarlo   *I'm sorry that I cannot meet*
antes de las once.   *him before eleven.*

Niego haber tomado su   *I deny that I took his book.*
libro.

(2) **Creer** used affirmatively does not take the subjunctive. When used interrogatively it may take the subjunctive if the expected reply is negative; i.e., the speaker expects the listener to share his doubt:

Creo que vendrá.	*I think he will come.*
No cree Ud. que vendrá?	*Don't you think he'll come?*
Cree Ud. que yo haga eso?	*Do you think that I would do that?*

(d) **Es importante que Ud. lo compre hoy.**   *It's important that you buy it today.*

Es preciso que Juan estudie mucho.   *It's necessary for John to study a great deal.*

Es lástima que no tenga amigos fieles.   *It's a pity that he doesn't have faithful friends.*

The subjunctive is used after such impersonal expressions as: **es preciso** (*it is necessary*); **es importante** (*it is important*); **es menester** (*it is necessary*); **es necesario** (*it is necessary*); **es posible** (*it is possible*); **es imposible** (*it is impossible*); **es probable** (*it is probable*); **es lástima** (*it's a pity*); **parece increíble** (*it is incredible*); **parece mentira** (*it is incredible*); **puede ser** (*it is possible*); **es natural** (*it is natural*).

NOTE:

(1) **Es cierto que viene.**   *It is certain that he will come.*

Es claro que puede ayudarnos.   *It is evident that he can help us.*

The subjunctive is not used after an impersonal expression that expresses certainty.

(2) **Es importante estudiar.**   *It is important to study.*

Es imposible hacerlo.   *It's impossible to do it.*

The subjunctive is not used after an impersonal expression. if the subject of the dependent verb is not a specific person or thing. The sentence then becomes a generalization.

50. *Estúdiese en el apéndice el presente de indicativo, el pretérito, el imperfecto, el futuro, el condicional y el presente de subjuntivo de los verbos irregulares andar, traer, valer.*

IV. Ejercicios

A. *Contéstense las preguntas siguientes usando oraciones completas en español:*

1. ¿Por qué no ha comprado los billetes José?
2. ¿Quiere Juan que se moleste el señor Ruiz?
3. ¿Dónde encontraron a los señores Ruiz?
4. ¿Por qué espera José que el señor Ruiz lleve a su señora?
5. ¿Qué se dice para presentar a una persona?
6. ¿Qué se dice después de ser presentado?
7. ¿Cómo se llama el amigo de José?
8. ¿Por qué quieren entrar antes de que empiece la comedia?
9. ¿Qué drama verán?
10. ¿Qué dramas españoles ha visto Juan en Nueva York?
11. ¿Quiénes escribieron estos dramas?
12. ¿Ha visto Ud. un drama español?
13. Nombre Ud. tres dramaturgos famosos del Siglo de Oro.
14. ¿Qué reflejan las obras de esos dramaturgos?
15. ¿Cuáles son los temas centrales en las obras de estos autores?

B. *Escríbase una pregunta en español con cada una de las «frases importantes» que siguen:*

1. apagar la luz
2. el día de estreno
3. levantarse el telón
4. así como
5. estar al corriente de

C. *Escríbase una oración completa en español con cada una de las «frases importantes» que siguen:*

1. ¡ojalá!
2. coger asientos
3. presentar a
4. delante de
5. buenas noches
6. estrenarse

D. *Cámbiense al singular los verbos de las oraciones siguientes:*

1. Traemos la ropa sucia a la lavandera.
2. Anduvimos por las calles de la ciudad.
3. Estas hoyas no valen mucho.
4. Andaban de Ceca en Meca.

5. Estos relojes no andan bien.
6. ¿Cuánto valdrán?
7. ¿Trajisteis el agua?
8. ¿Por qué andan Uds. tan despacio?

E. *Complétense las oraciones siguientes con la forma correspondiente del presente de subjuntivo:*

1. (ir)   No creo que ellos _____.
2. (ser)   No es posible que él _____ tan malo.
3. (estar)   Quiero que ellos _____ listos para salir.
4. (hablar)   Deseo que tú _____ con mi padre.
5. (vivir)   Su madre le aconseja que _____ en paz con todos.
6. (comprender)   Dudo que Ud. _____ lo que yo he dicho.
7. (traer)   Luis pide que Antonio _____ el libro.
8. (tener)   ¡Ojalá que _____ éxito la comedia!
9. (venir)   Teme que tú no _____ mañana.
10. (comer)   El doctor prohibe que Juan _____ dulces.
11. (llevar)   Antonio espera que el señor Ruiz _____ a su señora.
12. (andar)   Es necesario que al auto _____ bien.
13. (hacer)   Me alegro de que ellos lo _____.
14. (valer)   Es lástima que este billete no _____ nada.
15. (salir)   Es posible que Carlos _____.

F. *Póngase la forma correspondiente del verbo en las oraciones siguientes:*

1. (ser)   Él duda que nosotros _____ españoles.
2. (estudiar)   Es menester que ellos _____ más.
3. (poder)   Es imposible _____ hacerlo.
4. (venir)   Quiere _____ con nosotros.
5. (estar)   Es cierto que María _____ en su cuarto.
6. (ayudar)   Me piden que _____ a su familia.
7. (tener)   Es claro que no _____ el libro.
8. (venir)   Se alegra de que nosotros _____ a visitarla.
9. (leer)   Temo _____ el telegrama que me ha mandado mi familia.
10. (salir)   El capitán manda que los soldados _____.

11. (ir)   Prefiero _____ con mi padre.
12. (hacer)   Creo que Luis lo _____.
13. (comprar)   Es importante que Ud. _____ un auto nuevo.
14. (ser)   Niegan que el drama _____ original.
15. (dar)   Sienten que el señor Ruiz no les _____ los billetes.

G. *Escríbase una oración en español con cada uno de los verbos siguientes:*

1. permitir	6. pedir	11. creer
2. preferir	7. escribir	12. esperar
3. es difícil	8. es preciso	13. sentir
4. dudar	9. desear	14. decir
5. negar	10. rogar	15. valer

H. *Tradúzcase al español:*

1. Mr. and Mrs. Ruiz bought two tickets and the usher led them to their seats.
2. Luis hopes that the play will be sucessful.
3. They are afraid that we shall not see the curtain go up.
4. It is impossible to help them in this problem.
5. The Spanish playwrights of the Golden Age often treated theological themes.
6. It is evident that they do not like this play.
7. May I present my friend, Antonio Rivera? How do you do?
8. How do you like our city? I like it very much.
9. I hope that you will come again next year.
10. Oh, would that I could!

I. *Prepárese una composición oral de tres minutos empleando uno de los temas siguientes:*

1. En el teatro
2. En el metro
3. Los dramaturgos españoles

J. *Dictado tomado de la conversación «En el teatro», pp. 73–75.*

Lección Novena

EN EL RESTAURANTE

I. Conversación

[*Léase en voz alta varias veces y apréndase de memoria.*]

—¡Qué buen restaurante es éste! / What a fine restaurant this is!

—Es uno de los más lujosos de Madrid. / It's one of the most luxurious in Madrid.

—Y sus precios son los más altos, ¿no? / And its prices are the highest, aren't they?

—Quizás, pero aunque los precios sean altos no importa con tal que comamos bien. / Perhaps, but although the prices may be high is not important provided we eat well.

—Está bien, si pagas tú. / All right, if you pay the bill.

—¿Quieres un aperitivo primero? Te dará apetito. / Would you like an aperitif? It will give you an appetite.

—No, gracias, no necesito aperitivo porque ya tengo mucha hambre. / No, thanks, I don't need an aperitif because I'm already very hungry.

—Bueno, todo te gustará entonces porque como dice el refrán, «el hambre es la mejor salsa». / Good, you'll like everything then because as the proverb says, "hunger is the best sauce."

—Aquí viene el camarero con la lista. / Here comes the waiter with the menu.

—A ver, ¿qué hay de bueno? / Let's see, what's good?

—Hay algunos de mis entre- / There are a few of my favorite

meses favoritos, anchovas en
aceite, salmón escabechado,
coctel de camarones o cangrejo. . . .

appetizers, anchovies in oil,
pickled salmon, shrimp or crab
cocktail. . . .

—Nunca he visto tantos platos
en un menú. Mira, biftec con
hongos fritos, chuletas de
cerdo, costillas de ternera,
rosbif. . . .

I've never seen so many dishes
on a menu. Look, beefsteak with
fried mushrooms, pork chops,
veal cutlets, roast beef. . . .

—Yo voy a tomar un coctel de
almejas, sopa de cebolla, y en
vez de carne voy a tomar
pescado.

I'm going to have a clam cocktail, onion soup, and instead of
meat I'll have fish.

—¿Por qué no pruebas una
paella valenciana?

Why don't you try a "paella
valenciana?"

—¿Cómo la preparan?

How do they prepare it?

—Con arroz, pollo, almejas,
camarones, pimientos y gui-
santes; todo cocido al horno.

With rice, chicken, clams,
shrimp, red peppers, peas, and
it's baked.

—Parece muy sabrosa. Sí, voy a
probarlo.

It sounds very tasty. Yes, I'll
try it.

—Yo tomo solamente pavo asado
y una ensalada de lechuga
con tomate porque estoy a
régimen.

I'm having roast turkey and a
lettuce and tomato salad only
because I'm on a diet.

—Una buena comida necesita un
buen vino, ¿verdad? ¿ Qué
deseas, vino blanco o vino
tinto?

A good meal deserves some good
wine, doesn't it? What will you
have, white or red wine?

—Según los gastrónomos, vino
tinto con la carne y vino
blanco con el pescado y el
pollo, ¿no es así?

According to the gourmets, red
wine goes with meat and white
wine with fish and chicken, isn't
it so?

—Creo que sí. Entonces vino
blanco para los dos.

I think so. Then white wine for
the both of us.

—¿Qué postre deseas, helado,
pastel de manzana, torta de
queso, o fruta fresca?

What dessert do you want, ice
cream, apple pie, cheese cake, or
fresh fruit?

—Fruta fresca, sandía o melón si lo tienen.	Fresh fruit, watermelon or melon if they have it.

. . .   . . .

—¡Ah, sí que ha sido una comida sabrosísima!	Oh boy, that certainly was a very tasty meal!
—Y ahora déme la cuenta.	And now give me the check.
—No, no, pago yo.	No, no, I'm paying.
—Está bien, entonces yo dejo la propina.	All right, I'll leave the tip then.

II. Frases Importantes

[*Apréndanse de memoria.*]

a ver	let's see
al horno	in the oven
carne asada	roast meat
cocido al horno	baked
con tal que; siempre que	provided that
el bisté (biftec, bistec), coctel, rosbif	the beefsteak, cocktail, roast beef (*words borrowed from English*)
el menú; la lista	the menu
estar a régimen	to be on a diet
fruta fresca	fresh fruit (*eaten at the end of the meal in many countries*)
¿no? (¿no es verdad?)	isn't it so? aren't they?
para los dos	for the two (of us, of them)
pescado frito	fried fish
¿qué hay de bueno?	what's good?
tener calor	to be hot (warm)
tener frío	to be cold
tener (mucha) hambre	to be (very) hungry
tener miedo	to be afraid
tener sed	to be thirsty
vino blanco (tinto)	white (red) wine

Gramaticales

...rito imperfecto de subjuntivo (Imperfect subjunctive)

PRETERITE			IMPERFECT SUBJUNCTIVE		
hablarøn	hablara	or	hablase	(that)	I might speak
	hablaras		hablases	"	you might speak
	hablara		hablase	"	he, she, you might speak
	habláramos		hablásemos	"	we might speak
	hablarais		hablaseis	"	you might speak
	hablaran		hablasen	"	they, you might speak
comprendierøn	comprendiera	or	comprendiese		
	comprendieras		comprendieses		
	comprendiera		comprendiese		
	comprendiéramos		comprendiésemos		
	comprendierais		comprendieseis		
	comprendieran		comprendiesen		
vivierøn	viviera	or	viviese		
	vivieras		vivieses		
	viviera		viviese		
	viviéramos		viviésemos		
	vivierais		vivieseis		
	vivieran		viviesen		
dijerøn	dijera	or	dijese		
	dijeras		dijeses		
	dijera		dijese		
	dijéramos		dijésemos		
	dijerais		dijeseis		
	dijeran		dijesen		
fuerøn	fuera	or	fuese		
	fueras		fueses		
	fuera		fuese		
	fuéramos		fuésemos		
	fuerais		fueseis		
	fueran		fuesen		

tuvier**ø**n	tuvie*ra*	or	tuvie*se*
	tuvie*ras*		tuvie*ses*
	tuvie*ra*		tuvie*se*
	tuvié*ramos*		tuvié*semos*
	tuvie*rais*		tuvie*seis*
	tuvie*ran*		tuvie*sen*

The imperfect subjunctive has two forms which may be used interchangeably.* The imperfect subjunctive of all verbs, regular or irregular, is formed by changing the –ron ending of the third person plural of the preterite indicative to –ra, –ras, –ra, –ramos, –rais, –ran or –se, –ses, –se, –semos, –seis, –sen.

52. **El subjuntivo en cláusulas relativas** (Subjunctive in relative—adjective—clauses)

Busco un cocinero que sepa preparar una buena paella.	*I'm looking for a cook who can prepare a good paella.*
Busco un restaurante que tenga comidas sabrosas.	*I'm looking for a restaurant which has tasty meals.*
No tengo a nadie con quien yo pueda contar.	*I have no one I can rely on.*
No hay nadie que quiera ayudarme.	*There is no one who wishes to help me.*
Antonio se sentía capaz de comer todos los platos que hubiera en el menú.	*Anthony felt capable of eating all the dishes which were on the menu.*

The subjunctive is used in an adjective clause † when the noun or pronoun it modifies is indefinite or nonexistent.

NOTE: The pronouns **cualquiera** and **quienquiera** are, because of their indefinite nature, always followed by the subjunctive:

Cualquiera que sea su decisión la aceptaré.	*Whatever his decision may be I'll accept it.*
Quienquiera que venga, déjelo entrar.	*Whosoever may come, let him enter.*

* For exception see pp. 98–99, section 57 (a); p. 100, section 58 (d).
† An adjective clause is one that modifies a noun or a pronoun and is introduced by a relative pronoun.

53. El subjuntivo en cláusulas adverbiales (Subjunctive in adverbial clauses) *

(a) Purpose

Te he traído a este restaurante para que comas bien.	*I've brought you to this restaurant so that you may eat well.*
Se sentaron de manera que pudieran ver los transeúntes.	*They sat so that they could see the passers-by.*
Llamó al sereno a fin de que abriese la puerta.	*He called the night watchman in order that he might open the door.*

The subjunctive is used in adverbial clauses to express purpose. These clauses are usually introduced by the following conjunctions: **a fin de que, a que, para que** (*in order that*), **de manera que** (*so as, so that*), **de modo que** (*so that, in order that*).

(b) Negative Result

Se fué sin que su madre lo viese.	*He left without his mother seeing him.*
Nada ocurría en el pueblo que no se supiese inmediatamente.	*Nothing happened in the town without its being known immediately.*

The subjunctive is used in adverbial clauses to express negative result. These clauses are usually introduced by the conjunctions **sin que** (*without*), and **que no** (*without*) after a negative.

(c) Temporal

Le daré tus recuerdos cuando lo vea.	*I shall give him your regards when I see him.*
No podemos hacer nada más que esperar hasta que llegue un tranvía.	*We cannot do anything more than wait until a trolley comes.*
No quería esperar hasta que llegase el ómnibus.	*She didn't want to wait until the bus arrived.*
Se lo diré tan pronto como lo vea.	*I shall tell him as soon as I see him.*

* An adverbial clause is one which modifies a verb and is introduced by a conjunctive adverb.

The subjunctive is used in adverbial clauses to express future time in relation to the main clause.

NOTE: The indicative is used in adverbial clauses when the time expressed is present or past:

Cuando viene se sienta en esta mesa.	*When he comes he sits at this table.*
Se lo dije cuando lo ví.	*I told it to him when I saw him.*
Esperamos hasta que llegó el tranvía.	*We waited until the trolley arrived.*

(d) Proviso and Supposition

Iré al cine con tal que me acompañes.	*I'll go to the movies provided that you accompany me.*
Terminará la lección siempre que sus amigos no vayan a interrumpirlo.	*He will finish the lesson, provided his friends don't interrupt him.*
En caso de que venga dígale que lo esperamos en el café.	*In case he comes tell him we're waiting for him in the café.*

The subjunctive is used in adverbial clauses of proviso and supposition. These clauses are usually introduced by the following conjunctions: **con tal que, siempre que** (*provided that*), **a condición de que** (*on condition that*), **dado que, en caso de que** (*in case*) **a menos que, a no ser que** (*unless*), **excepto que** (*except that*), **salvo que** (*save that*), **supuesto que, supóngase que** (*supposing*).

(e) Concession

Tendré que estudiar esta noche aun cuando no tenga ganas.	*I'll have to study tonight even though I may not feel like it.*
No podrá cenar con nosotros aunque él quiera.	*He cannot come to supper with us although he wants to.*

The subjunctive is used in adverbial clauses of concession after the following conjunctions: **aunque, bien que, por más que** (*although*), **aun cuando** (*even though*), **a pesar de que** (*in spite of*).

NOTE: The indicative is used in an adverbial clause of concession when it expresses a fact:

No quiso cenar con nosotros aunque lo invitamos muchas veces.	*He didn't want to sup with us although we invited him many times.*

54. **La correlación de los tiempos del subjuntivo** (Sequence of tenses of the subjunctive) *

Quiero (querré) que él venga con nosotros.	*I want (shall want) him to come with us.*
Quería (quise) que él viniese con nosotros.	*I wanted him to come with us.*
Querría que él viniese con nosotros.	*I should want him to come with us.*

In general, when the verb in the main clause is in the present or future indicative, the verb of the dependent clause will be in the present subjunctive. When the verb of the main clause is in a past tense of the indicative or in the conditional, the verb of the dependent clause will be in the imperfect subjunctive.

NOTE: It is possible, however (when the action of the dependent clause has already occurred), to have an imperfect subjunctive follow a present tense in the main clause:

Siento que él no viniese con nosotros.	*I'm sorry that he didn't come with us.*

55. *Estúdiese en el apéndice el presente de indicativo, el pretérito, el imperfecto, el futuro, el condicional, el presente de subjuntivo y el pretérito imperfecto de subjuntivo de los verbos irregulares* conducir, oír.

IV. Ejercicios

A. *Contéstense las preguntas siguientes usando oraciones completas en español:*

1. ¿Cómo son los precios de un restaurante lujoso?
2. ¿Quién pagó la última vez que Ud. fué a un restaurante?
3. ¿Toma Ud. un aperitivo antes de comer? ¿Por qué?
4. ¿Cuál es la mejor salsa?

* See also p. 98, section 56 (c).

5. ¿Qué quiere decir el refrán, «el hambre es la mejor salsa»?
6. ¿Qué es un menú?
7. ¿Cómo se llama el que da la lista a los amigos?
8. ¿Cuáles son sus entremeses favoritos de Ud.?
9. ¿Cuál le gusta a Ud. más, carne o pescado?
10. ¿Cuál es su plato favorito?
11. ¿Cómo se prepara una paella valenciana?
12. ¿Qué toma el amigo que está a régimen?
13. ¿Qué necesita una buena comida?
14. ¿Qué dicen los gastrónomos?
15. ¿Qué postre le gusta a Ud. más?
16. Antes de salir del restaurante, ¿qué da Ud. al camarero?

B. *Escríbase una pregunta en español con cada una de las «frases importantes» que siguen:*

1. carne asada
2. tener sed
3. cocido al horno
4. fruta fresca
5. tener calor
6. estar a régimen

C. *Escríbase una oración completa en español con cada una de las «frases importantes» que siguen:*

1. con tal que
2. pescado frito
3. tener hambre
4. tener miedo
5. tener frío
6. vino tinto
7. para los dos
8. al horno

D. *Complétense las oraciones siguientes con la forma correcta del verbo entre paréntesis:*

1. (venir)   Quise que él _viniera_ conmigo.
2. (estar)   No creía que ellos _estuvieran_ en casa.
3. (ir)   Era preciso que tú _fueras_ la oficina.
4. (ser)   Buscaba un hombre que _fuera_ honorable.
5. (tener)   Temía que yo no _tuviera_ éxito.
6. (comprar) Querría que Uds. _____ los libros. _comprara_
7. (hacer)   Su padre le dió el dinero para que _____ el viaje. _hiciera_
8. (querer)   Dudaba que vosotros _quisierais_ acompañarle.
9. (dar)   Pidieron que ella les _____ la dirección. _dieran_

10. (saber)   Buscaba un muchacho que _____ *supiera* hablar español.
11. (poder)   Se sentó de manera que _____ *pudiera* ver la gente salir.
12. (poner)   No quería que tú _____ *pusieras* la mesa allí.
13. (decir)   Se fueron antes de que yo les *dijera* nada.
14. (salir)   Me despertó para que yo *saliera* temprano.
15. (llegar)   No querían esperar hasta que *llegara* el ómnibus.
16. (oír)   Quería que yo *oyera* los poemas que había escrito.
17. (conducir) Era importante que el director *condujera* los negocios.
18. (leer)   No creo que Carlos *lea* esta novela.

E. *Cámbiense los verbos de las oraciones siguientes a los tiempos pasados:*

1. Quiere que yo salga. *Quiso — saliera*
2. Dudo que él sepa la verdad. *Dudaba ... fuera*
3. Es necesario que tú estudies más. *Era ... estudiara*
4. Mi padre escribe que yo deba economizar. *escribió ... debera*
5. Promete venir al cine con tal que nosotros compremos los billetes. *Prometió ... compraramos*
6. Busco un señor que hable español. *Buscaba ... hablara*
7. Te doy el dinero para que pagues tus deudas. *daba ... pagara*
8. Puede salir sin que nadie lo vea. *Pudo ... viera*
9. Aunque los precios son altos no importa porque comemos bien. *importaba comiera*
10. Es importante que una buena comida tenga un buen vino. *Era - tuviera*
11. Quiero que oigas toda la verdad. *Quiso — oyeras*
12. Busco un hombre que conozca la ciudad. *Busqué — conociera*

F. *Complétense las oraciones siguientes en español:*

1. Le hablaré (when I see him).
2. Háblele (before he leaves).
3. Iré al teatro (even though I may not have) el dinero.
4. Estudió toda la noche (even though he didn't feel like it).
5. Busca una criada que (knows how to cook).
6. Tenemos una criada que (knows how to cook very well).

7. ¿Hay alguien que (will help me)?
8. Salió (without his father seeing him).
9. Esperó (until his friend arrived).
10. Esperaremos (until the trolley arrives).
11. No hay nadie que (drives the car well).
12. (Although he heard) la misma canción no la recordó.

G. *Tradúzcase al español:*

1. These prices are high aren't they? No, I don't think so.
2. He is afraid that the prices will be too high.
3. I'll go to that luxurious restaurant, provided you pay the bill.
4. I was hungry and I ate everything, although I was on a diet.
5. The menu offered many tasty dishes.
6. They stopped in order to have a beer because they were very thirsty.
7. I'm looking for a maid who is not afraid to work.
8. There is no one who can cook like my mother.
9. We shall leave as soon as he finishes his meal.
10. My father didn't allow (permit) us to leave the table.
11. I am going to have a clam cocktail, onion soup, a steak with fried mushrooms, ice cream and coffee.
12. When I pay the bill, I always leave the waiter a good tip.
13. I called him but I am sure that he didn't hear me.
14. Do you want me to conduct the group to the restaurant?

H. *Prepárese una composición oral de tres minutos usando uno de los temas siguientes:*

1. En el restaurante
2. La comida en mi casa

I. *Dictado tomado de la conversación* «En el restaurante», pp. 83–85.

Lección Décima

EL MUSEO DEL PRADO

I. Conversación

[*Léase en voz alta varias veces y apréndase de memoria.*]

—¡Qué mal tiempo!

What bad weather!

—Por eso he traído mi paraguas y mi impermeable.

That's why I brought my umbrella and my raincoat.

—Sería mejor posponer nuestra visita al Prado para otro día.

It would be better to postpone our trip to the Prado.

—Aunque llueva todo el día iré de todos modos.

Although it rains all day I shall go anyway.

—¡Pero, hombre, si llueve a cántaros! Podremos ir mañana.

But, man, it's raining cats and dogs! We can go tomorrow.

—Y si lloviese mañana, y pasado mañana, y toda la semana no podría ver nada según tú modo de pensar.

And if it should rain tomorrow, and the day after, and all week, I would not be able to see anything, according to your way of thinking.

—¡Qué prisa, qué afán, cálmete! Hay bastante tiempo para todo!

What hurry, what anxiety, calm down! There's enough time for everything!

—¡Ojalá que tuviese tiempo! Tengo solamente un par de semanas.

Oh would that there were enough time! I only have a couple of weeks.

—Ahora comprendo porque la enfermedad del corazón mata más personas en los Estados Unidos que cualquier otra.

Now I understand why heart disease kills more persons in the United States than any other.

—Vamos, quizás el cielo se despeje.

Let's go, perhaps it will clear up.

—Sí, vamos, . . . tú a sufrir un ataque cardíaco y yo a coger una pulmonía.

Yes, let's go, . . . you to get a heart attack and I to catch pneumonia.

. . .

—Éste es uno de los museos más famosos del mundo ¿verdad?

This is one of the most famous museums in the world, right?

—El más famoso y me alegro de que tú, un extranjero, lo reconozcas.

The most famous and I'm glad that you, a foreigner, admit it.

—Estos dibujos, ¿de quién son?

Whose drawings are these?

—En el primer piso se ven los aguafuertes y los cuadros de Goya.

On the first floor are seen the etchings and paintings of Goya.

—¿De qué tratan?

What are they about?

—Se pueden considerar sátiras sociales contra el egoísmo y la hipocresía de los hombres y los desastres de la guerra.

We can say that they are social satires on the egoism and hypocrisy of man and the disasters of war.

—Aquél parece un cuadro de una familia importante.

That one seems to be the portrait of an important family.

—Sí, se titula «La Familia de Carlos IV».

Yes, it's entitled "The Family of Charles IV."

—¡Qué caras estúpidas y vacuas!

What stupid and vacuous faces!

—Tienes razón. Goya se mostró muy atrevido al pintar a la familia real con tanta exactitud. No cabe duda que fué el artista más grande del siglo XVIII.

You're right. Goya showed great courage in painting the royal family with such exactitude. There is no doubt that he was the greatest artist of the eighteenth century.

—¿Qué cuadros hay arriba?

What paintings are there upstairs?

—En el segundo piso hay las pinturas de Velázquez, El Greco, y otros.

On the second floor there are the paintings of Velázquez, El Greco, and others.

—Aquel cuadro es «las Meninas», ¿verdad?

That painting is "The Ladies in Waiting," right?

—Sí, la obra maestra de Velázquez.

Yes, the masterpiece of Velázquez.

—¡Qué originalidad! ¡Qué naturalidad! Parece que estamos observando nosotros al
pintor trabajando en su cuarto
del palacio real.

What originality! What naturalness! It seems as if we're observ-
ing the painter working in his
room in the royal palace.

—Sí, es verdad. Han dicho que
Velázquez representa en la
pintura el realismo español y
El Greco el alma religiosa de
España.

Yes, it's true. They have said
that Velázquez portrays in painting Spanish realism and El Greco
the religious soul of Spain.

—Conozco las obras de El Greco.
Él también es muy original
pero mucho más espiritual que
los otros.

I know the works of El Greco.
He too is very original but much
more spiritual than the others.

—Los otros cuadros de Murillo,
Ribera, Ticiano, Rubens, y
Tintoretto tendremos que ver-
los mañana.

The other paintings of Murillo,
Ribera, Titian, Rubens, and
Tintoretto, we'll have to see to-
morrow.

—¡Dale tú con ese «mañana»!

There you go again with tomorrow!

—¡Y tú con quererlo hacer todo
en un día!

And you with wanting to do all
in one day!

II. Frases Importantes

[Apréndanse de memoria.]

caber duda; no cabe duda	to be in doubt (*lit.*, **caber** *means* to fit); there is no doubt
coger un resfriado	to catch (a) cold
coger una pulmonía	to catch pneumonia
dale tú	there you go again
despejarse (el cielo)	to clear up
de todos modos	anyway, anyhow
el modo de pensar	the view, the way of thinking
enfermedad del corazón	heart trouble
hace buen tiempo (hacer buen [mal] tiempo)	it's good (weather), it's a fair (nice) day (to be good [bad] weather)

hacer calor	to be hot (warm
hacer fresco	to be cool
hacer frío	to be cold
hacer sol	to be sunny
hacer viento	to be windy
llover a cántaros	to pour, to come down in buckets, to rain cats and dogs
la obra maestra	the masterpiece
un ataque cardíaco	a heart attack
un ataque de apoplejía	a heart attack, apoplexy

III. Puntos Gramaticales

56. **Los tiempos compuestos del subjuntivo** (Compound tenses of the subjunctive)

   (a) **El pretérito perfecto de subjuntivo** (Present perfect subjunctive)

haya		(that)	I may have spoken (understood, lived), etc.
hayas	hablado		
haya	(comprendido,		
hayamos	vivido)	(that)	I have spoken
hayáis			(understood, lived),
hayan			etc.

   The present perfect subjunctive is formed by the present subjunctive of **haber** plus the past participle of the main verb.

   (b) **El pretérito pluscuamperfecto de subjuntivo** (pluperfect subjunctive)

hubiera		(that)	I might have spoken, (understood, lived), etc.
(hubiese)			
hubieras			
(hubieses)		(that)	I had spoken,
hubiera	hablado		(understood, lived),
(hubiese)	(comprendido,		etc.
hubiéramos	vivido)		
(hubiésemos)			
hubierais			
(hubieseis)			
hubieran			
(hubiesen)			

The pluperfect subjunctive is formed by the imperfect subjunctive of **haber** plus the past participle of the main verb. The imperfect subjunctive of **haber**, like that of all other verbs, has two forms which may be used interchangeably.

(c) **La correlación de los tiempos del subjuntivo** (Sequence of tenses of the subjunctive)

Siento que él salga.	*I'm sorry that he is leaving (will leave).*
Siento que haya salido.	*I'm sorry that he has left.*
Sentí que él saliese.	*I was sorry that he left.*
Sentí que hubiese salido.	*I was sorry that he had left.*

The present perfect subjunctive is used in a subordinate clause after the present indicative, future, and imperative in the main clause to show past action in relation to the verb of the main clause. The pluperfect subjunctive is used in a subordinate clause after a past tense or a conditional in the main clause to show action prior to that of the verb in the main clause.

57. El uso del subjuntivo en oraciones condicionales (Use of subjunctive in conditional sentences)

(a) **Si tuviera (tuviese) tiempo iría (fuera) contigo a la corrida.**

If I had time, I would go with you to the bullfight.

Si fuera (fuese) rico, vistaría (visitara) a España todos los veranos.

If I were rich, I would visit Spain every summer.

Si lloviera (lloviese) mañana no iríamos (fueramos) a la playa.

If it should rain tomorrow, we should not go to the beach.

Si tuviera (tuviese) la oportunidad, lo haría (hiciera) con mucho gusto.

If I had the opportunity, I would do it gladly.

Si hubiera (hubiese) tenido tiempo habría (hubiera) ido contigo a la corrida.

If I had had time, I would have gone with you to the bullfight.

Si ella hubiera (hubiese) hablado a tiempo, nunca se habrían (hubieran) enfadado.

If she had spoken in time, they would never have been offended.

The subjunctive is used in contrary to fact conditions; that is, in clauses that express something which is untrue or impossible of becoming true. In these sentences, when the time expressed is present, either form of the imperfect subjunctive is used in the *if* clause, and the conditional or the –ra form of the imperfect subjunctive is used in the result clause.

When the time expressed is in the past, then either form of the pluperfect subjunctive is used in the *if* clause, and the conditional perfect or the –ra form of the pluperfect subjunctive is used in the result clause.

(b) **Si Juan está allí, le hablaré.**   *If John is there, I shall speak to him.*

Si fueron al teatro, no los ví.   *If they went to the theatre, I did not see them.*

The subjunctive is not used in a conditional sentence which merely states a fact or which does not wish to imply impossibility, improbability or doubt. In this case the indicative is used in both the *if* clause and the result clause.

(c) **¡Ojalá que sea la verdad!**   *Oh would that it be the truth!*
¡Ojalá que estuviera aquí él!   *Oh would that he were here!*
¡Ojalá que hubiera (hubiese) estado aquí!   *Oh would that he had been here!*

¡Ojalá que (*would that*)! is used to express a hope or wish. If the hope or wish is thought of as possible of fulfilment, the present or the present perfect subjunctive follows **ojalá;** if the wish or hope is thought of as impossible of fulfilment, the imperfect or the pluperfect subjunctive follows **ojalá.**

Ojalá may be followed by the present subjunctive, present perfect subjunctive, or the imperfect subjunctive to refer to present time, and by the pluperfect subjunctive to relate to past time.

58. **El uso del subjuntivo en oraciones independientes** (Use of subjunctive in independent sentences)

(a) **Quizás no esté abierto el museo a esta hora.**   *Perhaps the museum is not open at this hour.*

Tal vez no sea importante el asunto.   *Maybe the matter isn't important.*

The subjunctive is used in independent clauses after such phrases as **quizá(s), acaso, tal vez, por ventura** (*perhaps,* *maybe*). It is to be noted that these expressions in themselves imply uncertainty.

(b)   ¡Dios te bendiga!   *May God bless you!*
     ¡Que lo pase bien!   *Good luck!*
     ¡Viva el presidente Ribera!   *Long live President Ribera!*
     ¡Válgame Dios!   *Heaven help me!*
     ¡Alabado sea Dios!   *God be praised!*

The subjunctive * is also used in exclamations that express a wish. These expressions are independent clauses. Probably they were originally subordinate to a main clause (expressing a wish) which has disappeared and/or is implied. «Alabado sea Dios» really means «Espero que Dios sea alabado».

(c)   Que entre el prisionero.   *Let the prisoner enter.*
     Que venga con nosotros.   *Let him come with us.*

The subjunctive † is used in independent clauses to express an indirect command.

(d)   Quisiera ver al señor director.   *I should like to see the director.*
     ¿Pudiera Ud. decirme dónde   *Could you tell me where the*
     está la Biblioteca Nacional?   *National Library is?*

The —ra form of the imperfect subjunctive is often used in independent clauses with poder, querer, deber, preferir, and other verbs to soften the tone of a request. This form is often called "softened assertion." It is to be noted that the conditional can also be used instead of the subjunctive.

59. *Estúdiese en el apéndice el presente de indicativo, el pretérito, el imperfecto, el futuro, el condicional, el presente de subjuntivo y el pretérito imperfecto de subjuntivo de los verbos irregulares* caber, conocer, haber.

IV. Ejercicios

A. *Contéstense las preguntas siguientes usando oraciones completas en español:*

1. ¿Qué tiempo hace hoy?
2. ¿Qué tiempo hizo ayer?
3. ¿Qué hace Ud. cuando llueve?
4. Si lloviese mañana, ¿qué haría Ud.?

---

* This is called the optative subjunctive.
† This is called the hortatory subjunctive.

5. ¿En qué estación del año llueve más?
6. ¿Qué lleva Ud. cuando hace mal tiempo?
7. ¿Adónde van los dos amigos?
8. ¿Por qué tiene prisa el norteamericano?
9. ¿Qué dice el español acerca de la enfermedad del corazón?
10. ¿Cuál es uno de los museos más famosos del mundo?
11. ¿Dónde está?
12. ¿De qué tratan los aguafuertes de Goya?
13. ¿Quién pintó a la familia de Carlos IV?
14. ¿Comó pintó Goya la familia de Carlos IV?
15. ¿Quién era el padre de Carlos IV?
16. ¿En qué piso del museo están las pinturas de Velázquez y El Greco?
17. ¿Cuál es la obra maestra de Velázquez?
18. ¿Qué representa Velázquez en la pintura española?
19. ¿Quién es el pintor del alma religiosa española?
20. Mencione Ud. otros pintores famosos.
21. Describa Ud. la diferencia entre el norteamericano y el español en la conversación.

B. *Escríbase una pregunta en español con cada una de las «frases importantes» que siguen:*

1. hacer calor
2. hacer buen tiempo
3. hacer fresco
4. hacer sol
5. un ataque de apoplejía

C. *Escríbase una oración completa en español con cada una de las «frases importantes» que siguen:*

1. coger un resfriado
2. caber duda
3. de todos modos
4. obra maestra
5. llover a cántaros
6. hacer viento
7. enfermedad del corazón
8. dale tú

D. *Dése la forma correspondiente del verbo:*

1. (ver)   Si Juan le _____, le dará el paraguas.
2. (tener)   Si ellos _____ el dinero, habrían ido a España.
3. (conocer) Me alegro de que tú _____ las obras de Velázquez.

4. (llover)   Si _____ toda la semana no podría ver nada.
5. (ser)   ¡Ojalá que _____ interesante!
6. (ir)   Si no hubiese llovido, mis padres _____ al museo.
7. (volver)   Era preciso que ella _____ inmediatamente.
8. (llegar)   Quizás _____ los muchachos mañana.
9. (venir)   ¡Que _____ con nosotros!
10. (salir)   Siento que él _____ ayer.
11. (hacer)   Iríamos a dar un paseo si no _____ mal tiempo
12. (comprar)   Tal vez mis amigos _____ esta casa.
13. (hablar)   No conozco a nadie que _____ portugués.
14. (decir)   Si María me lo _____ yo lo hubiera hecho.
15. (comprender) Si los estudiantes estudian, _____ la lección.

E. *Tradúzcanse las frases entre paréntesis al español:*

1. Me alegro de que (he has come).
2. Me alegro de que (he is coming).
3. Me alegré de que (he came).
4. Me alegré de que (he had come).
5. Puede decírmelo cuando (you arrive).
6. Se lo dije cuando (he arrived).
7. Buscábamos un taxi que (would take us) al museo.
8. Tomó un tranvía que (took him) al hotel.
9. No creo que ellos (have seen) los cuadros.
10. No creía que (they had seen) los cuadros, antes de su visita al museo.
11. (If he had been there) lo habría visto.
12. (If you had studied) no hubiera fracasado.
13. (If it rains) nos quedaremos en casa.
14. (If it should rain) no iríamos a la playa.
15. Siento que (you have not met) al señor Torres.
16. No creo que toda la ropa (fits) en el baúl.

F. *Tradúzcase al español:*

1. How is the weather? It's raining but I think that it will clear up.
2. Oh would that I had brought my umbrella!
3. Don't worry, calm down, tomorrow will be sunny.

4. At least when it rains it's cool.
5. If I were you, I would not go out tonight.
6. If he would study, he would not fail.
7. Velázquez is the painter of Spanish realism.
8. El Greco has painted the religious soul of Spain.
9. I don't know the works of Ribera.
10. The masterpiece of El Greco is perhaps the "Burial (entierro) of the Count of Orgaz."
11. There is no doubt that the Prado is the most famous museum in the world.
12. I'm glad that you like Goya's etchings.
13. Goya showed great courage to paint the royal family with such exactitude.
14. "The Ladies in Waiting" by Velázquez shows great originality and naturalness.
15. If I had had more time, I would have seen the works of the other great Spanish painters.

G. *Prepárese una composición oral de unos tres minutos empleando uno de los temas siguientes:*

1. El Museo del Prado
2. El museo de esta ciudad
3. Los pintores españoles
4. Los pintores modernos

I. *Dictado tomado de la conversación* «**El museo del Prado**», pp. 94–96.

Lección Once

EN UNA LIBRERÍA

I. Conversación

[*Léase en voz alta varias veces y apréndase de memoria.*]

(Al salir del Prado)

(On leaving the Prado Museum)

—¿Quieres volver al hotel?

Do you want to go back to the hotel?

—No, debería comprar unos regalos para mi familia. ¿Están abiertas las tiendas?

No, I ought to buy some presents for my family. Are the stores open?

—Todavía no. Cierran por la siesta y se abren de nuevo a las tres.

Not yet. They close for the siesta and they open again at three.

—Faltan solamente unos minutos a las tres. Paseémonos un poquito.

There are only a few minutes till three. Let's walk a bit.

—Vamos. ¿Qué quieres comprar?

Let's go. What do you want to buy?

—Unos juguetes y unos libros para mis hijos.

Some toys and some books for my children.

—¿Les gusta leer?

Do they like to read?

—A mi hija sí, pero no a mi hijo. Cuando lee lo hace solamente por miedo al maestro.

My daughter does but not my son. When he reads he does it only through fear of the teacher.

—¡No te olvides de comprar algo para la señora!

Don't forget to buy something for your wife!

104

—No te apures, nunca me atrevería a olvidar una cosa tan importante.

Don't worry, I'd never dare forget so important a matter.

—Por la Avenida José Antonio encontraremos muchas tiendas.

—Allí está una librería. Entremos.

Along José Antonio Street we'll find many stores.

There is a bookstore. Let's go in.

—El dependiente está detrás del mostrador, allí al fondo.

The clerk is behind the counter in the rear.

—Buenas tardes, señores. Entren. ¿En qué puedo servirles?

Good afternoon, gentlemen. Come in. What can I do for you?

—Quisiera ver unos libros de poesías.

I should like to see some books of poetry.

—Con mucho gusto. Venga Ud. por aquí. En este estante tenemos las obras escritas por los poetas románticos, Espronceda, Bécquer, Zorrilla; por los místicos, San Juan de la Cruz, Fray Luis de León; y también por los más modernos, Machado, Darío, García Lorca, Ramón Jiménez y otros.

Gladly. Come this way. On this shelf we have the works written by the romantic poets, Espronceda, Bécquer, Zorrilla; by the mystics, Saint John of the Cross, Fray Luis de León; and even those by the more modern ones, Machado, Darío, García Lorca, Ramón Jiménez, and others.

—Déjeme Ud. ver ese tomo, «Las Cien Mejores Poesías Líricas de la Lengua Castellana». ¿Son verdaderamente las mejores?

Let me see that volume, *The Hundred Best Lyric Poems of the Spanish Language.* Are they really the best?

—Fueron escogidas por Menéndez y Pelayo, el rítico más grande que ha tenido España.

They were chosen by Menéndez y Pelayo, the greatest critic that Spain has produced.

—Quisiera también ver una buena edición de El Quijote.

I should also like to see a good edition of Don Quijote.

—Tenemos varias. Ésta encuadernada en tela es muy hermosa.

We have several. This one bound in cloth is very beautiful.

—¿Cuánto cuesta?

How much is it?

—Ésta se la puedo dar por ciento

I can give you this for one hun-

cincuenta pesetas, ésta en rústica por cien pesetas, y ésta en piel por trescientas.

dred fifty pesetas, this paperbound one for a hundred pesetas, and this one in leather for three hundred.

—Los precios son un poquito altos.

The prices are a little high.

—Ni por sueño, señor; nuestros precios son al menos diez por ciento más bajos que los de cualquier otra librería en Madrid.

Not at all, sir; our prices are at least ten per cent lower than those of any other bookstore in Madrid.

—Está bien. Para un regalo es mejor gastar un poquito más. Déme la encuadernada en piel.

All right. It's better to spend a little more for a gift. Give me the leatherbound one.

—Quedará Ud. muy contento con esta edición, le durará muchos años.

You'll be very happy with this edition, it will last for many years.

II. Frases Importantes

[*Apréndanse de memoria.*]

al fondo
in the back, in the rear

al salir
upon(on) leaving (al + inf. = upon [on] + pres. part. in English)

atreverse a
to dare

¿cuánto me cobra?
how much (is it)?

de nuevo
again

El Quijote
the great novel by Cervantes. Its full title is «El Ingenioso Hidalgo Don Quijote de la Mancha»

encuadernado en rústica
paperbound

encuadernado en tela
clothbound

faltar
to lack, to be lacking (*used as gustar*)

ni por sueño
not at all, by no means

olvidarse de	to forget
pasearse	to stroll, to tal
por ciento	per cent
quedarse contento con	to be satisfied w
todavía no	not yet

III. Puntos Gramaticales

60. Los mandatos (Commands)

(a)
habla (tú)	comprende (tú)	vive (tú)
hablad (vosotros)	comprended (vosotros)	vivid (vosotros)
hable (Ud.)	comprenda (Ud.)	viva (Ud.)
hablen (Uds.)	comprendan (Uds.)	vivan (Uds.)

There are two forms of commands: the familiar (tú, vosotros) which is the imperative mood, and the polite (Ud., Uds.). The singular familiar command is the same as the third person singular of the present indicative. The plural familiar command is formed by replacing the –r of the infinitive ending of all verbs with a –d.

The polite commands are the same as the third person (singular and plural) of the present subjunctive.

(b)
no hables (tú)	no comprendas (tú)	no vivas (tú)
no habléis	no comprendáis	no viváis
(vosotros)	(vosotros)	(vosotros)
no hable (Ud.)	no comprenda (Ud.)	no viva (Ud.)
no hablen (Uds.)	no comprendan (Uds.)	no vivan (Uds.)

The negative forms of the familiar command are the same as the second person (singular and plural) of the present subjunctive. The polite commands retain the same form as in the affirmative.

The pronouns Ud. and Uds. are usually used with the polite command forms, whereas tú and vosotros are usually omitted with the familiar commands (except for emphasis).

(c) The following verbs have irregular familiar commands in the singular. The plural familiar commands are all regular:

decir:	di
hacer:	haz
ir:	ve

poner:	pon
salir:	sal
tener:	ten
venir:	ven

(d)

hablemos	*let us speak*
comprendamos	*let us understand*
vivamos	*let us live*

When the speaker includes himself in a command (i.e. English "let us"), the form used in Spanish is the same as the first person plural of the present subjunctive.

NOTE: In the case of the verb **ir**, nevertheless, **vamos** (*pres. ind.*) is used in place of the subjunctive **vayamos**.

61. Los mandatos y los pronombres personales (Commands and personal pronouns)

(a)

Háblele Ud. mañana.	*Speak to him tomorrow.*
Mándemela Ud.	*Send it to me.*
Levántense, señores.	*Get up, gentlemen.*
Lávate las manos, Pablo.	*Wash your hands, Paul.*
Levantaos, niños.	*Get up, children.*
Levantémonos.	*Let's get up.*
Vámonos.	*Let's go away.*
Idos.	*Go away.*
No me la mande Ud. por favor.	*Please, don't send it to me.*
No se levanten, señores.	*Don't get up, gentlemen.*
No os levantad, niños.	*Don't get up, children.*

The personal pronouns always follow and are attached to the verb in affirmative commands. In negative commands the personal pronouns precede the verb.

Levantad + os = Levantaos
Levantemos + nos = Levantémonos

When the reflexive pronoun **os** is attached to a command, the final –d of the verb is dropped (except for the verb **ir**). When the reflexive pronoun **nos** is attached to the command, the final –s of the verb is dropped.

(b) A written accent is added to an affirmative command in order to retain the original stress when the addition of a pronoun would otherwise alter the stress:

Hable! (*Speak!*)	follows the rule *—no written accent required.
Háblele (*Speak to him*)	placing the stress on the –a (where it originally was before the addition of **le**) now requires a written accent because **ha** is no longer the next to the last syllable.
Levantad	Stress is on last syllable according to the rule.
Levantaos	Stress is on next to the last syllable, also according to the rule, and therefore no written accent is needed.

62. Los usos de por y para (uses of **por** and **para**)

In general **por** refers to source or cause and **para** to destination or result. Specifically:

(a) **Por** is used to express:

1. agent

El libro fué escrito por mi hermano.	*The book was written by my brother.*
La comida fué preparada por la cocinera.	*The meal was prepared by the cook.*

2. manner or means

Llevó al niño por la mano.	*He led the child by the hand.*
Me sacó el dinero por fuerza.	*He got the money from me by (means of) force.*

3. reason or motive

Los misioneros sufren mucho por la fé.	*Missionaries suffer much for the faith.*
Por eso lo hice.	*That's why I did it.*

* According to the rules of accentuation, a word that ends in a vowel or **–n** and **–s** receives the stress on the next to the last syllable. A word that ends in a consonant (except **–n** or **–s**) receives the stress on the last syllable. Any word whose stress doesn't follow these rules must have a written accent.

4. opinion

Si lo tienen por tonto se equivocan.	*If they consider him a fool, they are making a mistake.*
A veces los locos pasan por sabios.	*At times crazy persons pass for wise men.*

5. exchange

Cambió el auto viejo por uno nuevo.	*He changed the old car for a new one.*
Pagamos cien pesos por el libro.	*We paid one hundred pesos for the book.*

6. place through or along which

El desfile no pasa por aquí.	*The parade doesn't pass by here.*
Corrió por las calles como una loca.	*She ran through the streets like a mad woman.*

7. time during which

Llegaron por la tarde.	*They arrived in the afternoon.*
Fueron a las montañas por el verano.	*They went to the mountains for the summer.*

8. in behalf of, for the sake of, in place of

Ruega por nosotros.	*Pray for us.*
El abogado habló por el acusado.	*The lawyer spoke for the accused.*

9. exclamation

¡Por amor de Dios!	*For the love of God!*
¡Por Dios!	*For heaven's sake!*

(b) Para is used to express:

1. purpose

Voy a Barcelona para ver a mis hijos.	*I'm going to Barcelona to see my children.*
Trabajo para ganarme la vida.	*I work to earn my bread.*

2. destination

Salió para su hacienda ayer.	*He left for his ranch yesterday.*
Este regalo es para ti.	*This gift is for you.*

3. use

Este cántaro es para el vino y ése para el agua.	*This pitcher is for the wine and that one for the water.*

4. a point in future time

Preparen la lección para el lunes.	*Prepare the lesson for Monday.*
Nos citamos para la próxima semana.	*We made an appointment for next week.*

5. comparison

Para un regalo no cuesta demasiado.	*For a gift it's not too expensive.*
Para un extranjero tú sabes mucho de nuestra literatura.	*For a foreigner you know quite a bit about our literature.*

IV. Ejercicios

A. *Contéstense las preguntas siguientes usando oraciones completas en español:*

1. ¿Por qué no quiere volver al hotel el señor Smith?
2. ¿Por qué están cerradas las tiendas?
3. ¿Qué regalos quiere comprar el señor Smith?
4. ¿A quién le gusta leer?
5. ¿Le gusta leer a Ud.?
6. ¿Cómo se titula el último libro que ha leído Ud.?
7. ¿Dónde se encuentran las tiendas?
8. ¿Adónde entran los dos amigos?
9. ¿Dónde está el dependiente?
10. ¿Qué pidió el señor Smith al dependiente?
11. ¿Quiénes son Espronceda, Bécquer y Zorrilla?
12. ¿De qué trata la poesía mística?

13. ¿Quiénes son algunos poetas modernos?
14. ¿Quién era Menéndez y Pelayo?
15. ¿Qué tomo quiere ver el señor Smith?
16. ¿Quién escribió «Don Quijote de la Mancha»?
17. ¿Qué le gusta a Ud. más un libro encuadernado en tela o en piel?
18. ¿Qué cuesta más un libro encuadernado en tela o en rústica?
19. ¿Qué dice el dependiente de los precios de su tienda?
20. ¿Cuánto cuesta el libro que compró el señor Smith?

B. *Escríbase una pregunta en español con cada una de las «frases importantes» que siguen:*

1. al fondo   3. encuadernado en tela   5. por ciento
2. atreverse a   4. olvidarse de   6. faltar

C. *Escríbase una oración completa en español con cada una de las «frases importantes» que siguen:*

1. al salir   3. ni por sueño   5. pasearse
2. de nuevo   4. encuadernado en rústica   6. todavía no

D. *Complétense las oraciones siguientes con la forma apropriada de los mandatos:*

1. (Comprar) tú la carne y el pan. *Compra*
2. (Ayudar) tú a Juanito. *ayuda*
3. (Entrar) Uds., señores. *Entren*
4. (Venir) aquí, muchachos. *Venid*
5. (Decir) la verdad, señor Ribera. *Diga*
6. (Levantarse) ahora, niños. *Levantaos* *Levantaos*
7. (Olvidarse) Ud. de ellos. *Olvídese*
8. (Abrir) Ud. la puerta, por favor. *abra*
9. (Tener) Ud. cuidado. *Tenga*
10. (Irse) a casa, muchacha, es tarde. *Váyase y vete*
11. (Poner) Ud. los libros en la mesa. *Ponga*
12. (Ser) buenos, chicos. *Sean*
13. (Salir) vosotros ahora, yo vengo más tarde. *Salid*
14. (Cerrar) tú la ventana. *Cierra*
15. (Hacer) Uds. el café. *Hagan*

E. *Conviértanse en negativos los mandatos en el ejercicio D.*

F. Tradúzcase al español:

1. Let's go. *Vamos*
2. Don't worry (tú) *Pierde Cuidado*
3. Send it to me (Ud.) *Mándemelo*
4. Don't write it (*f.*) now (tú). *No lo escribas ahora*
5. Tell it (*m.*) to them (Ud.). *Dígaselo*
6. Let's get up. *Levantémonos*
7. Don't speak to them (Ud.). *No les hable*
8. Give them to us (vosotros). *Dádnoslo*
9. Don't give it to him (Uds.).
10. Let's do it. *Hagámoslo*

G. Complétense las oraciones siguientes con la forma correcta de por o para:

1. Salieron *para* Barcelona ayer.
2. «Noche Oscura del Alma» fué escrita *por* San Juan de la Cruz.
3. Lo tienen *por* sabio.
4. Pagué doscientas pesetas *por* el libro.
5. Este regalo es *para* mi padre.
6. Lo hizo *por* miedo y no *por* amor.
7. La lección es *para* mañana.
8. Este plato es *para* la sopa.
9. La comida fué preparada *para* los invitados. (use)
10. La comida fué preparada *por* la cocinera. cook (by)
11. Fué a Sevilla *para* ver al famoso matador.
12. Nos dió un descuento de diez *por* ciento. per cent
    discount

H. Cámbiense al plural los sujetos y los verbos de las oraciones siguientes:

1. ¿Conoces tú las obras de Velázquez?
2. No sé si la camisa cabrá en la maleta.
3. De pronto oí sonar un clarín.
4. Aquel joven conducía demasiado de prisa.
5. He oído hablar tanto de la corrida que tengo muchas ganas de verla.
6. ¿Cuánto valía aquella corbata?
7. Conocí a los señores Ribera en casa de mi tía.
8. Oigo decir que el señor Moreno es riquísimo.

I. Tradúzcase al español:

1. The toy is for my son and the book of poetry for my daughter.
2. Don't get up, gentlemen, I'll sit down.

3. We went to the bookstore to buy a modern novel.
4. *Don Quijote*, written by Cervantes, is a great masterpiece.
5. For a gift, a clothbound book is better than a paperbound book.
6. In the morning they went to the museum and in the afternoon to the library.
7. He did everything for his children.
8. Please come in, I should like to introduce you to my family.
9. Our students do not like to read the poetry of the romantic poets.
10. In this bookstore the prices are at least fifteen per cent lower than in that one.

J. *Prepárese una composición oral de tres minutos usando uno de los temas siguientes:*

1. En la librería
2. Don Quijote de la Mancha
3. Nuestra biblioteca

K. *Dictado tomado de la conversación* «**En una librería**», pp. 104–106.

Lección Doce

DÍA DE FIESTA

I. Conversación

[Léase en voz alta varias veces y apréndase de memoria.]

(En el cuarto de Juan)   (In John's room)

—Juan, vamos, despiértate. Tenemos que salir temprano.
John, let's go, wake up. We have to leave early.

—¿Para qué?
For what?

—¡Cómo, para qué! No te recuerdas, vamos a ver la fiesta de San Francisco.
What do you mean, for what! Don't you remember, we're going to see the feast of Saint Francis.

—Ah, sí, ahora me acuerdo. Lo siento mucho, pero cuando me acuesto tarde nunca puedo levantarme temprano. Pues, siéntate.
Ah, yes, now I remember. I'm very sorry, but when I go to bed late I can't ever get up early. Well, sit down.

—No, para no perder más tiempo, mientras tú te vistes, yo voy a ver si el automóvil está listo.
No, in order not to lose any more time, while you dress, I'll go to see if the car is ready.

—¿Dónde lo tienes, en el garage?
Where do you have it, in the garage?

—Sí, el mecánico está cambiando unas bujías y revisando el acumulador y los frenos.
Yes, the mechanic is changing some sparkplugs and checking the battery and the brakes.

—¿Por qué, no anda bien?
Why, doesn't it run well?

115

—Hace algunos días que falla el motor. Pues, yo voy y vuelvo en un santiamén.

The motor has been missing for a few days. Well, I'll be back in a flash.

—Yo estaré listo en unos minutos.

I'll be ready in a few minutes.

—Estacionaré el coche a la acera. Te espero abajo.

I'll park the car at the curb. I'll wait for you downstairs.

—Está bien, hasta más tarde.

All right, I'll see you later.

(En el automóvil)

(In the car)

—¿Quieres manejar tú?

Do you want to drive?

—No, tú sabes el camino, yo no. ¿Dónde tiene lugar esta fiesta?

No, you know the road, I don't. Where does this feast take place?

—En un pueblo a unos kilómetros de aquí. Están festejando el día del santo patrón del pueblo.

In a town a few kilometers from here. They're celebrating the feast day of the patron saint of the town.

—¿Cómo se celebra este día?

How do they celebrate this day?

—Por la mañana todo el mundo se pone su traje más fino y va a la iglesia para oír Misa o para rezar frente a la estatua del santo.

In the morning everyone puts on his finest clothes and goes to the church to hear mass or to pray in front of the statue of the saint.

—¡Es una fiesta religiosa, entonces!

It's a religious feast, then!

—Sí, pero también es una oportunidad para la diversión popular. Por la tarde hay una corrida, hay música, bailes, y por la noche fuegos artificiales.

Yes, but it's also an opportunity for the people's enjoyment. In the afternoon, there is a bullfight, there is music, dancing, and at night fireworks.

—La gente se divierte mucho, al parecer.

The people enjoy themselves very much, apparently.

—Ah sí, el pueblo ha esperado todo el año para celebrar esta fiesta y cuando el día llega todo es animación, bullicio y alegría.

Oh yes, the town has waited the whole year to celebrate this holiday and when the day comes excitement, noise, and happiness reigns.

—¿Y es ésta una tradición local?
—No, esto ocurre en todos los pueblos de España. La parte más solemne es la procesión, cuando la imagen del santo es llevado en hombros por las calles del pueblo.
—Creo que la divinidad parece más humana andando entre el pueblo.
—Eso es. La relación entre el español devoto y el santo es muy personal y real. Mientras las campanas suenan y la banda toca, la imagen pasa lentamente ante la muchedumbre. Va escoltada por las autoridades eclesiásticas y civiles y dos filas de fieles llevan cirios encendidos.
—La escena debe ser muy emocionante.
—Sí, porque se nota en las caras de la gente una sincera y honda emoción, un sentimiento de humildad, gratitud y amor.

And is this a local tradition? No, this occurs in all the towns of Spain. The most solemn part is the procession, when the image of the saint is carried on the shoulders by the faithful through the streets of the town.
I think that the divinity seems more human going out among the people.
That's it. The relationship between the devout Spaniard and the Saint is very personal and real. While the church bells ring and the band plays, the statue passes slowly in front of the crowd. It is escorted by the ecclesiastical and civil authorities and two rows of the faithful carry lighted candles.
The scene must be very moving.

Yes, because one notices in the faces of the people a sincere and deep emotion, a feeling of humility, gratitude and love.

II. Frases Importantes

[*Apréndanse de memoria.*]

a unos kilómetros de aquí — a few kilometers from here
cambiar las bujías — to change the sparkplugs
celebrar una fiesta — to celebrate a feast
divertirse — to amuse one's self, to have a good time, to enjoy oneself
el parabrisas — the wind shield
el volante (de dirección) — the steering wheel
estacionar el coche — to park the car

fallar (el motor)	to fail, to miss (a motor)
festejar	to entertain, to feast, to celebrate
fuegos artificiales	fireworks
los frenos	the brakes
llevar en hombros	to carry on one's shoulders
manejar	to manage, to drive (a car)
perder tiempo	to lose time, to waste time
revisar el acumulador	to check the battery
tocar	to touch, to play (*an instrument*)

III. Puntos Gramaticales

63. **Verbos que cambian la raíz** (Radical changing verbs)

Radical changing verbs can be grouped into three classes:

(a) First Class

cerrar   e > ie

PRESENT INDICATIVE: **cierro, cierras, cierra, cerramos, cerráis, cierran**

PRESENT SUBJUNCTIVE: **cierre, cierres, cierre, cerremos, cerréis, cierren**

IMPERATIVE: **cierra, cerrad**

volver   o > ue

PRESENT INDICATIVE: **vuelvo, vuelves, vuelve, volvemos, volvéis, vuelven**

PRESENT SUBJUNCTIVE: **vuelva, vuelvas, vuelva, volvamos, volváis, vuelvan**

IMPERATIVE: **vuelve, volved**

In the first class belong all −ar and −er verbs that are radical changing. These verbs change the −e of the root to −ie and the −o to −ue in all of the singular and the third person plural of the present indicative, present subjunctive and the imperative singular.

Among the verbs which change like **cerrar** are: **comenzar, despertar**(se), **empezar, entender, negar, pensar, perder, sentar**(se).

Among the verbs which change like **volver** are: **acordar**(se), **acostar**(se), **almorzar, contar, costar, encontrar, llover, mostrar, mover, recordar, rogar, sonar, soñar, volar.**

(b) Second Class

sentir   e > ie,i

PRESENT INDICATIVE: **siento, sientes, siente, sentimos, sentís, sienten**

PRESENT SUBJUNCTIVE: **sienta, sientas, sienta, sintamos, sintáis, sientan**

IMPERATIVE: **siente, sentid**

PRETERITE INDICATIVE: **sentí, sentiste, sintió, sentimos, sentisteis, sintieron**

IMPERFECT SUBJUNCTIVE: **sintiera, sintieras, sintiera, sintiéramos, sintierais, sintieran** or **sintiese, sintieses, sintiese, sintiésemos, sintieseis, sintiesen**

PRESENT PARTICIPLE: **sintiendo**

dormir   o > ue,u

PRESENT INDICATIVE: **duermo, duermes, duerme, dormimos, dormís, duermen**

PRESENT SUBJUNCTIVE: **duerma, duermas, duerma, durmamos, durmáis, duerman**

IMPERATIVE: **duerme, dormid**

PRETERITE INDICATIVE: **dormí, dormiste, durmió, dormimos, dormisteis, durmieron**

IMPERFECT SUBJUNCTIVE: **durmiera, durmieras, durmiera, durmiéramos, durmierais, durmieran** or **durmiese, durmieses, durmiese, durmiésemos, durmieseis, durmiesen**

PRESENT PARTICIPLE: **durmiendo**

In the second class are found only –ir verbs. These verbs change –e of the root to –ie and –o to –ue as in the first class (that is, in all of the singular and the third person plural of the present indicative, the present subjunctive, and the imperative singular). They also change –e to –i and –o to –u in the first and second persons plural of the present subjunctive, in the third person singular and plural of the preterite, throughout the imperfect subjunctive, and in the present participle. Verbs which change like **sentir** are: **advertir, consentir, convertir(se), divertir(se), mentir, preferir, referir;** like **dormir: morir.**

(c) Third Class

pedir   e > i

PRESENT INDICATIVE: **pido, pides, pide, pedimos, pedís, piden**

PRESENT SUBJUNCTIVE: **pida, pidas, pida, pidamos, pidáis, pidan**

PRETERITE INDICATIVE: **pedí, pediste, pidió, pedimos, pedisteis, pidieron**

IMPERFECT SUBJUNCTIVE: **pidiera, pidieras, pidiera, pidiéramos, pidierais, pidieran** or
pidiese, pidieses, pidiese, pidiésemos, pidieseis, pidiesen

IMPERATIVE: **pide, pedid**

PRESENT PARTICIPLE: **pidiendo**

The third class consists also of –ir verbs. These verbs change the –e of the root to –i in all of the singular and the third person plural of the present indicative, throughout the present subjunctive, in the third person singular and plural of the preterite, throughout the imperfect subjunctive, in the imperative singular, and in the present participle. Other verbs which change like **pedir** are: **corregir, despedirse, elegir, gemir, impedir, repetir, seguir, servir, vestir.**

64. La voz pasiva (Passive voice)

A verb is said to be in the passive voice when the subject, instead of performing the action, receives the action of the verb.

(a) **La fiesta será celebrada por los aldeanos.**   *The feast will be celebrated by the villagers.*

Estos artículos fueron escritos por un joven autor.   *These articles were written by a young author.*

La puerta fué abierta por la criada.   *The door was opened by the servant.*

The passive voice may be expressed by the proper tense of the verb **ser** plus the past participle of the main verb (if the agent of the action is stated or implied). In this case the past participle agrees in gender and number with the subject. The agent (doer of the action) is usually introduced by **por.**

(b) **La fiesta se celebra cada año.**   *The feast is celebrated every year.*

A lo lejos se oyó la bocina del coche.   *The horn of the car was heard in the distance.*

When no agent is expressed the Spaniard avoids the passive and favors an active construction. In such a situation, the reflexive form of the verb substitutes for the passive.

(c) **La puerta estaba cerrada.**   *The door was closed.*

El coche está estacionado a la acera.   *The car is parked at the curb*

The verb **estar** is used with a past participle to describe a state or condition rather than an action. The past participle in this case is an adjective and agrees in gender and number with the subject.

IV. Ejercicios

A. *Contéstense las preguntas siguientes usando oraciones completas en español:*

1. ¿Qué hace Juan cuando entra su amigo?
2. ¿Por qué tienen que salir temprano?
3. ¿Por qué no puede levantarse temprano Juan?
4. ¿A qué hora se acuesta Ud.?
5. ¿A qué hora se levanta Ud.?
6. ¿Tiene Ud. un automóvil?
7. ¿Dónde lo estaciona Ud.?
8. ¿Por qué no anda bien el auto del amigo de Juan?
9. ¿Por qué no quiere manejar Juan?
10. ¿Sabe Ud. manejar?
11. ¿Dónde tendrá lugar la fiesta?
12. ¿Qué están celebrando?
13. ¿Qué tipo de fiesta es?
14. ¿Cómo se divierte la gente?
15. ¿Cuántas veces al año celebran esta fiesta?
16. ¿Cuál es la parte más solemne de la fiesta?
17. ¿Cómo llevan la estatua del santo?

B. *Escríbase una pregunta en español con cada una de las «frases importantes» que siguen:*

1. cambiar las bujías
2. fuegos artificiales
3. celebrar una fiesta
4. manejar
5. divertirse

C. *Escríbase una oración completa en español con cada una de las «frases importantes» que siguen:*

1. estacionar el coche
2. festejar
3. llevar en hombros
4. perder tiempo
5. revisar el acumulador
6. fallar el motor

D. *Dése la forma correcta del presente de indicativo de cada verbo:*

1. yo (volver, cerrar, dormir, sentir)
2. tú (sentarse, servir, rogar, dormir)
3. él (divertirse, pensar, seguir, celebrar)
4. nosotros (sonar, despedirse, morir, pensar)
5. ellos (entender, morir, pedir, contar)
6. vosotros (empezar, preferir, elegir, costar)

E. *Dése la forma apropriada del presente de subjuntivo de cada verbo:*

1. yo (negar, dormir, esperar, festejar)
2. Ud. (recordar, tener, seguir, costar)
3. Uds. (costar, comprender, vestir, perder)
4. ella (cerrar, hablar, servir, poder)
5. nosotros (despertarse, manejar, abrir, comprar)
6. vosotros (acordarse, morir, cerrar, levantarse)

F. *Dése la forma apropriada del pretérito de indicativo y del imperfecto de subjuntivo de cada verbo:*

1. yo (dormir, pedir, cerrar)
2. ellos (morir, seguir, rogar)
3. tú (sentir, vestirse, soñar)
4. él (consentir, servir, acordarse)
5. Uds. (advertir, impedir, volver)
6. nosotros (acostarse, gemir, encontrar)

G. *Complétense las oraciones siguientes en español:*

1. Juan (opened) la puerta.
2. La puerta fué (opened) por Juan.
3. La fiesta (is celebrated) cada año.
4. La escuela (opens) en septiembre.
5. Mi hermano (will be punished) por mi padre.
6. Aquí (is spoken) español.
7. Lope de Vega (wrote) esta comedia.
8. Este poema (was written) por un joven autor.
9. Las bujías (are changed) por el mecánico.
10. Estos regalos (were sent) por su tía.

H. *Tradúzcase al español:*

1. Get up, John. We have to leave early.
2. When he goes to bed late, he can never get up on time.
3. Don't you remember, you promised to take me to see the feast of Saint Francis.
4. Where is the car parked? At the curb.
5. Do you want me to drive? Yes, because I don't know the road.
6. This car doesn't run very well.
7. Do you want the mechanic to check it?
8. Yes, I want him to change the sparkplugs too.
9. Where is the feast being celebrated?
10. When will the procession take place?
11. The doors of the church were opened by the crowd.
12. There was joy and happiness everywhere.
13. The statue was carried on the shoulders of the faithful.
14. On the feast day of Saint Francis, everyone puts on his finest clothes and goes to the church to hear mass.
15. In the evening, fireworks are seen.

I. *Prepárese una composición oral de cuatro minutos sobre uno de los temas siguientes:*

1. Día de fiesta en España
2. Día de fiesta en los Estados Unidos
3. Nuestro automóvil

J. *Dictado tomado de la conversación* «**Día de fiesta**», *pp. 115–117.*

Lección Trece

EL CINE

I. Conversación

[Léase en voz alta varias veces y apréndase de memoria.]

—¿Qué dice aquel cartel al lado del Teatro Internacional?

What does that sign on the side of the International Theatre say?

—Estreno del gran espectáculo cinematográfico, «La Hija del Mar», interpretado por las más brillantes estrellas del cine español.

First showing of the great cinematographic spectacle, *The Daughter of the Sea*, interpreted by the most brilliant stars of Spanish movies.

—Según esos anuncios nunca han hecho una mala película.

According to those advertisements they have never made a bad film.

—No soy apasionado del cine pero si quieres verla, te acompaño.

I'm not fond of movies but if you wish to see it, I'll go with you.

—Me gustaría ver una película española. Estoy cansado de ver esas tonterías que impresionan en Hollywood.

I should like to see a Spanish film. I'm tired of seeing that nonsense that they film in Hollywood.

—¿Sabes que se exhiben aquí también, dobladas en español?

Do you know that they are shown here, dubbed in Spanish?

—¿Y les gustan a los españoles?

And do the Spaniards like it?

—Sí, sobre todo las comedias musicales en tecnicolor y los dibujos de muñecos.

Yes, especially the musical comedies in technicolor and the cartoons.

—A ver esta obra maestra, pero

Let's go see this masterpiece, but

124

esta vez me toca a mí convidarte a ti.
—No seas tonto. Tú eres mi huésped en Madrid.
—De ninguna manera. No quiero que sigas pagando por todo.
—Eso no importa, vamos, que la función está para empezar.

(Al salir del cine)

—¿Qué te pareció?
—No me gustó tanto. La trama era bastante trillada.
—Sí, trataron de mezclar los elementos de una tragedia griega con los de una novela regional.
—Sin embargo las escenas que retrataban la vida de los pescadores eran muy interesantes.
—La actriz era hermosísima pero le faltaba la honda emoción que el papel necesitaba.
—Tienes razón, el protagonista trabajó mejor que ella.
—Sí, pero el actor más hábil de todos era el que hizo el papel del tendero.
—Estoy de acuerdo. Ese personaje resultó más completo, más creíble.
—A veces me pareció un poco exagerada la cosa. Por ejemplo cuando la cogió por los cabellos y la echó al suelo.

it's my turn to treat you this time.
Don't be silly. You're my guest in Madrid.
Not at all. I don't want you to keep paying for everything.
That doesn't matter, let's go, because the program is about to begin.

(On leaving the movies)

How did you like it?
I didn't like it so much. The plot was rather hackneyed.
Yes, they tried to combine the elements of a Greek tragedy with those of a regional novel.
Nevertheless the scenes which depicted the life of the fishermen were very interesting.
The actress was very beautiful but she lacked the deep emotion that the role required.
You're right, the hero acted better than she did.
Yes, but the best actor of all was the one who took the role of the storekeeper.
I agree. That character turned out fuller, more believable.
At times the thing seemed a bit exaggerated. For example when he took her by the hair and threw her to the ground.

—¡Qué rara esa mujer! Cuanto más él la despreciaba tanto más ella le quería.

What a strange woman! The more he disdained her the more she loved him.

—No es tan rara, muchas son así.

Not so strange, many women are like that.

—A pesar de todo la película fué más divertida de lo que yo esperaba.

In spite of everything the film was more amusing than I expected.

II. Frases Importantes

[*Apréndanse de memoria.*]

a pesar de	in spite of
al lado de	on the side of, beside
comedias musicales	musical comedies
de ninguna manera	not at all
dibujos de muñecos	cartoons
doblado en español	dubbed in Spanish (*with a Spanish sound track*)
el argumento; la trama	the plot
eso no importa	that doesn't matter
hacer el papel	to play (act) the role
impresionar	to film, to shoot (*a film*)
me toca a mí	it's my turn
no seas tonto	don't be silly
¡qué raro!	how strange!
ser apasionado de	to be fond of
sin embargo	nevertheless
tocar a uno	to be one's turn

III. Puntos Gramaticales

65. **Los verbos con cambios ortográficos** (Orthographic-changing verbs)

Orthographic-changing verbs are those which undergo a change in spelling (orthography) in order to maintain the sound of the final consonant of the infinitive. These changes are as follows:

(a) sacar   c > qu

PRET. IND. saqué, sacaste, sacó, sacamos, sacasteis, sacaron
PRES. SUBJ. saque, saques, saque, saquemos, saquéis, saquen

Verbs ending in –car change –c to –qu before the vowel –e.
Other verbs that change like **sacar** are: **tocar, colocar, picar, buscar.**

(b) pagar   g > gu

PRET. IND. pagué, pagaste, pagó, pagamos, pagasteis, pagaron
PRES. SUBJ. pague, pagues, pague, paguemos, paguéis, paguen

Verbs ending in –gar change –g to –gu before the vowel –e.
Other verbs that change like **pagar** are: **llegar, negar, vengar.**

(c) gozar   z > c

PRET. IND. gocé, gozaste, gozó, gozamos, gozasteis, gozaron
PRES. SUBJ. goce, goces, goce, gocemos, gocéis, gocen

Verbs ending in –zar change –z to –c before the vowel –e.
Other verbs that change like **gozar** are: **almorzar, alzar, aterrizar, comenzar, empezar, rezar.**

(d) averiguar   gu > gü

PRET. IND. averigüé, averiguaste, averiguó, averiguamos, averiguasteis, averiguaron
PRES. SUBJ. averigüe, averigües, averigüe, averigüemos, averigüéis, averigüen

Verbs ending in –guar change –gu to –gü before the vowel –e.
Atestiguar changes like **averiguar.**

(e) 1. vencer   c > z

PRES. IND. venzo, vences, vence, vencemos, vencéis, vencen
PRES. SUBJ. venza, venzas, venza, venzamos, venzáis, venzan

Verbs ending in a consonant + –cer or –cir usually change the –c to –z before the vowels –o and –a. Other verbs which change like **vencer** are: **convencer, esparcir.**

2. conocer   c > zc

PRES. IND. conozco, conoces, conoce, conocemos, conocéis, conocen
PRES. SUBJ. conozca, conozcas, conozca, conozcamos, conozcáis, conozcan

Verbs ending in a vowel + –cer or –cir change **c** to **zc** before the vowels –o or –a. Other verbs of this type are: **crecer, lucir, merecer, nacer, parecer, producir, ofrecer.**

NOTE: **cocer** (*to cook*) and **mecer** (*to rock*) are exceptions to rule 2 above. These verbs are conjugated like **vencer.**

(f) **escoger   g > j**
PRES. IND. **escojo, escoges, escoge, escogemos, escogéis, escogen**
PRES. SUBJ. **escoja, escojas, escoja, escojamos, escojáis, escojan**

Verbs ending in –ger or –gir change the –g to –j before the vowels –o and –a. Other verbs that change like **escoger** are: **coger, dirigir.**

(g) **seguir   gu > g**
PRES. IND. **sigo, sigues, sigue, seguimos, seguís, siguen**
PRES. SUBJ. **siga, sigas, siga, sigamos, sigáis, sigan**

Verbs ending in –guir change –gu to –g before the vowels –o and –a. **Distinguir** changes like **seguir.**

(h) **delinquir   qu > c**
PRES. IND. **delinco, delinques, delinque, delinquimos, delinquís, delinquen**
PRES. SUBJ. **delinca, delincas, delinca, delincamos, delincáis, delincan**

Verbs ending in –quir change –qu to –c before the vowels –o and –a.

66. **Adjetivos comparativos** (Comparative of adjectives)

(a)		
alegre	**más alegre**	**el (la) más alegre**
happy	*happier*	*the happiest*
difíciles	**menos difíciles**	**los (las) menos difíciles**
difficult	*less difficult*	*the least difficult*

The comparative of an adjective is formed by placing **más** (*more*) or **menos** (*less*) before the adjective. The superlative is the same as the comparative except that the appropriate definite article is placed before it.

(b)		
bueno	**mejor**	**el (la) mejor**
good	*better*	*best*

malo	peor	el (la) peor
bad	*worse*	*worst*
pequeño	**menor**	**el (la) menor**
small	(*smaller*), *younger*	(*smallest*), *youngest*
grande	**mayor**	**el (la) mayor**
large, (*great*)	(*larger, greater*),	(*largest, greatest*),
	older	*oldest*

In addition to the regular comparative forms, the above adjectives may also be compared irregularly. Generally **pequeño** and **grande** are compared regularly (**más pequeño, más grande**) to express size; irregularly (**menor, mayor**) to express age or importance.

(c) **Juan es más alto que su hermano.** — *John is taller than his brother.*

Esta novela es menos interesante que ésa. — *This novel is less interesting than that one.*

Su hermana es mayor que la mía. — *Her sister is older than mine.*

Tengo menos de diez dólares. — *I have less than ten dollars*

But:

No vale más que cinco pesetas. — *It's not worth more than five pesetas.*

In comparatives of inequality *than* is expressed by **que** except before a number. In the latter case **de** must be used. However, to express *no more than* before a number **no más que** is used.

(d) **Mi madre me mandó más ropa de la que yo necesitaba.** — *My mother sent me more clothing than I needed.*

Este actor es mejor del que vimos la semana pasada. — *This actor is better than the one we saw last week.*

Me dió menos libros de los que yo le di a él. — *He gave me fewer books than I gave him.*

Esta película es más divertida de lo que yo me esperaba. — *This film is more amusing than I expected.*

When the comparison is expressed in two clauses and is based upon a noun, **del que** (**de los que, de la que, de las que**) is used to express *than*. If the comparison concerns the whole idea of the principal clause and is based upon an adjective or an adverb, then **de lo que** must be used.

(e) **Felipe es tan inteligente como su hermano.**   *Philip is as intelligent as his brother.*

No escribe tan a menudo como debiera.   *He doesn't write as often as he should.*

No tiene tanto dinero como Uds. creen.   *He doesn't have as much money as you think.*

Ha leído tantas novelas como el profesor.   *She read as many novels as the professor.*

The comparison of equality may be expressed by **tan** + *adj.* (or *adv.*) + **como** (*as, so . . . as*) or **tanto(a)**, **tantos(as)** + *noun* + **como** (*as much, as many . . . as*).

67. El superlativo absoluto (Absolute superlative)

grande	*large*	**muy grande**	**grandísimo**	*very large*
útil	*useful*	**muy útil**	**utilísimo**	*very useful*
rico	*rich*	**muy rico**	**riquísimo**	*very rich*
largo	*long*	**muy largo**	**larguísimo**	*very long*
amable	*kind*	**muy amable**	**amabilísimo**	*very kind*
mucho	*much*	. . .	**muchísimo**	*very much*

The absolute superlative is another type of superlative. It merely names the quality as being in a very high degree. It does not express any real comparison. It is formed by placing **muy** before the adjective or by adding **ísimo(a)** to the adjective. Adjectives ending in a vowel drop the vowel before –**ísimo(a)** is added. Adjectives ending in –**co** or –**go** change –**c** to –**qu** and –**g** to –**gu** respectively in order to retain the sound of the positive form of the adjective. Adjectives ending in –**ble** become –**bilísimo**.

NOTE: **Mucho** has only one form: **muchísimo**.

68. Los adverbios (Adverbs)

(a)   ADJECTIVE   ADVERB

     alegre (*happy*)   **alegremente** (*happily*)

     claro,–a (*clear*)   **claramente** (*clearly*)

     fácil (*easy*)   **fácilmente** (*easily*)

     rápido,–a (*rapid*)   **rápidamente** (*rapidly*)

Many adverbs are formed in Spanish by adding –mente to the feminine singular form of the adjective. If the adjective has a written accent, that accent is retained after –mente has been added.

(b) **Hablaba clara y lentamente.**   *He spoke clearly and slowly.*

When more than one adverb ending in –mente are used in a sentence, only the last one retains the –mente. The others have the feminine form of the adjective.

(c) **Adverbios comparativos** (Comparative of adverbs)

1. **cerca** (*near*)   **más cerca** (*nearer*)
   despacio (*slowly*)   **menos despacio** (*less slowly*)

   The comparative of an adverb is formed in the same way as the adjective, by placing **más** (*more*) or **menos** (*less*) before the adverb.

   NOTE: The superlative is usually formed by placing **lo más** (**menos**) before the adverb and **posible** after it: **lo más fácilmente** (**posible**) *as easily as possible* (i.e. most easily).

2. The following are compared irregularly:

   bien (*well*)   **mejor** (*better, best*)
   mal (*badly*)   **peor** (*worse, worst*)
   mucho (*much*)   **más** (*more, most*)
   poco (*little*)   **menos** (*less, least*)

(d) **Cuanto más gana tanto más gasta.**   *The more he earns the more he spends.*

In comparing clauses, *the more* (*less*) . . . *the more* (*less*) is expressed in Spanish by **cuanto más** (**menos**) + *verb* + **tanto más** (**menos**) + *verb*. **Mientras** may be used in place of **cuanto**. When so used, **tanto** may be omitted.

IV. Ejercicios

A. *Contéstense las preguntas siguientes usando oraciones completas en español:*

1. ¿Qué dice el cartel al lado del Teatro Internacional?
2. ¿Cuál es el título de la película?

3. ¿Es Ud. apasionado del cine?
4. ¿Qué tipos de películas le gustan más a Ud.?
5. ¿No ha visto Ud. nunca una película española?
6. ¿Qué quiere decir la palabra doblada?
7. ¿Qué tipos de películas de Hollywood les gustan a los españoles?
8. ¿Cómo se dice en español: "The program is about to begin?"
9. ¿Cómo era la trama de la película que vieron los dos amigos?
10. ¿Cuáles escenas eran interesantes?
11. ¿Qué es una novela regional?
12. ¿Cómo era la actriz?
13. ¿Qué le faltaba a la actriz?
14. ¿Quién era el actor más hábil?
15. ¿Qué pareció exagerado?
16. A pesar de todo, ¿cómo fué la película?

B. *Escríbase una pregunta en español con cada una de las «frases importantes» que siguen:*

1. al lado de
2. dibujos de muñecos
3. la trama
4. comedias musicales
5. de ninguna manera
6. eso no importa

C. *Escríbase una oración completa en español con cada una de las «frases importantes» que siguen:*

1. a pesar de
2. hacer el papel
3. tocar a uno
4. doblado en español
5. ser apasionado de
6. sin embargo

D. *Dése la forma correcta del presente de subjuntivo de cada verbo:*

1. yo	sacar	10. vosotros	llegar
2. tú	tocar	11. nosotros	rezar
3. Ud.	colocar	12. tú	aterrizar
4. él	buscar	13. ellos	vencer
5. Uds.	pagar	14. ella	coger
6. nosotros	vengar	15. yo	conocer
7. ella	gozar	16. Ud.	seguir
8. yo	almorzar	17. él	dirigir
9. Ud.	averiguar	18. ellas	nacer

E. *Dése la forma correcta del presente de indica*
   de indicativo de cada verbo:

1. yo	conocer	10. nosotros		
2. ella	crecer	11. Ud.		
3. yo	escoger	12. yo		
4. él	ofrecer	13. vosotros	gozar
5. Uds.	dirigir	14. yo	averiguar
6. yo	seguir	15. ellas	llegar
7. tú	pagar	16. yo	buscar
8. ellos	sacar	17. tú	tocar
9. yo	distinguir	18. yo	alzar

F. *Complétense las oraciones siguientes:*

1. Esta lección es (better than) aquélla. *mejor que*
2. Ganó (more than) quinientas pesetas el mes pasado. *más de*
3. Juan es (older than) Carlos. *mayor que*
4. Antonio es (the eldest) de mis hijos. *el mayor, más grande*
5. El Brasil es el país (largest) de las Américas. *el mayor*
6. No tengo (more than) tres dólares. *no más que*
7. El señor García es (very rich). *muy rica — riquísimo*
8. Me gustó la película (very much). *muchísimo*
9. Paquito es (the younger) de los dos hermanos. *menor*
10. El tren anda (more slowly than) el coche. *más despacio que*
11. Compré más libros (than I needed). *de los que necesitaba*
12. Tiene (less) habilidad (than) nosotros hasta ahora. *menos que*
13. Ana es (as pretty as) su hermana. *tan bonita como*
14. Luis escribió (as many letters as) Pablo. *tantas cartas como*
15. Antonio habla español (worse than) yo. *peor que*

G. *Tradúzcase al español:*

1. The sign in front of the movie house announces a new film.
2. She is one of the best actresses in the world.
3. The role that I liked most was that of the storekeeper.
4. Yes, he was a better actor than the star.
5. What a strange man he was!
6. I never did find out how he died.
7. While you are in Madrid I don't want you to pay for anything.

no más que - only

am not very fond of the movies but I do like the cartoons.

The show is about to begin, let's go in.

10. In spite of its many faults, the movie was more amusing than I expected.

H. *Prepárese una composición oral de cuatro minutos usando uno de los temas siguientes:*

1. «La Hija del Mar»
2. Las películas de Hollywood
3. Un gran actor

I. *Dictado tomado de la conversación «El cine», pp. 124–126.*

2. Ella es una del mejor actrices en el mundo.

3. Me gustó más el papel del tendero.

4. Sí, Era un mejor actor que la estrella.

5. Qué ~~rara~~ ~~se~~ ~~hombre~~ hombre tan rara

10. A pesar de sus muchas faltas, la película era más, divertido de la que espere.

Lección Catorce

PREPARATIVOS PARA EL VIAJE

I. Conversación

[*Léase en voz alta varias veces y apréndase de memoria.*]

—Mañana me despido de ti y de Madrid.

Tomorrow I take leave of you and of Madrid.

—¡Qué lástima que no puedes quedarte unos días más!

What a pity that you can't remain a few days more!

—¡Ojalá que pudiera! Pero es imposible, tengo que visitar nuestra sucursal en Barcelona.

Oh how I wish I could! But it's impossible, I have to visit our branch office in Barcelona.

—¿Cuándo volverás?

When will you come back?

—¡Quien sabe! De Barcelona voy a París en avión, y después a Roma, Londres e Irlanda.

Who knows! From Barcelona I'm going to Paris by plane, and then to Rome, London and Ireland.

—¡Cuánta suerte tienes!

How lucky you are!

—El viajar es muy interesante pero también cansa mucho. Antes de salir tengo que hacer unas cositas.

Traveling is very interesting but it is also very tiring. Before departing I have to do a few little things.

—Manos a la obra, entonces. ¿Qué tienes que hacer?

Let's get to work, then. What do you have to do?

—Quisiera primero cobrar este cheque porque necesito dinero y después, echar al correo unas cartas.

First I should like to cash this check because I need money and then, mail a few letters.

—La oficina de correos está solamente a dos cuadras de aquí.

The post office is only two blocks from here.

—Bueno, primero vamos allí y después iremos al banco.

Fine, first we'll go there and then we'll go to the bank.

—Vengo contigo. Quiero comprar unos sellos.

I'm coming with you. I want to buy some stamps.

(En la oficina de correos)

(In the post office)

—Buenos días, señor.

Good morning, sir.

—Buenos días. Esta carta contiene unos papeles importantes y no quiero que se pierda.

Good morning. This letter contains some important papers and I don't want it to go astray.

—Le aconsejo que la certifique. Para las cartas certificadas tendrá que ir a la otra ventanilla.

I advise you to register it. For registered letters you'll have to go to the other window.

—¿Y para remitir un paquete por correo aéreo?

And to send a package by airmail?

—Eso se puede hacer aquí. ¿Cuánto pesa?

That can be taken care of here. How much does it weigh?

—No lo he pesado.

I haven't weighed it.

—Páselo a través de la ventanilla por favor, lo peso aquí . . . un kilo y cuarto.

Pass it through the window please, I'll weigh it here . . . one kilogram and a quarter.

—¿Cuánto me costará el franqueo?

How much will the postage be?

—Ciento treinta y cinco pesetas.

One hundred and thirty-five pesetas.

—Muy bien, aquí las tiene. Gracias. José, ¿has comprado los sellos?

Very well, here you are. Thanks. Joseph, did you buy your stamps?

—Sí, vamos al banco.

Yes, let's go to the bank.

—¿Cree Ud. que me harán efectivo este cheque?

Do you think that they will cash this check?

—Creo que sí, pero si hay alguna dificultad lo puedo endosar yo.

I think so, but if there is any problem I can endorse it.

—¿Te conocen?   Do they know you?

—Sí, yo tengo una cuenta co-   Yes, I have an account there.
rriente allí.

—Muy bien. ¡Qué hubiera   Fine. What would I have done
hecho yo en Madrid sin ti!   in Madrid without you!

II. Frases Importantes

[*Apréndanse de memoria.*]

certificar una carta	to register a letter
cobrar un cheque; hacer efectivo un cheque	to cash a check
¡cuánta suerte tienes!	how lucky you are!
despedirse de	to take leave of, to say good-by to
echar al correo	to mail
el franqueo	the postage
en avión	by plane
endosar un cheque	to endorse a check
¡manos a la obra!	let's get to work; let's go!
por correo aéreo	(by) airmail
¡quién sabe!	who knows!
remitir un paquete	to send a package (*by mail*)
una cuenta corriente	a bank account

III. Puntos Gramaticales

69. **Usos del infinitivo** (Uses of the infinitive)

(a) **Después de besar a su madre salió.**

After kissing his mother he went out.

Se puso en marcha temprano para llegar al mercado antes de las ocho.

He started early in order to reach the market before eight o'clock.

Al cerrar la puerta se lastimó el dedo pulgar.

On closing the door he hurt his thumb.

The infinitive is used in Spanish after a preposition.

(b) **Comprar cosas que uno no necesita es una tontería.**

To buy things one doesn't need is foolish.

El comer demasiado es peligroso para la salud.

Eating too much is dangerous to one's health.

Saber es poder.	*Knowledge is power.*
Al pasar delante de la escuela se oía el cantar de los alumnos.	*On passing in front of the school the students' singing was heard.*
No le gustaba el constante ir y venir de la gente.	*She didn't like the constant going and coming of the people.*

The infinitive may be used in Spanish as a verbal noun. It may be the subject or the object of the verb.

(c) 1.

Quiere vernos.	*He wants to see us.*
La oí cantar.	*I heard her sing.*
No puede venir ahora.	*He can't come now.*
Saben jugar al tenis.	*They know how to play tennis.*

The infinitive may be used to complete the meaning of another verb. When so used, it is called the dependent infinitive.

2.

Vino a invitarnos al baile.	*He came to invite us to the dance.*
Empezó a correr cuando vió al policía.	*He began to run when he saw the policeman.*
Aprendió a manejar el coche dentro de pocos días.	*He learned to drive the car in a few days.*
Carlos me enseñó a patinar.	*Charles taught me how to skate.*

Verbs of motion and verbs that express beginning, learning, and teaching require a before a dependent infinitive.*

(d) The infinitive is sometimes used after impersonal expressions. See p. 79, section 49 (d).

(e) The infinitive is sometimes used in place of the subjunctive in noun clauses. See p. 78, section 49 (c).

70. Los usos del participio pasivo (Uses of the past participle)

(a) The past participle is used to form compound tenses. See pp. 65–67; 97–98.

* See appendix for a complete list of verbs which require a preposition before a dependent infinitive.

(b) 1. La niña estaba sentada cerca   *The girl was seated near*
     de su madre.   *her mother.*

     Éste es un libro muy cono-   *This is a well-known book.*
     cido.

     Tenía los codos apoyados en   *He had his elbows resting*
     la mesa.   *on the table.*

The past participle may be used as an adjective. When so used, it agrees in gender and number with the word it modifies.

2. Acabada la lección, salieron   *The lesson having ended,*
    de la clase.   *they left the room.*

    Vistas las nubes, decidieron   *Having seen the clouds, they*
    regresar a casa.   *decided to go back home.*

The past participle may be used in an absolute clause detached from the rest of the sentence.

71. El gerundio (Gerund)

(a) hablar   hablando   *speaking*
    comprender   comprendiendo   *understanding*
    vivir   viviendo   *living*

The gerund or present participle is formed by adding **–ando** to the root of **–ar** verbs, and **–iendo** to the root of **–er** and **–ir** verbs.

(b) 1. Están escribiendo la carta.   *They are writing the letter.*
    Estaba fregando los platos.   *She was washing the dishes.*

The gerund is used with **estar** to form the progressive construction.

2. Siguió estudiando aunque sus   *He continued studying al-*
    compañeros hacían mucho   *though his friends made*
    ruido.   *a great deal of noise.*

    Continúa trabajando en   *He keeps working in that*
    aquella fábrica.   *factory.*

The gerund is used with **seguir** and **continuar** to indicate continuity of action.

3. Dándome cuenta de que no   *Realizing that he wasn't*
    venía, fuí a buscarlo.   *coming, I went to look for*
                                     him.

Vió al niño corriendo calle   *She saw the boy running up*
arriba.   *the street.*

The gerund may act as a modifier of a subject or an object.

72. **Los pronombres personales después de preposiciones** (Personal
prepositional pronouns)

(a) The personal prepositional pronouns have the following forms:

mí	*me*	nosotros(as)	*us*
ti	*you* (fam.)	vosotros(as)	*you* (fam.)
él	*him*	ellos	*them* (m.)
ella	*her*	ellas	*them* (f.)
Usted	*you*	Ustedes	*you*
ello	*it*		

(b) Sin ellos no podemos hacer   *Without them we cannot do*
nada.   *anything.*
Me habló a menudo de Ud.   *He spoke often to me about*
you.

Seguramente querrá venir con   *She surely will want to come*
nosotros.   *with us.*
Para mí es lo mismo.   *It's all the same to me.*

The personal prepositional pronouns are used as direct objects
of prepositions.

(c) No quiso venir **conmigo** a la   *He didn't want to come with*
tertulia.   *me to the gathering.*
¿No asistieron **contigo** a la   *Didn't they attend the meeting*
reunión?   *with you?*

With the preposition **con**, the pronouns **mí** and **ti** combine to
become **conmigo, contigo.**

(d) Podremos salvarnos solamente   *We can save ourselves only*
si la situación económica   *if the economic situation*
cambia; en ello pongo mis   *changes; I am placing my*
últimas esperanzas.   *last hope on it.*

The neuter form **ello** refers only to a general situation and not
to a particular thing.

(e) **Siempre compra cosas para sí.**   *He is always buying things for himself.*

Lo quiero para mí.   *I want it for myself.*

Tú lo haces para ti.   *You do it for yourself.*

Se lo llevó consigo.   *He took it with him.*

Mí, ti, sí are reflexive prepositional pronouns. They are used only when the object of the sentence is the same as the subject. The reflexive pronoun **sí** combines with **con** to become **consigo.**

(f) **No se lo di a él, sino a Ud.**   *I did not give it to him, but to you.*

Te atreves a decirme eso a mí.   *You dare say that to me.*

A ellos no les gustó el drama.   *They didn't like the play.*

Al muchacho no le gusta estudiar.   *The boy doesn't like to study.*

The prepositional form may appear in a sentence in addition to other personal pronouns or nouns for the sake of clarity or for emphasis.

IV. Ejercicios

A. *Contéstense las preguntas siguientes usando oraciones completas en español:*

1. ¿Cuándo se despide Juan de su amigo?
2. ¿Por qué no puede quedarse en Madrid?
3. ¿Qué tomará para ir a París?
4. ¿Adónde irá después de París?
5. ¿Por qué es interesante viajar?
6. ¿Qué ciudades ha visitado Ud.?
7. ¿Qué tiene que hacer Juan en el banco?
8. ¿Qué quiere decir «cobrar un cheque»?
9. ¿Dónde se compran sellos?
10. ¿Por qué quiere Juan certificar la carta?
11. ¿Cuánto pesa el paquete?
12. ¿Cuánto cuesta un sello de correo aéreo?
13. ¿Dónde se cobra un cheque?
14. ¿Cómo se endosa un cheque?
15. ¿Por qué le conocen a José en el banco?

B. *Escríbase una pregunta en español con cada una de las «frases importantes» que siguen:*

1. certificar una carta
2. hacer efectivo un cheque
3. despedirse de

4. en avión
5. el franqueo

C. *Escríbase una oración completa en español con cada una de las «frases importantes» que siguen:*

1. cobrar un cheque
2. endosar un cheque
3. remitir un paquete

4. echar al correo
5. por correo aéreo
6. una cuenta corriente

D. *Complétense las oraciones siguientes en español:*

1. Roberto (was studying) cuando entré.
2. (Smoking) es peligroso para la salud.
3. (To err) es una cosa muy común entre los hombres.
4. Se fué (without closing) la puerta.
5. Vino para (to take leave of us).
6. (Upon entering) vió a todos sus compañeros.
7. No puede (learn) a manejar el coche.
8. Aprendió (to speak) español dentro de pocos meses.
9. Queremos (to see) toda la ciudad.
10. (The lesson finished) salieron de la clase.
11. (Having read) el periódico, se lo puso en el bolsillo.
12. Cuando llegamos vimos que la puerta (was closed) y las ventanas (were open).

E. *Complétense las oraciones siguientes en español:*

1. Juan (took leave of him) y de Madrid.
2. Después de (traveling) a Roma, Juan irá a Londres.
3. (Traveling) es muy interesante pero cansa mucho.
4. Vendré (with you) porque quiero comprar unos sellos.
5. Antonio (was sending) un paquete por correo aéreo cuando entré en la oficina de correos.
6. ¿Qué hubiera hecho Ud. en Madrid (without me)?
7. Mi amigo (taught me) patinar.
8. Vinieron (to see us) antes de (leaving) para Irlanda.

9. Las niñas (were seated) cerca de la ventana.
10. Sus padres (keep working) en aquella fábrica.
11. El profesor castiga (him but not her).
12. Ella lo hizo (for herself).
13. (She doesn't like) el drama.

F. *Hágase una oración, en español, con el presente y el futuro de cada uno de los verbos siguientes:*

1. valer	5. caber
2. reconocer	6. consentir
3. devolver	7. pagar
4. ofrecer	8. gozar

G. *Tradúzcase al español:*

1. What a pity, tomorrow I have to take leave of you.
2. I'm sorry that you cannot stay a few more days.
3. Oh, would that I could! I must leave for Paris today.
4. You're going by plane, aren't you?
5. Why don't you come back afterwards?
6. Having finished my vacation, I have to return to New York.
7. Where can I cash this check?
8. At the bank. Do you have an account there?
9. Will you come with me to the post office? I want to register this letter and mail this package.
10. Are you going to send those letters by airmail?
11. Stamps are sold at that window.
12. The postage on this package will be one hundred pesetas.
13. If you had not endorsed the check, I don't know what I would have done.

H. *Prepárese una composición oral de dos minutos usando uno de los temas siguientes:*

1. En la oficina de correos
2. En el banco

I. *Dictado tomado de la conversación* «**Preparativos para el viaje**», pp. 135–137.

Lección Quince

LA DESPEDIDA

I. Conversación

[*Léase en voz alta varias veces y apréndase de memoria.*]

(En el cuarto de Juan)

—Se acabó. Éste es el último día de mi estancia en Madrid.

—¡No sabes cuánto lo siento!

—Muchas gracias por tus atenciones. Has sido tan amable.

—¡Oh, no es nada! Fué un placer para mí. ¿Has hecho las maletas?

—Sí; oh, aquí está otra corbata.

—¿Cuál es la valija en la cual tienes las corbatas?

—La que está al lado del armario. No te molestes, la abro yo.

—¿Estás seguro de que has empaquetado todo . . . el cepillo de dientes, el peine, la maquinilla de afeitar?

—Sí, todo. Sabes que me he divertido un mundo. ¡Qué

(In John's room)

It's all over. This is the last day of my stay in Madrid.

You don't know how sorry I am!

Many thanks for your consideration. You've been very kind.

Oh, it's nothing! It was a pleasure for me. Have you packed the suitcases?

Yes; oh, here is another tie.

In which valise do you have the ties?

The one that is beside the bureau. Don't bother, I'll open it.

Are you sure you packed everything . . . the toothbrush, the comb, the safety razor?

Yes, everything. Do you know that I've enjoyed myself im-

144

interesante fueron la corrida, el drama, la fiesta!

—Me alegro de eso.

—Pero lo que me gustó más fué la cortesía de la gente.

—Muchas gracias. Creo que es tiempo de ponernos en marcha.

—Pues, andando.

(Más tarde, en la estación de ferrocarriles)

—¿A qué hora sale el tren?

—A las trece y cinco, según el horario.

—No hay que darse prisa entonces; son las doce y veinte.

—¿Quieres comer algo antes de partir?

—No tengo hambre ahora. Este tren tiene un coche comedor y tomaré algo allí.

—Mientras tú sacas el pasaje yo voy a facturar el equipaje.

—Gracias, pero deja ese maletín porque quiero llevarlo conmigo.

. . .

—Aquí tienes las contraseñas. Cuidado de no perderlas.

—Gracias. Creo que nos dejarán subir al tren ahora. Vamos.

—Los vagones de primera clase están allá.

—Aquí hay un compartimiento vacío. ¡Sube!

mensely. How interesting were the bullfight, the play, the feast!

I'm happy about that.

But what I liked most was the courtesy of the people.

Thank you very much. I think it's time to start out.

Well, let's go.

(Later, in the railroad station)

At what time does the train leave?

At five after one, according to the timetable.

There is no need to hurry, then; it's twelve-twenty now.

Do you want to eat something before leaving?

I'm not hungry now. This train has a dining car and I'll have something there.

While you get the ticket I'll check the baggage.

Thank you, but leave that small valise because I want to take it with me.

. . .

Here are the stubs. Be careful not to lose them.

Thanks. I think that they will let us get on the train now. Let's go.

The first-class cars are further on.

Here is an empty compartment. Get in!

—Pues, adiós, Juan. **Toma esta tarjeta. He escrito el nombre y la dirección de un amigo mío que vive en Barcelona. Si necesitas algo, pídeselo a él.**

Well, good-by, John. Take this card. I've written the name and address of a friend of mine who lives in Barcelona. If you need anything, ask him.

—**Mil gracias, José. No sabes lo agradecido que estoy.**

Many thanks, Joseph. You don't know how grateful I am.

—**No hay de qué. Feliz viaje. No te olvides de escribir.**

You're welcome. Pleasant journey. Don't forget to write.

—**Recuerdos a la familia.**

Regards to your family.

—**Adiós.**

Good-by.

II. Frases Importantes

[Apréndanse de memoria.]

cuidado de + *inf.*	take care to
darse prisa	to hurry
divertirse un mundo	to enjoy oneself immensely
el cepillo de dientes	the toothbrush
el coche cama	the Pullman, the sleeper
el coche comedor	the dining car
el vagón de primera clase	the first-class car (*Trains in Spain have first, second, and third classes.*)
facturar el equipaje	to check the baggage
hacer las maletas	to pack the suitcases
has sido tan amable	you've been so kind
la maquinilla de afeitar	the safety razor
lo agradecido que estoy	how thankful I am
mil gracias	a thousand thanks, many thanks
no es nada	it's nothing
no sabes cuánto lo siento	you don't know how sorry I am
ponerse en marcha	to start out, to start
recuerdos	regards
sacar el pasaje	to get the ticket
se acabó	it's ended, it's all over, it's finished

III. Puntos Gramaticales

73. **Pronombres y adjetivos relativos** (Relative pronouns and adjectives)

Relative pronouns and adjectives refer to and connect the dependent clause to a noun or pronoun in the main clause.

(a)
La señora que vino aquí era alta.	*The lady who came here was tall.*
No leyó el libro que le presté.	*He didn't read the book I lent him.*
¿Dónde está la revista que estaba leyendo?	*Where is the magazine I was reading?*

Que (*who, whom, which, that*) is the most common relative pronoun. It is invariable, refers to persons or things, and can be used as the subject or object of a verb. It cannot be omitted as is often the case in English.

(b)
El coche con que voy a la universidad es de mi padre.	*The car with which I go to the university belongs to my father.*
No me gusta el apartamento en que vivo.	*I don't like the apartment in which I live.*
El muchacho con quien hablaba es mi primo.	*The boy with whom I was speaking is my cousin.*

Que (*which*) is used as the object of a preposition when the antecedent is a thing. **Quien** (*whom*) is used after a preposition to refer to persons.

(c)
Se los entregué al señor quien estaba a la puerta.	*I handed them to the gentleman who was at the door.*
El dependiente quien le vendió esa corbata está de vacaciones.	*The clerk who sold you that tie is on vacation.*

The relative pronoun **quien** (*who*) refers only to persons. Its main use is as the direct object of a preposition relating to a person. (See [b] above.) The plural of **quien** is **quienes**.

(d)
¿Dónde está la maleta en la cual puse las camisas?	*Where is the suitcase in which I put the shirts?*

Nos llevaron a un cuarto en el cual había dos camas viejas.	*They took us to a room in which there were two old beds.*
La criada del señor Ribera, el cual se fué a Santiago, podrá ayudarte.	*Mr. Ribera's maid, who went to Santiago, will be able to help you.*

The relative pronouns **el cual, los cuales, la cual, las cuales** (*who, which, that*) may refer to both persons and things. They are generally used after long prepositions and also in place of **que** to distinguish between two antecedents.

NOTE: The simple relative **el que** (**los que, la que, las que**) may replace **el cual.**

(e) Este trabajo es muy duro, lo cual no me gusta.	*This work is very hard, which I don't like.*
La situación política es muy peligrosa, lo que me preocupa mucho.	*The political situation is very dangerous, which worries me a great deal.*

The relative pronouns **lo cual** (*which*) and **lo que** (*which, what, that which*) are invariable. They refer to an idea or to a situation and not to a particular noun.

(f) José es el que tiene la culpa.	*Joseph is the one who is to blame.*
Los que vinieron se divirtieron.	*Those who came enjoyed themselves.*
Lo que Ud. oyó es la pura verdad.	*What (that which) you heard is the pure truth.*

The relative pronouns **el que, la que** (*he who, she who, the one who, the one that*), **los que, las que** (*those who, the ones that*) are compound relatives which contain their own antecedents. **Lo que** (*what, that which*) is a neuter relative pronoun which refers to an idea or to a situation and not to a particular noun.

(g) La Señora González, cuyas hijas pertenecen al círculo, vino a la reunión.	*Mrs. Gonzales, whose daughters belong to the club, came to the meeting.*
El profesor Morenos, cuya erudición es bien conocida, será mi consejero.	*Professor Morenos, whose knowledge is well known, will be my adviser.*

Cuyo, cuyos, cuya, cuyas (*whose, of which*) are relative adjectives. They precede the nouns they modify and agree with them in gender and number.

(h) El doctor hizo **cuanto** pudo y después mandó llamar al cura.

The doctor did all he could and then sent for the priest.

Antes de salir le di **cuantos** libros tenía.

Before leaving I gave him all the books that I had.

Cuanto, cuantos, cuanta, cuantas (*all, all that, all those who*) may be used as pronouns or as adjectives. They refer to both persons or things. Like **el que,** they contain their own antecedents.

(i) Allí está el almacén **donde** trabaja Paquito.

There is the department store where Frankie works.

Pronto sabremos **de donde** viene.

Soon we shall know from where he comes.

Donde (*where, in what place*) and its derivatives, a **donde, de donde, en donde,** are relative adverbs indicating place.

74. Los pronombres y adjetivos interrogativos (Interrogative pronouns and adjectives)

(a) **¿Qué** quieren Uds.?
¿Qué hizo él ayer?
¿Qué es el cubismo?

What do you want?
What did he do yesterday?
What is cubism?

The interrogative pronoun **¿qué?** (*what?*), invariable in form, may be used as the subject or object of a verb. When used with **ser** it requests a definition.

(b) **¿Qué** libros ha leído Ud.?
¿Qué novela desea Carlos?

Which books have you read?
Which novel does Charles wish?

The interrogative adjective **¿qué?** has the meaning of *which?, which one(s)?*

(c) **¿Cuál** de los dos prefiere Ud.?

Which of the two do you prefer?

¿Cuál es la montaña más alta del mundo?

Which is the highest mountain in the world?

¿Cuáles de tus hijos van a ser abogados?	*Which of your sons are going to become lawyers?*

¿Cuál?, ¿cuáles? (*which?, which one(s)?*) refer to persons or things. They are used to distinguish one person or thing from another.

(d)
¿Quién es aquel señor?	*Who is that gentleman?*
¿Con quién hablabas?	*With whom were you speaking?*
¿A quién dió Ud. el billete?	*To whom did you give the ticket?*
¿De quiénes son esas maletas?	*Whose suitcases are those?*

¿Quién? (**¿quiénes?**) is used as a pronoun which refers to persons only. In addition to the meaning *who?*, it is used as the object of most prepositions to mean *whom?* and with the preposition **de** to mean *whose?*

(e)
¿Cuánto vale?	*How much is it worth?*
¿Cuántos libros hay en esta biblioteca?	*How many books are there in this library?*
¿Cuántas personas vendrán?	*How many people will come?*

¿Cuánto? (**–a, –os, –as**) means *how much?* or *how many?* It may be used as a relative pronoun or a relative adjective.

(f)
¿Dónde está tu sobrina?	*Where is your niece?*
¿Cómo ocurrió?	*How did it happen?*
¿Cuándo viene?	*When is he coming?*

¿Dónde? (*where?*), **¿cómo?** (*how?*), **¿cuándo?** (*when?*) are interrogative adverbs.

75. Dejar y salir

Deje Ud. la maleta aquí.	*Leave the suitcase here.*
Déjalo hablar.	*Let him speak.*
El tren sale a las cinco.	*The train leaves at five o'clock.*
Salió de la casa.	*He left the house.*
Salieron a la calle.	*They went out into the street.*

Dejar means *to let, to allow, to leave behind.* **Salir** means *to depart, to go out of, to go out to.*

76. *Estúdiese en el apéndice los verbos* continuar, enviar, huir, reír.

IV. Ejercicios

A. *Contéstense las preguntas siguientes usando oraciones completas en español:*

1. ¿Para dónde sale el señor Smith?
2. ¿Qué se olvidó de empaquetar?
3. ¿Dónde está la valija?
4. ¿Ha empaquetado todo el señor Smith?
5. ¿Qué le gustó más al señor Smith?
6. ¿A qué hora sale el tren?
7. ¿Dónde está la estación de ferrocarriles?
8. ¿Qué ciudades ha visitado Ud.?
9. ¿Qué medio de transporte prefiere Ud.?
10. ¿Dónde se come en un tren?
11. ¿Qué hace José mientras que Juan saca el pasaje?
12. ¿Dónde están los vagones de primera clase?
13. ¿Por qué le dió José al señor Smith la dirección de un amigo suyo en Barcelona?
14. ¿Por qué está agradecido el señor Smith?

B. *Escríbase una pregunta en español con cada una de las «frases importantes» que siguen:*

1. darse prisa
2. divertirse un mundo
3. el coche cama
4. el vagón de primera clase
5. facturar el equipaje
6. ponerse en marcha
7. sacar el pasaje
8. se acabó

C. *Escríbase una oración completa en español con cada una de las «frases importantes» que siguen:*

1. cuidado de
2. el cepillo de dientes
3. el coche comedor
4. hacer las maletas
5. la maquinilla de afeitar
6. lo agradecido que estoy
7. no sabes cuánto lo siento

D. *Complétense las oraciones siguientes en español:*

1. El muchacho (who) está allí es mi primo.
2. (He who) estudia aprende.
3. (What) me gustó más fué la corrida.

4. La señora (to whom) hablaba era muy amable.
5. El compartimiento (in which) estábamos era muy pequeño.
6. Me falta dinero (which) me preocupa.
7. (Those who) llegaron tarde perdieron el tren.
8. La fiesta (to which) nos invitaron fué muy divertida.
9. La hija del señor Moreno, (who) está enferma, no pudo venir.
10. Tú eres (the one who) tiene la culpa.

E. *Complétense las oraciones siguientes en español:*

1. ¿(Which one) de los dos prefiere Ud.?
2. ¿(Whose) son estas maletas?
3. ¿(To whom) dió Ud. las contraseñas?
4. ¿(How much) dinero te falta?
5. ¿(What) quieren ellos?
6. ¿(How many) libros leyó Ud. durante el verano?
7. ¿(Which ones) son los más inteligentes?
8. ¿(Whose) es esta novela?
9. ¿(Who) llamaron a la puerta?
10. ¡(Leave) esta casa en seguida!
11. ¡(Leave) esta valija aquí!
12. No quiero (leave) para la oficina ahora.

F. *Cámbiense los verbos subrayados al presente de indicativo:*

1. Huí con toda prisa de aquel lugar lúgubre.
2. Nos envió unos regalos bonitos.
3. Ella continuó trabajando todo el día.
4. Mi padre quería que yo estudiase con más ahinco.
5. La conocí desde hace mucho tiempo.
6. Se rieron de los pobres campesinos.
7. Seguí contemplando el cuadro.
8. Ya saqué el pasaje.
9. No querían que yo pagase la comida.
10. ¿A qué hora salió el tren?

G. *Tradúzcase al español:*

1. My stay in Madrid was very pleasant.
2. Now I must leave for Rome.

3. What I don't like is to leave my friends behind.
4. You don't know how sorry I am.
5. Which one of these suitcases are you taking with you?
6. The one that is on the bureau.
7. Don't forget to pack the toothbrush, the shirts, and the ties.
8. Mrs. Moreno's son, whom you met at the theatre, will accompany us.
9. Whose address is this? It's ours.
10. The one who took us to the railroad station is very kind.
11. What is a dining car?
12. Where are the first-class cars? They are further on.

H. *Prepárese una composición oral usando uno de los temas siguientes:*

1. La despedida
2. Mi último viaje a la capital
3. Los medios de transporte

I. *Dictado tomado de la conversación* «**La despedida**», pp 144–146.

APPENDIX

77. Los verbos regulares (Regular verbs)

I –ar	II –er	III –ir

INFINITIVE

hablar *to speak*	comprender *to understand*	vivir *to live*

PRESENT PARTICIPLE

hablando *speaking*	comprendiendo *understanding*	viviendo *living*

PAST PARTICIPLE

hablado *spoken*	comprendido *understood*	vivido *lived*

INDICATIVE MOOD

PRESENT

I speak, do speak, am speaking, etc.	*I understand, do understand, am understanding*, etc.	*I live, do live, am living*, etc.
hablo	comprendo	vivo
hablas	comprendes	vives
habla	comprende	vive
hablamos	comprendemos	vivimos
habláis	comprendéis	vivís
hablan	comprenden	viven

IMPERFECT

I was speaking, used to speak, spoke, etc.	*I was understanding, used to understand, understood*, etc.	*I was living, used to live, lived*, etc.
hablaba	comprendía	vivía
hablabas	comprendías	vivías
hablaba	comprendía	vivía
hablábamos	comprendíamos	vivíamos
hablabais	comprendíais	vivíais
hablaban	comprendían	vivían

PRETERITE

I spoke, did speak, etc.	I understood, did understand, etc.	I lived, did live, etc.
hablé	comprendí	viví
hablaste	comprendiste	viviste
habló	comprendió	vivió
hablamos	comprendimos	vivimos
hablasteis	comprendisteis	vivisteis
hablaron	comprendieron	vivieron

FUTURE

I shall (will) speak, etc.	I shall (will) understand, etc.	I shall (will) live, etc.
hablaré	comprenderé	viviré
hablarás	comprenderás	vivirás
hablará	comprenderá	vivirá
hablaremos	comprenderemos	viviremos
hablaréis	comprenderéis	viviréis
hablarán	comprenderán	vivirán

CONDITIONAL

I should (would) speak, etc.	I should (would) understand, etc.	I should (would) live, etc.
hablaría	comprendería	viviría
hablarías	comprenderías	vivirías
hablaría	comprendería	viviría
hablaríamos	comprenderíamos	viviríamos
hablaríais	comprenderíais	viviríais
hablarían	comprenderían	vivirían

IMPERATIVE MOOD

Speak, etc.	Understand, etc.	Live, etc.
habla (tú)	comprende (tú)	vive (tú)
hable Ud.	comprenda Ud.	viva Ud.
hablemos (nosotros)	comprendamos (nosotros)	vivamos (nosotros)
hablad (vosotros)	comprended (vosotros)	vivid (vosotros)
hablen Uds.	comprendan Uds.	vivan Uds.

Subjunctive Mood

Present

(that) I may speak, etc.	*(that) I may under-stand,* etc.	*(that) I may live,* etc.
hable	comprenda	viva
hables	comprendas	vivas
hable	comprenda	viva
hablemos	comprendamos	vivamos
habléis	comprendáis	viváis
hablen	comprendan	vivan

Imperfect (−se form)

(that) I might (should) speak, etc.	*(that) I might (should) understand,* etc.	*(that) I might (should) live,* etc.
hablase	comprendiese	viviese
hablases	comprendieses	vivieses
hablase	comprendiese	viviese
hablásemos	comprendiésemos	viviésemos
hablaseis	comprendieseis	vivieseis
hablasen	comprendiesen	viviesen

Imperfect (−ra form)

hablara	comprendiera	viviera
hablaras	comprendieras	viveras
hablara	comprendiera	viviera
habláramos	comprendiéramos	viviéramos
hablarais	comprendierais	vivierais
hablaran	comprendieran	vivieran

Compound Tenses

The compound tenses of all verbs are formed by adding the past participle of the main verb to the proper form of the auxiliary verb **haber.**

Perfect Infinitive

haber hablado *to have spoken*	**haber comprendido** *to have understood*	**haber vivido** *to have lived*

Perfect Participle

habiendo hablado *having spoken*	**habiendo comprendido** *having understood*	**habiendo vivido** *having lived*

INDICATIVE MOOD

PRESENT PERFECT

I have spoken (understood, lived), etc.

he
has
ha
hemos
habéis
han
} hablado (comprendido, vivido)

PLUPERFECT

I had spoken (understood, lived), etc.

había
habías
había
habíamos
habíais
habían
} hablado (comprendido, vivido)

PRETERITE PERFECT

I had spoken (understood, lived), etc.

hube
hubiste
hubo
hubimos
hubisteis
hubieron
} hablado (comprendido, vivido)

FUTURE PERFECT

I shall have spoken (understood, lived), etc.

habré
habrás
habrá
habremos
habréis
habrán
} hablado (comprendido, vivido)

CONDITIONAL PERFECT

I should have spoken (understood, lived), etc.

habría
habrías
habría
habríamos
habríais
habrían
} hablado (comprendido, vivido)

SUBJUNCTIVE MOOD

PRESENT PERFECT

(that) I may have spoken (understood, lived), etc.

haya
hayas
haya
hayamos
hayáis
hayan
} hablado (comprendido, vivido)

PLUPERFECT (–se, –ra)

(that) I might (should) have spoken (understood, lived), etc.

hubiese (hubiera)
hubieses (hubieras)
hubiese (hubiera)
hubiésemos (hubiéramos) } hablado
hubieseis (hubierais)   (comprendido, vivido)
hubiesen (hubieran)

78. Los verbos que cambian la raíz (Radical-changing verbs)

A radical-changing verb is one whose radical vowel (–e or –o) changes when the tonic accent (voice stress) falls upon them. There are three classes of radical-changing verbs:

(a) First Class   e > ie; o > ue
In this class belong only –ar and –er verbs. These verbs change –e of the root to –ie and –o to –ue in all of the singular and the third person plural of the present indicative, present subjunctive, and the imperative singular.

cerrar *to close*

PRES. IND. **cierro, cierras, cierra, cerramos, cerráis, cierran**
PRES. SUBJ. **cierre, cierres, cierre, cerremos, cerréis, cierren**
IMPERATIVE **cierra, cerrad**

volver *to return*

PRES. IND. **vuelvo, vuelves, vuelve, volvemos, volvéis, vuelven**
PRES. SUBJ. **vuelva, vuelvas, vuelva, volvamos, volváis, vuelvan**
IMPERATIVE **vuelve, volved**

(b) Second Class   e > ie, i; o > ue, u
In this class are found only –ir verbs. These verbs change –e of the root to –ie and –o to –ue as in the First Class (that is, in all of the singular and the third person plural of the present indicative, the present subjunctive, and the imperative singular). They also change –e to –i and –o to –u in the first and second persons plural of the present subjunctive, in the third person singular and plural of the preterite, throughout the imperfect subjunctive, and in the present participle.

sentir *to feel, to regret, to be sorry*

PRES. IND. **siento, sientes, siente, sentimos, sentís, sienten**
PRES. SUBJ. **sienta, sientas, sienta, sintamos, sintáis, sientan**
IMPERATIVE **siente, sentid**
PRET. IND. **sentí, sentiste, sintió, sentimos, sentisteis, sintieron**

IMPERF. SUBJ. (–ra form) sintiera, sintieras, sintiera, sintiéramos, sintierais, sintieran

(–se form) sintiese, sintieses, sintiese, sintiésemos, sintieseis, sintiesen

PRES. PART. sintiendo

dormir *to sleep*

PRES. IND. duermo, duermes, duerme, dormimos, dormís, duermen

PRES. SUBJ. duerma, duermas, duerma, durmamos, durmáis, duerman

IMPERATIVE duerme, dormid

PRET. IND. dormí, dormiste, durmió, dormimos, dormisteis, durmieron

IMPERF. SUBJ. (–ra form) durmiera, durmieras, durmiera, durmiéramos, durmierais, durmieran

(–se form) durmiese, durmieses, durmiese, durmiésemos, durmieseis, durmiesen

PRES. PART. durmiendo

(c) Third Class   e > i

This class also consists only of –ir verbs. These verbs change the –e of the root to –i in all of the singular and the third person plural of the present indicative, throughout the present subjunctive, in the third person singular and plural of the preterite, throughout the imperfect subjunctive, in the imperative singular, and in the present participle.

pedir *to ask* (*for*)

PRES. IND. pido, pides, pide, pedimos, pedís, piden

PRES. SUBJ. pida, pidas, pida, pidamos, pidáis, pidan

IMPERATIVE pide, pedid

PRET. IND. pedí, pediste, pidió, pedimos, pedisteis, pidieron

IMPERF. SUBJ. (–ra form) pidiera, pidieras, pidiera, pidiéramos, pidierais, pidieran

(–se form) pidiese, pidieses, pidiese, pidiésemos, pidieseis, pidiesen

PRES. PART. pidiendo

79. Los verbos con cambios ortográficos (Orthographic-changing verbs)

Orthographic-changing verbs are those which undergo a change in spelling (orthography) in order to maintain the sound of the final consonant of the infinitive. These changes occur as follows:

(a) Verbs in –car   c > qu

sacar *to take out*

PRET. IND. saqué, sacaste, sacó, sacamos, sacasteis, sacaron

PRES. SUBJ. saque, saques, saque, saquemos, saquéis, saquen

Verbs ending in –car change –c to –qu before the vowel –e.

(b) Verbs in –gar   g > gu
pagar *to pay*
PRET. IND. pagué, pagaste, pagó, pagamos, pagasteis, pagaron
PRES. SUBJ. **pague, pagues, pague, paguemos, paguéis, paguen**
Verbs ending in –gar change –g to –gu before the vowel –e.

(c) Verbs in –zar   z > c
gozar *to enjoy*
PRET. IND. gocé, gozaste, gozó, gozamos, gozasteis, gozaron
PRES. SUBJ. goce, goces, goce, gocemos, gocéis, gocen
Verbs ending in –zar change –z to –c before the vowel –e.

(d) Verbs ending in –guar   gu > gü
averiguar *to ascertain*
PRET. IND. **averigüé, averiguaste, averiguó, averiguamos, averi-guasteis, averiguaron**
PRES. SUBJ. **averigüe, averigües, averigüe, averigüemos, averigüéis, averigüen**
Verbs ending in –guar change –gu to –gü before the vowel –e.

(e) Verbs in –cer and –cir, preceded by a consonant   c > z
vencer *to conquer*
PRES. IND. **venzo, vences, vence, vencemos, vencéis, vencen**
PRES. SUBJ. **venza, venzas, venza, venzamos, venzáis, venzan**

esparcir *to scatter*
PRES. IND. **esparzo, esparces, esparce, esparcimos, esparcís, esparcen**
PRES. SUBJ. **esparza, esparzas, esparza, esparzamos, esparzáis, esparzan**
Verbs ending in –cer and –cir preceded by a consonant usually change –c to –z before the vowels –o and –a.

(f) Verbs in –cer and –cir, preceded by a vowel   c > zc
conocer *to know*
PRES. IND. **conozco, conoces, conoce, conocemos, conocéis, conocen**
PRES. SUBJ. **conozca, conozcas, conozca, conozcamos, conozcáis, conozcan**

producir *to produce*
PRES. IND. **produzco, produces, produce, producimos, producís, producen**
PRES. SUBJ. **produzca, produzcas, produzca, produzcamos, produzcáis, produzcan**
Verbs ending in –cer and –cir preceded by a vowel change –c to –zc before the vowels –o and –a.

(g) Verbs in –ger and –gir   g > j
escoger *to choose, to select*
PRES. IND. **escojo, escoges, escoge, escogemos, escogéis, escogen**
PRES. SUBJ. **escoja, escojas, escoja, escojamos, escojáis, escojan**

dirigir *to direct*
PRES. IND. dirijo, diriges, dirige, dirigimos, dirigís, dirigen
PRES. SUBJ. dirija, dirijas, dirija, dirijamos, dirijáis, dirijan
Verbs ending in –ger and –gir change –g to –j before the vowels
–o and –a.

(h) Verbs in –guir   gu > g
seguir *to follow, to continue*
PRES. IND. sigo, sigues, sigue, seguimos, seguís, siguen
PRES. SUBJ. siga, sigas, siga, sigamos, sigáis, sigan
Verbs ending in –guir change –gu to –g before the vowels –o and –a.

(i) Verbs in –quir   qu > c
delinquir *to do wrong, to be delinquent*
PRES. IND. delinco, delinques, delinque, delinquimos, delinquís, delinquen
PRES. SUBJ. delinca, delincas, delinca, delincamos, delincáis, delincan
Verbs ending in –quir change –qu to –c before the vowels –o and –a.

(j) Verbs in –iar and –uar   i > í; u > ú
enviar *to send*
PRES. IND. envío, envías, envía, enviamos, enviáis, envían
PRES. SUBJ. envíe, envíes, envíe, enviemos, enviéis, envíen
IMPERATIVE envía, enviad

continuar *to continue*
PRES. IND. continúo, continúas, continúa, continuamos, continuáis, continúan
PRES. SUBJ. continúe, continúes, continúe, continuemos, continuéis, continúen
IMPERATIVE continúa, continuad
Some verbs ending in –iar and all verbs in –uar (except –guar) require a written accent on the –i and –u respectively throughout the singular and the third person plural of the present indicative and present subjunctive. The accent also appears in the singular of the familiar imperative.

80. **Verbos con otros cambios** (Other verbal irregularities)

(a) Verbs in –uir
huir *to flee*
PRES. IND. huyo, huyes, huye, huimos, huís, huyen
PRES. SUBJ. huya, huyas, huya, huyamos, huyáis, huyan
PRET. IND. huí, huiste, huyó, huimos, huisteis, huyeron
IMPERF. SUBJ. (–ra) huyera, huyeras, huyera, huyéramos, huyerais, huyeran
        (–se) huyese, huyeses, huyese, huyésemos, huyeseis, huyesen
IMPERATIVE huye, huid

PRES. PART. **huyendo**
Verbs ending in **–uir** (except **–guir, –quir**) insert **–y** before **–a, –o,**
and **–e,** and replace an unstressed **–i** between vowels by **–y.**

(b) Verbs in **–eír**
reír to laugh
PRES. IND. **río, ríes, ríe, reímos, reís, ríen**
PRES. SUBJ. **ría, rías, ría, riamos, riáis, rían**
PRET. IND. **reí, reíste, rió, reimos, reísteis, rieron**
IMPERF. SUBJ. (**–ra**) **riera, rieras, riera, riéramos, rierais, rieran**
  (**–se**) **riese, rieses, riese, riésemos, rieseis, riesen**
IMPERATIVE **ríe, reíd**
PRES. PART. **riendo**
PAST. PART. **reído**
Verbs ending in **–eír** belong to the third class of radical-changing
verbs (like **pedir**). The initial **i** of an ending of a verb beginning
with **ie** or **io** is dropped.

81. **Verbos con preposición delante de un infinitivo** (Verbs requiring a preposition before a dependent infinitive)

(a) The following are the most common verbs that require the preposition **a** before an infinitive:

acertar	*to manage, succeed* (*in*)
acostumbrarse	*to accustom oneself, get used to*
acudir	*to hurry, hasten*
aprender	*to learn*
apresurarse	*to hasten*
atreverse	*to dare*
ayudar	*to help*
bajar	*to come* (*go*) *down*
comenzar	*to begin*
correr	*to run*
disponerse	*to prepare, make onself ready*
echar(se)	*to start*
empezar	*to begin*
enseñar	*to teach*
entrar	*to enter*
enviar	*to send*
invitar	*to invite*
ir	*to go*
llegar	*to arrive*
negarse	*to refuse*
obligar	*to compel*
pasar	*to pass, go by*
persuadir	*to persuade*

ponerse	*to start*
proceder	*to proceed*
subir	*to go (come) up*
tornar	*to turn, return, do again*
venir	*to come*
volar	*to fly*
volver	*to return, do again*

(b) The following are the most common verbs that require the preposition de before an infinitive:

acabar	*to have just*
acordarse	*to remember*
alegrarse	*to be glad*
avergonzarse	*to be ashamed*
cesar	*to cease*
concluir	*to finish*
dejar	*to discontinue*
encargarse	*to undertake, take on oneself*
extrañarse	*to be surprised*
gozar	*to enjoy*
olvidarse	*to forget*
tratar	*to try*

(c) The following are the most common verbs that require the preposition en before an infinitive:

acordar	*to agree upon*
complacerse	*to take pleasure in*
consentir	*to consent (to)*
empeñarse	*to insist (on)*
insistir	*to insist (on)*
pensar	*to think (of)*
persistir	*to persist (in)*
quedar	*to agree, decide*
tardar	*to be slow (to), delay*
vacilar	*to hesitate (to)*

(d) The following are the most common verbs that require the preposition con before an infinitive:

contar	*to count on, rely on*
soñar	*to dream (of)*

82. Los verbos irregulares (Irregular verbs)

andar *to walk, to go, to run*
PRES. IND. ando, andas, anda, andamos, andáis, andan
PRES. SUBJ. ande, andes, ande, andemos, andéis, anden

IMPERF. IND. andaba, andabas, andaba, andábamos, andabais, **andaban**
FUT. IND. andaré, andarás, andará, andaremos, andaréis, andarán
COND. andaría, andarías, andaría, andaríamos, andaríais, andarían
PRET. IND. anduve, anduviste, anduvo, anduvimos, anduvisteis, anduvieron
IMPERF. SUBJ. (–ra) anduviera, anduvieras, anduviera, anduviéramos,
anduvierais, anduvieran
  (–se) anduviese, anduvieses, anduviese, anduviésemos, anduvieseis,
anduviesen
IMPERATIVE anda, andad
PRES. PART. andando
PAST PART. andado

caber *to fit, to be contained in*
PRES. IND. quepo, cabes, cabe, cabemos, cabéis, caben
PRES. SUBJ. quepa, quepas, quepa, quepamos, quepáis, quepan
IMPERF. IND. cabía, cabías, cabía, cabíamos, cabíais, cabían
FUT. IND. cabré, cabrás, cabrá, cabremos, cabréis, cabrán
COND. cabría, cabrías, cabría, cabríamos, cabríais, cabrían
PRET. IND. cupe, cupiste, cupo, cupimos, cupisteis, cupieron
IMPERF. SUBJ. (–ra) cupiera, cupieras, cupiera, cupiéramos, cupierais,
cupieran.
  (–se) cupiese, cupieses, cupiese, cupiésemos, cupieseis, cupiesen
IMPERATIVE cabe, cabed
PRES. PART. cabiendo
PAST PART. cabido

caer *to fall*
PRES. IND. caigo, caes, cae, caemos, caéis, caen
PRES. SUBJ. caiga, caigas, caiga, caigamos, caigáis, caigan
IMPERF. IND. caía, caías, caía, caíamos, caíais, caían
FUT. IND. caeré, caerás, caerá, caeremos, caeréis, caerán
COND. caería, caerías, caería, caeríamos, caeríais, caerían
PRET. IND. caí, caíste, cayó, caímos, caísteis, cayeron
IMPERF. SUBJ. (–ra) cayera, cayeras, cayera, cayéramos, cayerais, cayeran
  (–se) cayese, cayeses, cayese, cayésemos, cayeseis, cayesen
IMPERATIVE cae, caed
PRES. PART. cayendo
PAST PART. caído

conducir *to conduct*
PRES. IND. conduzco, conduces, conduce, conducimos, conducís, conducen
PRES. SUPJ. conduzca, conduzcas, conduzca, conduzcamos, conduzcáis, con-
duzcan
IMPERF. IND. conducía, conducías, conducía, conducíamos, conducíais,
conducían
FUT. IND. conduciré, conducirás, conducirá, conduciremos, conduciréis,
conducirán

COND. conduciría, conducirías, conduciría, conduciríamos, conduciríais, conducirían

PRET. IND. conduje, condujiste, condujo, condujimos, condujisteis, condujeron

IMPERF. SUBJ. (–ra) condujera, condujeras, condujera, condujéramos, condujerais, condujeran
(–se) condujese, condujeses, condujese, condujésemos, condujeseis, condujesen

IMPERATIVE conduce, conducid

PRES. PART. conduciendo

PAST PART. conducido

conocer *to know, to be acquainted with*

PRES. IND. conozco, conoces, conoce, conocemos, conocéis, conocen

PRES. SUBJ. conozca, conozcas, conozca, conozcamos, conozcáis, conozcan

IMPERF. IND. conocía, conocías, conocía, conocíamos, conocíais, conocían

FUT. IND. conoceré, conocerás, conocerá, conoceremos, conoceréis, conocerán

COND. conocería, conocerías, conocería, conoceríamos, conoceríais, conocerían

PRET. IND. conocí, conociste, conoció, conocimos, conocisteis, conocieron

IMPERF. SUBJ. (–ra) conociera, conocieras, conociera, conociéramos, conocierais, conocieran
(–se) conociese, conocieses, conociese, conociésemos, conocieseis, conociesen

IMPERATIVE conoce, conoced

PRES. PART. conociendo

PAST PART. conocido

creer *to believe*

PRES. IND. creo, crees, cree, creemos, creéis, creen

PRES. SUBJ. crea, creas, crea, creamos, creáis, crean

IMPERF. IND. creía, creías, creía, creíamos, creíais, creían

FUT. IND. creeré, creerás, creerá, creeremos, creeréis, creerán

COND. creería, creerías, creería, creeríamos, creeríais, creerían

PRET. IND. creí, creíste, creyó, creímos, creísteis, creyeron

IMPERF. SUBJ. (–ra) creyera, creyeras, creyera, creyéramos, creyerais, creyeran
(–se) creyese, creyeses, creyese, creyésemos, creyeseis, creyesen

IMPERATIVE cree, creed

PRES. PART. creyendo

PAST PART. creído

dar *to give*

PRES. IND. doy, das, da, damos, dais, dan

PRES. SUBJ. dé, des, dé, demos, deis, den

IMPERF. IND. daba, dabas, daba, dábamos, dabais, daban

FUT. IND. daré, darás, dará, daremos, daréis, darán
COND. daría, darías, daría, daríamos, daríais, darían
PRET. IND. di, diste, dió, dimos, disteis, dieron
IMPERF. SUBJ. (–ra) diera, dieras, diera, diéramos, dierais, dieran
    (–se) diese, dieses, diese, diésemos, dieseis, diesen
IMPERATIVE da, dad
PRES. PART. dando
PAST PART. dado

decir *to say, to tell*
PRES. IND. digo, dices, dice, decimos, decís, dicen
PRES SUBJ. diga, digas, diga, digamos, digáis, digan
IMPERF. IND. decía, decías, decía, decíamos, decíais, decían
FUT. IND. diré, dirás, dirá, diremos, diréis, dirán
COND. diría, dirías, diría, diríamos, diríais, dirían
PRET. IND. dije, dijiste, dijo, dijimos, dijisteis, dijeron
IMPERF. SUBJ. (–ra) dijera, dijeras, dijera, dijéramos, dijerais, dijeran
    (–se) dijese, dijeses, dijese, dijésemos, dijeseis, dijesen
IMPERATIVE di, decid
PRES. PART. diciendo
PAST PART. dicho

estar *to be*
PRES. IND. estoy, estás, está, estamos, estáis, están
PRES. SUBJ. esté, estés, esté, estemos, estéis, estén
IMPERF. IND. estaba, estabas, estaba, estábamos, estabais, estaban
FUT. IND. estaré, estarás, estará, estaremos, estaréis, estarán
COND. estaría, estarías, estaría, estaríamos, estaríais, estarían
PRET. IND. estuve, estuviste, estuvo, estuvimos, estuvisteis, estuvieron
IMPERF. SUBJ. (–ra) estuviera, estuvieras, estuviera, estuviéramos, estu-
vierais, estuvieran
    (–se) estuviese, estuvieses, estuviese, estuviésemos, estuvieseis,
estuviesen
IMPERATIVE está, estad
PRES. PART. estando
PAST PART. estado

haber *to have*
PRES. IND. he, has, ha, hemos, habéis, han
PRES. SUBJ. haya, hayas, haya, hayamos, hayáis, hayan
IMPERF. IND. había, habías, había, habíamos, habíais, habían
FUT. IND. habré, habrás, habrá, habremos, habréis, habrán
COND. habría, habrías, habría, habríamos, habríais, habrían
PRET. IND. hube, hubiste, hubo, hubimos, hubisteis, hubieron
IMPERF. SUBJ. (–ra) hubiera, hubieras, hubiera, hubiéramos, hubierais,
hubieran
    (–se) hubiese, hubieses, hubiese, hubiésemos, hubieseis, hubiesen

IMPERATIVE. he, habed
PRES. PART. habiendo
PAST PART. habido

hacer *to do, to make*
PRES. IND. hago, haces, hace, hacemos, hacéis, hacen
PRES. SUBJ. haga, hagas, haga, hagamos, hagáis, hagan
IMPERF. IND. hacía, hacías, hacía, hacíamos, hacíais, hacían
FUT. IND. haré, harás, hará, haremos, haréis, harán
COND. haría, harías, haría, haríamos, haríais, harían
PRET. IND. hice, hiciste, hizo, hicimos, hicisteis, hicieron
IMPERF. SUBJ. (–ra) hiciera, hicieras, hiciera, hiciéramos, hicierais, hicieran
(–se) hiciese, hicieses, hiciese, hiciésemos, hicieseis, hiciesen
IMPERATIVE haz, haced
PRES. PART haciendo
PAST PART. hecho

ir *to go*
PRES. IND. voy, vas, va, vamos, vais, van
PRES. SUBJ. vaya, vayas, vaya, vayamos, vayáis, vayan
IMPERF. IND. iba, ibas, iba, íbamos, ibais, iban
FUT. IND. iré, irás, irá, iremos, iréis, irán
COND. iría, irías, iría, iríamos, iríais, irían
PRET. IND. fuí, fuiste, fué, fuimos, fuisteis, fueron
IMPERF. SUBJ. (–ra) fuera, fueras, fuera, fuéramos, fuerais, fueran
(–se) fuese, fueses, fuese, fuésemos, fueseis, fuesen
IMPERATIVE ve, id
PRES. PART. yendo
PAST PART. ido

leer *to read*
PRES. IND. leo, lees, lee, leemos, leéis, leen
PRES. SUBJ. lea, leas, lea, leamos, leáis, lean
IMPERF. IND. leía, leías, leía, leíamos, leíais, leían
FUT. IND. leeré, leerás, leerá, leeremos, leeréis, leerán
COND. leería, leerías, leería, leeríamos, leeríais, leerían
PRET. IND. leí, leíste, leyó, leímos, leísteis, leyeron
IMPERF. SUBJ. (–ra) leyera, leyeras, leyera, leyéramos, leyerais, leyeran
(–se) leyese, leyeses, leyese, leyésemos, leyeseis, leyesen
IMPERATIVE lee, leed
PRES. PART. leyendo
PAST PART. leído

oír *to hear*
PRES. IND. oigo, oyes, oye, oímos, oís, oyen
PRES. SUBJ. oiga, oigas, oiga, oigamos, oigáis, oigan
IMPERF. IND. oía, oías, oía, oíamos, oíais, oían

FUT. IND. oiré, oirás, oirá, oiremos, oiréis, oirán
COND. oiría, oirías, oiría, oiríamos, oiríais, oirían
PRET. IND. oí, oíste, oyó, oímos, oísteis, oyeron
IMPERF. SUBJ. (−ra) oyera, oyeras, oyera, oyéramos, oyerais, oyeran
    (−se) oyese, oyeses, oyese, oyésemos, oyeseis, oyesen
IMPERATIVE oye, oíd
PRES. PART. oyendo
PAST PART. oído

poder *to be able*
PRES. IND. puedo, puedes, puede, podemos, podéis, pueden
PRES. SUBJ. pueda, puedas, pueda, podamos, podáis, puedan
IMPERF. IND. podía, podías, podía, podíamos, podíais, podían
FUT. IND. podré, podrás, podrá, podremos, podréis, podrán
COND. podría, podrías, podría, podríamos, podríais, podrían
PRET. IND. pude, pudiste, pudo, pudimos, pudisteis, pudieron
IMPERF. SUBJ. (−ra) pudiera, pudieras, pudiera, pudiéramos, pudierais,
  pudieran
    (−se) pudiese, pudieses, pudiese, pudiésemos, pudieseis, pudiesen
IMPERATIVE ——, ——
PRES. PART. pudiendo
PAST PART. podido

poner *to put, to place*
PRES. IND. pongo, pones, pone, ponemos, ponéis, ponen
PRES. SUBJ ponga, pongas, ponga, pongamos, pongáis, pongan
IMPERF. IND. ponía, ponías, ponía, poníamos, poníais, ponían
FUT. IND. pondré, pondrás, pondrá, pondremos, pondréis, pondrán
COND. pondría, pondrías, pondría, pondríamos, pondríais, pondrían
PRET. IND. puse, pusiste, puso, pusimos, pusisteis, pusieron
IMPERF. SUBJ. (−ra) pusiera, pusieras, pusiera, pusiéramos, pusierais,
  pusieran
    (−se) pusiese, pusieses, pusiese, pusiésemos, pusieseis, pusiesen
IMPERATIVE pon, poned
PRES. PART. poniendo
PAST PART. puesto

querer *to wish, to want*
PRES. IND. quiero, quieres, quiere, queremos, queréis, quieren
PRES. SUBJ. quiera, quieras, quiera, queramos, queráis, quieran
IMPERF. IND. quería, querías, quería, queríamos, queríais, querían
FUT. IND. querré, querrás, querrá, querremos, querréis, querrán
COND. querría, querrías, querría, querríamos, querríais, querrían
PRET. IND. quise, quisiste, quiso, quisimos, quisisteis, quisieron
IMPERF. SUBJ. (−ra) quisiera, quisieras, quisiera, quisiéramos, quisierais,
  quisieran
    (−se) quisiese, quisieses, quisiese, quisiésemos, quisieseis, quisiesen

IMPERATIVE quiere, quered
PRES. PART. queriendo
PAST PART. querido

saber *to know, to know how*
PRES. IND. sé, sabes, sabe, sabemos, sabéis, saben
PRES. SUBJ. sepa, sepas, sepa, sepamos, sepáis, sepan
IMPERF. IND. sabía, sabías, sabía, sabíamos, sabíais, sabían
FUT. IND. sabré, sabrás, sabrá, sabremos, sabréis, sabrán
COND. sabría, sabrías, sabría, sabríamos, sabríais, sabrían
PRET. IND. supe, supiste, supo, supimos, supisteis, supieron
IMPERF. SUBJ. (–ra) supiera, supieras, supiera, supiéramos, supierais, supieran
  (–se) supiese, supieses, supiese, supiésemos, supieseis, supiesen
IMPERATIVE sabe, sabed
PRES. PART. sabiendo
PAST PART. sabido

salir *to go out, to leave*
PRES. IND. salgo, sales, sale, salimos, salís, salen
PRES. SUBJ. salga, salgas, salga, salgamos, salgáis, salgan
IMPERF. IND. salía, salías, salía, salíamos, salíais, salían
FUT. IND. saldré, saldrás, saldrá, saldremos, saldréis, saldrán
COND. saldría, saldrías, saldría, saldríamos, saldríais, saldrían
PRET. IND. salí, saliste, salió, salimos, salisteis, salieron
IMPERF. SUBJ. (–ra) saliera, salieras, saliera, saliéramos, salierais, salieran
  (–se) saliese, salieses, saliese, saliésemos, salieseis, saliesen
IMPERATIVE sal, salid
PRES. PART. saliendo
PAST PART. salido

ser *to be*
PRES. IND. soy, eres, es, somos, sois, son
PRES. SUBJ. sea, seas, sea, seamos, seáis, sean
IMPERF. IND. era, eras, era, éramos, erais, eran
FUT. IND. seré, serás, será, seremos, seréis, serán
COND. sería, serías, sería, seríamos, seríais, serían
PRET. IND. fuí, fuiste, fué, fuimos, fuisteis, fueron
IMPERF. SUBJ. (–ra) fuera, fueras, fuera, fuéramos, fuerais, fueran
  (–se) fuese, fueses, fuese, fuésemos, fueseis, fuesen
IMPERATIVE sé, sed
PRES. PART. siendo
PAST PART. sido

tener *to have*
PRES. IND. tengo, tienes, tiene, tenemos, tenéis, tienen
PRES. SUBJ. tenga, tengas, tenga, tengamos, tengáis, tengan
IMPERF. IND. tenía, tenías, tenía, teníamos, teníais, tenían

FUT. IND. tendré, tendrás, tendrá, tendremos, tendréis, tendrán
COND. tendría, tendrías, tendría, tendríamos, tendríais, tendrían
PRET. IND. tuve, tuviste, tuvo, tuvimos, tuvisteis, tuvieron
IMPERF. SUBJ. (–ra) tuviera, tuvieras, tuviera, tuviéramos, tuvierais, tuvieran
(–se) tuviese, tuvieses, tuviese, tuviésemos, tuvieseis, tuviesen
IMPERATIVE ten, tened
PRES. PART. teniendo
PAST PART. tenido

traer *to bring*
PRES. IND. traigo, traes, trae, traemos, traéis, traen
PRES. SUBJ. traiga, traigas, traiga, traigamos, traigáis, traigan
IMPERF. IND. traía, traías, traía, traíamos, traíais, traían
FUT. IND. traeré, traerás, traerá, traeremos, traeréis, traerán
COND. traería, traerías, traería, traeríamos, traeríais, traerían
PRET. IND. traje, trajiste, trajo, trajimos, trajisteis, trajeron
IMPERF. SUBJ. (–ra) trajera, trajeras, trajera, trajéramos, trajerais, trajeran
(–se) trajese, trajeses, trajese, trajésemos, trajeseis, trajesen
IMPERATIVE trae, traed
PRES. PART. trayendo
PAST PART. traído

valer *to be worth*
PRES. IND. valgo, vales, vale, valemos, valéis, valen
PRES. SUBJ. valga, valgas, valga, valgamos, valgáis, valgan
IMPERF. IND. valía, valías, valía, valíamos, valíais, valían
FUT. IND. valdré, valdrás, valdrá, valdremos, valdréis, valdrán
COND. valdría, valdrías, valdría, valdríamos, vadríais, valdrían
PRET. IND. valí, valiste, valió, valimos, valisteis, valieron
IMPERF. SUBJ. (–ra) valiera, valieras, valiera, valiéramos, valierais, valieran
(–se) valiese, valieses, valiese, valiésemos, valieseis, valiesen
IMPERATIVE val (vale), valed
PRES. PART. valiendo
PAST PART. valido

venir *to come*
PRES. IND. vengo, vienes, viene, venimos, venís, vienen
PRES. SUBJ. venga, vengas, venga, vengamos, vengáis, vengan
IMPERF. IND. venía, venías, venía, veníamos, veníais, venían
FUT. IND. vendré, vendrás, vendrá, vendremos, vendréis, vendrán
COND. vendría, vendrías, vendría, vendríamos, vendríais, vendrían
PRET. IND. vine, viniste, vino, vinimos, vinisteis, vinieron
IMPERF. SUBJ. (–ra) viniera, vinieras, viniera, viniéramos, vinierais, vinieran
(–se) viniese, vinieses, viniese, viniésemos, vinieseis, viniesen

IMPERATIVE **ven, venid**
PRES. PART. **viniendo**
PAST PART. **venido**

ver *to see*
PRES. IND. **veo, ves, ve, vemos, veis, ven**
PRES. SUBJ. **vea, veas, vea, veamos, veáis, vean**
IMPERF. IND. **veía, veías, veía, veíamos, veíais, veían**
FUT. IND. **veré, verás, verá, veremos, veréis, verán**
COND. **vería, verías, vería, veríamos, veríais, verían**
PRET. IND. **vi, viste, vió, vimos, visteis, vieron**
IMPERF. SUBJ. (–ra) **viera, vieras, viera, viéramos, vierais, vieran**
　　　　(–se) **viese, vieses, viese, viésemos, vieseis, viesen**
IMPERATIVE **ve, ved**
PRES. PART. **viendo**
PAST PART. **visto**

VOCABULARIES

ABBREVIATIONS

adj.	adjective
adv.	adverb
cond.	conditional
conj.	conjunction
def. art.	definite article
dem. adj.	demonstrative adjective
dem. pron.	demonstrative pronoun
dir. obj.	direct object
f.	feminine
fam.	familiar
fut.	future
gram.	grammar
indir. obj.	indirect object
inf.	infinitive
interr.	interrogative
m.	masculine
n.	noun
past part.	past participle
pers. pron.	personal pronoun
pl.	plural
poss.	possessive
prep.	preposition
pres. part.	present participle
pron.	pronoun
rel. pron.	relative pronoun
sing.	singular
subj.	subjunctive
vb.	verb

VOCABULARY: SPANISH–ENGLISH

a at, to, in, on; *with* **el = al**

abajo below, down, underneath, downstairs; **calle abajo** down the street; **por allí abajo** down there

abogado *m.* lawyer

abonar to guarantee, to recommend, to speak for, to justify; **abonar los derechos de matrícula** to pay the tuition fees

abono *m.* guarantee, subscription, allowance, discount, receipt; **billete de abono** *m.* commutation ticket

abril *m.* April

abrir to open

absoluto, –a absolute

absurdo, –a absurd

acabar to finish, to end; **acabar de +** *inf.* to have just + *past part.;* **se acabó** it's ended, it's all over, it's finished

acalorado, –a heated, fiery, excited

acaso perhaps, maybe

aceite *m.* oil

aceptar to accept

acera *f.* sidewalk, curb

acerca de about, concerning

acercarse (a) to draw near, to approach

acomodador *m.* usher

acompañar to accompany, to go with

Aconcagua *highest mountain in America*

aconsejar to advise

acontecimiento *m.* event, happening

acordarse (ue) (de) to remember

acostar (ue) to put to bed, to lay; **acostarse** to go to bed, to lie down

actitud *f.* attitude, position

acto *m.* act, action

actor *m.* actor

actriz *f.* actress

acuerdo *m.* accord, agreement; **estar de acuerdo** to agree, to be in agreement with; **de acuerdo** agreed, in accord, in agreement

acumulador *m.* battery; **revisar el acumulador** to check the battery

acusado, –a *n. or adj.* defendant, accused

adiós good-by

adjetivo *m.* adjective

administrador *m.* administrator, manager, director

¿adónde? where? (*to what place?*)

aduana *f.* customhouse

adverbial adverbial

adverbio *m.* adverb

advertir (ie, i) to warn, to notify

aéreo, –a aerial, air; **por correo aéreo** (by) airmail

aeroplano *m.* airplane

afán *m.* anxiety, eagerness

afeitar(se) to shave; **maquinilla de afeitar** *f.* safety razor

afueras *f. pl.* outskirts, suburbs
agitado, –a agitated, excited
agosto *m.* August
agradable pleasant, agreeable, pleasing
agradecer to be thankful for; **lo agradecido que estoy** how thankful I am
agua *f.* water
aguafuerte *f.* etching
ahí there
ahinco *m.* earnestness, eagerness, ardor
ahora now; **ahora mismo** just now, right now, this very minute
aire *m.* air
alabar to praise; **¡alabado sea Dios!** God be praised!
albedrío *m.* will, free will
aldeano *m.* villager
alegrarse de to be glad
alegre gay, happy
alegremente happily
alegría *f.* rejoicing, happiness, gaiety
Alfonso Alphonse
algo *pron.* something, anything; *adv.* somewhat, rather
algodón *m.* cotton
alguacil *m.* bailiff, constable
alguien someone, somebody, anyone, anybody
algún, alguno, –a *adj.* some, any; *pl.* a few; *pron.* someone, some
alma *f.* soul
almacenes *m. pl.* department store
almeja *f.* clam
almorzar (ue) to have lunch, to eat lunch
alojarse to live, to lodge, to take up lodgings
alto, –a tall, high, expensive (*in price*); **en alto** up (on) high; **en voz alta** aloud
alumno *m.* pupil, student
alzar to raise; **alzarse** to rise
allá there, over there
allí there
amable kind, lovely, amiable, affable;

has sido tan amable you've been very kind
amarillo, –a yellow
ambos, –as both
América *f.* America
amiga *f.* friend
amigo *m.* friend
amor *m.* love
Ana Anna
anchova *f.* anchovy
andando let's go
andar to walk, to go, to run (*a machine*)
andén *m.* platform
animación *f.* animation, liveliness, excitement
animal *m.* animal
anoche last night
anochecer *m.* nightfall, dusk
ansia *f.* anxiety, longing, yearning
ante before
anterior anterior, preceding; **pretérito anterior** preterite perfect
antes *adv.* before, formerly; **antes de** *prep.* before; **antes (de) que** *conj.* before
Antonio Anthony
anunciar to announce, to advertise
anuncio *m.* announcement, notice, advertisement, ad
año *m.* year
apagar to put out; **apagar la luz** to put out the light
aparato *m.* apparatus, machine; **aparato fotográfico** *m.* camera
apartamento *m.* apartment
apasionado, –a passionate, devoted, fond; **ser apasionado de** to be fond of
apenas hardly, scarcely; as soon as
apéndice *m.* appendix
aperitivo *m.* aperitif
apetito *m.* appetite
apoplejía *f.* apoplexy; **ataque de apoplejía** *m.* heart attack, apoplexy
apoyar to support, to lean, to rest

aprender to learn; **aprender de memoria** to learn by heart, to memorize

aprobado, –a pass in an examination; **resultar aprobado** to pass (*an examination*)

apropriado, –a appropriate

apurarse to worry, to fret, to grieve; **no te apures** don't worry

aquel, aquella *adj.* that; *pl.* those; *pron.* **aquél, aquélla, aquello** that (one), the former; *pl.* those, the former

aquí here; **por aquí** this way, around here, through here

Argentina *f.* Argentina

argumento *m.* argument, plot (*of a play or novel*)

armario *m.* cabinet, bookcase, bureau, closet

armonía *f.* harmony

arte *m. or f.* art; *bellas artes f.* fine arts

artículo *m.* article

artista *m. or f.* artist

arreglar to arrange

arriba up, upstairs, above

arroz *m.* rice

asado, –a roasted; **carne asada** roast meat

ascensor *m.* elevator

asegurar to reassure, to assure, to affirm

así thus, so, like that; **así como** as well as; **así que** so, so that; as soon as; **¿no es así?** isn't it so?

asiento *m.* seat; **coger asientos** to get seats

asignatura *f.* subject (*of study*)

asistir (a) to attend, to be present at

asunto *m.* matter, affair, subject

ataque *m.* attack; **ataque cardíaco** *m.* heart attack; **ataque de apoplejía** *m.* heart attack, apoplexy

atención *f.* attention, kindness, consideration

aterrizar to land

atestiguar to give evidence, to attest

atreverse (a) to dare

atrevido, –a bold, daring, fearless, insolent

aun, aún even, still; **aun cuando** even though

aunque although, even though

auto *m.* automobile

automóvil *m.* automobile

autor *m.* author

autoridad *f.* authority

averiguar to find out, to inquire

avión *m.* airplane; **en avión** by plane

avisar to notify, to warn, to inform

aviso *m.* advertisement, warning, notice

ayer yesterday

ayudar to help

bailarín *m.;* **bailarina** *f.* dancer

baile *m.* dance

bajar to get off, to descend, to go down

bajo, –a *adj.* low, short; *adv.* underneath, below; *prep.* under

balompié *m.* soccer, football

banco *m.* bank

banda *f.* band

banderilla *f.* **banderilla** (*a dart, with a steel point, about three feet in length*)

banderillero *m. bullfighter who places the banderilla into the flanks of the bull*

bañar(se) to bathe, to take a bath

barbaridad *f.* barbarity, nonsense, foolishness

barbero *m.* barber

bastante enough, rather; **bastante bien** all right, pretty well

baúl *m.* trunk, chest

beber to drink

bebida *f.* drink, beverage

Bécquer, Gustavo Adolfo *famous poet of 19th century* (*1836–1870*) bello, -a beautiful; **bellas artes** *f.* fine arts

bendecir to bless; ¡**que Dios te bendiga!** may God bless you!

bendito, –a blessed, darn, cursed

besar to kiss

biblioteca *f.* library

bien well, all right; **bastante bien** all right, pretty well; **bien que** although

biftec *m.* beefsteak

billete *m.* ticket, bill (*paper money*); **billete al sol** ticket in the sun; **billete a la sombra** ticket in the shade (*at a bullfight*); **billete de abono** commutation ticket; **billete de ida y vuelta** round trip ticket; **billete sencillo** one-way ticket

bisté *m.* beefsteak

bistec *m.* beefsteak

blanco, –a white

bocina *f.* horn

boda *f.* wedding

bolsillo *m.* pocket, purse, pocketbook

bondad *f.* kindness, goodness

bonito, –a pretty

Brasil *m.* Brazil

bravo, –a brave, fearless; ¡**bravo!** bravo!, hurrah!

brillante brilliant, bright

buen(o), –a good; *adv.* fine, all right; **buenas noches** good evening, good night; **buenos días** good morning; **muy buenos** good morning; ¿**qué hay de bueno?** what's good?

Buenos Aires *capital of Argentina*

bujía *f.* candle, candlestick, spark plug; **cambiar las bujías** to change the spark plugs

bullicio *m.* noise, bustle

buscar to look (for)

butaca *f.* armchair, orchestra seat

caballo *m.* horse; **a caballo** on horseback; **ir a caballo** to go on horseback, to go horseback riding

cabello *m.* hair; *pl.* hair

caber to fit; **caber duda** to be in doubt; **no cabe duda** there is no doubt

cada each, every

caer to fall; **caerse** to fall (down), to drop

café *m.* coffee, café; **tomar un café** to have a cup of coffee

calcetín *m.* sock

Calderón de la Barca, Pedro *Spanish dramatist of the Siglo de Oro* (*1600–1681*)

calma *f.* calm, calmness, tranquility

calmar to calm

calor *m.* heat; **hacer calor** to be hot (warm) (*weather*); **tener calor** to be hot (warm) (*person*)

callar(se) to be silent, to keep silent

calle *f.* street; **calle abajo** down the street; **calle arriba** up the street

cama *f.* bed; **coche cama** *m.* Pullman, sleeper

camarero *m.* waiter

camarón *m.* shrimp

cambiar to change; **cambiar las bujías** to change the spark plugs

cambio *m.* change, exchange

camino *m.* road, highway, path

camisa *f.* shirt

campana *f.* bell

campesino *m.* peasant, farmer

canción *f.* song

cangrejo *m.* crab

cansado, –a tired

cansar to tire; **cansarse** to get tired

cantar to sing

cántaro *m.* large pitcher; **llover a cántaros** to pour, to come down *in* buckets, to rain cats and dogs

capa *f.* cape, cloak, mantle

capaz capable

capital *f.* capital (*city*)

capitán *m.* captain

capítulo *m.* chapter

cara *f.* face

cardenal cardinal (*eccl.*)

cardinal cardinal

cardíaco, –a cardiac; **ataque cardíaco** *m.* heart attack

Carlos Charles; **Carlos IV** *king of Spain* (*1748–1819*)

carne *f.* meat

caro, –a dear, expensive

carta *f.* letter; **carta certificada** *f.* registered letter

cartel *m.* poster, placard, handbill

casa *f.* house, home, firm; **a casa** (**to**) home; **en casa** at home; **ir a casa** to go home

casi almost, nearly

caso *m.* case; **en caso** (**de**) **que** in case

castellano, –a Castilian, Spanish

castigar to punish

catedrático *m.* professor

católico, –a Catholic

catorce fourteen

cebolla *f.* onion

ceca *f.* mint; **de Ceca en Meca** to and fro, from place to place

celebrar to celebrate, to take place; **celebrar una fiesta** to celebrate a feast

cena *f.* dinner, supper

cenar to dine, to have supper

central central

centro *m.* center, middle; **en el centro** in the city, in town, downtown

cepillo *m.* brush; **cepillo de dientes** toothbrush

cerca (**de**) near, about

cerdo *m.* hog; **chuleta de cerdo** *f.* pork chop

cero zero

certificar to certify, to attest, to register; **certificar una carta** to register a letter

Cervantes *Spanish novelist and author of* Don Quijote (*1547–1616*)

cerrar (**ie**) to close, to shut

cielo *m.* sky, heaven(s)

ciencia *f.* science

cien(**to**) a hundred; **por ciento** *m.* per cent

ciento uno, –a a hundred one

cierto, –a a certain, sure; *adv.* sure; **es cierto** it is certain

cigarrillo *m.* cigarette

cinco five

cincuenta fifty

cine *m.* movie(s), movie house

cinematográfico, –a cinematographic

círculo *m.* club

cirio *m.* wax taper, candle

citarse to make an appointment with, to arrange to meet, to make a date

ciudad *f.* city

civil civil, polite, courteous

claramente clearly

clarín *m.* bugle, trumpet

claro, –a clear, light; ¡**claro**! of course!, sure!; **es claro** it is evident

clase *f.* class, classroom, type, kind

cláusula *f.* clause

clavar to nail, to drive in, to pierce, to gore

clima *m.* climate

cobrar to recover, to collect, to cash; **cobrar un cheque** to cash a check; ¿**cuánto me cobra?** how much (is it)?

cocer to cook

cocido, –a boiled, baked; **cocido al horno** baked

cocinar to cook

cocinero *m.*; **cocinera** *f.* cook

coctel *m.* cocktail

coche *m.* automobile, car, carriage, coach; **coche cama** *m.* Pullman, sleeper; **coche comedor** *m.* dining car

codazo *m.* blow with the elbow; **a codazos** by blows with the elbow

codo *m.* elbow

coger to seize, to catch, to pick (up), to gather; **coger asientos** to get seats; **coger un resfriado** to catch

(a) cold; **coger una pulmonía** to catch pneumonia

cola *f.* tail; **hacer cola** to form a line, to get in line, to stand in line

colegio *m.* (*private*) college, secondary school

colocar to place, to put

color *m.* color

comedia *f.* play, comedy; **comedias musicales** musical comedies

comedor *m.* dining room; **coche comedor** *m.* dining car

comenzar (ie) to begin, to start

comer to eat; **dar de comer** to feed

comida *f.* meal, dinner; **cuarto y comidas** room and board

como as; how, since; **¡como no!** why not!, of course!; **tan pronto como** as soon as

¿cómo? how? **¿cómo está Ud.?** how are you?

cómodo, –a comfortable

compañero *m.* companion, friend

comparativo, –a comparative

compartimiento *m.* compartment

compatriota *m.* compatriot

completar to complete

completo, –a complete

composición *f.* composition

compra *f.* purchase; **de compras** shopping; **hacer compras** to make purchases, to shop; **ir de compras** to shop, to go shopping

comprar to buy

comprender to understand

compuesto, –a composed, compound

común common

con with; **con tal que** provided that

conceder to concede, to grant, to admit

conde *m.* count, earl

condición *f.* condition; **a condición de que** on condition that

condicional conditional

conferencia *f.* conference, lecture; **dar (las) conferencias** to lecture

confianza *f.* confidence, trust

conjugación *f.* conjugation

conmigo (**con** + **mí**) with me

conocer to know, to be acquainted with, to meet

conocido, –a known, well known, famous

consejero *m.* counsellor, adviser

consentir (ie, i) to consent, to allow, to permit

considerar to consider

consigo (**con** + **sí**) with himself, herself, yourself, one's self, themselves, yourselves

constante constant, continued

contar (ue) to count, to tell, to relate; **contar con** to count on, to rely on

contemplar to look upon, to contemplate

contener to contain, to restrain

contento, –a contented, glad, happy; **quedarse contento con** to be satisfied with

contigo (**con** + **ti**) with you

continuar to keep on, to continue

contra against

contracción *f.* contraction

contribución *f.* contribution

contrario, –a contrary; **al contrario** on the contrary

contraseña *f.* tag, stub, check (*luggage*)

convencer to convince; **convencerse** to become convinced

conversación *f.* conversation

convertir(se) (ie, i) to convert, to change

convidar (a) to invite

coraje *m.* courage, bravery

corazón *m.* heart; **enfermedad del corazón** *f.* heart trouble

corbata *f.* necktie

corte *m.* cut; *f.* court

cortés courteous, civil, polite

cortesía *f.* courtesy

corto, –a short

correcto, –a correct
corregir (i) to correct
correlación *f.* correlation, sequence (*of tenses*)
correo *m.* mail; **echar al correo** to mail; **oficina de correos** post office; **por correo aéreo** (by) airmail
correr to run
correspondiente corresponding, respective, suitable
corrida (de toros) *f.* bullfight, bullfighting
corridor *m.* corridor
corriente current, running, common; **cuenta corriente** *f.* bank account; **estar al corriente de** to be informed about, to be up on
cosa *f.* thing
cosita *f.* little thing
costar (ue) to cost; **¿cuánto cuesta?** how much is it?, how much does it cost?
costilla *f.* rib, cutlet, chop
costoso, –a expensive, costly, dear
costumbre *f.* custom, habit; **de costumbre** usually; **como de costumbre** as usual
crecer to grow
creer to believe, to think; **creer que sí (no)** to believe so (not), to think so (not)
creíble credible, believable
criado *m.;* **criada** *f.* servant (*maid*)
criticar to criticize, to find fault with
crítico *m.;* **crítica** *f.* critic
cruz *f.* cross, withers
cuaderno *m.* notebook
cuadra *f.* block (*of houses*); **a dos cuadras de aquí** two blocks from here
cuadro *m.* picture, painting
cual which, like; **el (la, lo) cual, los (las) cuales** who, which, whom **¿cuál?** (**¿cuáles?**) which (one, ones)?
cualidad *f.* quality

cualquier, –a (*pl.* **cualesquiera**) *adj.* and *pron.* any, anyone, whatever, whichever
cuando when; **aun cuando** even though; **¿cuándo?** when?; **¿desde cuándo?** how long? since when?
cuanto, –a all that, all those, as much as, how much; **cuanto más (menos) . . . tanto más (menos)** the more (less) . . . the more (less)
¿cuánto, –a? how much? (*pl.* how many?); **¿a cuántos estamos?** what is the date today?; **¿cuántos años tiene?** how old is he?; **¿cuánto cuesta?** (**¿cuánto me cobra?,** **¿cuánto vale?**) how much is it?; **¿cuánto tiempo?** how long?; **¡cuánto, –a, –os, –as!** how much! how many!
cuarenta forty
cuarto *m.* room, quarter (*of an hour*); **cuarto y comidas** room and board
cuarto, –a fourth
cuatro four
cuatrocientos, –as four hundred
cubismo *m.* cubism
cubrir to cover
cuello *m.* neck
cuenta *f.* bill, check (*restaurant*); **cuenta corriente** *f.* bank account; **darse cuenta de** to realize
cuento *m.* story, tale
cuero *m.* leather
cuidado *m.* care; **con cuidado** carefully; **cuidado de + inf.** take care to; **tener cuidado** to be careful
culpa *f.* fault, blame; **tener la culpa** to be to blame
cultural cultural
cuna *f.* cradle
cura *m.* priest
curso *m.* course; **cursos de verano** *m.* summer courses, summer school
cuyo, –a whose, of which

charla *f.* chat, talk

charlador *m.;* **charladora** *f.* talker, chatterbox

charlar to chat, to discuss (*informally*)

cheque *m.* check; **cobrar un cheque, hacer efectivo un cheque** to cash a check

chico *m.* boy; *pl.* children

chuleta *f.* chop, cutlet

dado, –a given, granted; **dado que** in case (that)

daño *m.* harm, injury, damage; **hacer daño a** to hurt

dar to give; **al dar** on (upon) giving; **dále tú** there you go again; **dar de comer** to feed; **dar gusto** to please; **dar noticias** to give news, to inform, to tell about; **darle pases** to make passes at him; **darse cuenta de** to realize; **darse prisa** to hurry; **me da gusto** it pleases me, I'm glad

Darío, Rubén *Nicaraguan poet of the 19th and 20th centuries (1867–1916)*

de of, from, about, with, as; *with* **el = del**

deber to owe; ought to, must; **deber de + *inf.*** ought, must, probably

decano *m.* dean

decidir to decide

décimo, –a tenth

decir to say, to tell; **¡no me digas!** you don't say!; **querer decir** to mean

decisión *f.* decision

dedo *m.* finger; **dedo pulgar** *m.* thumb

defender (ie) to defend, to protect

definido, –a definite

dejar to leave, to let, to allow, to let go

delante (de) before, in front of, ahead

delinquir to do wrong, to be delinquent, to transgress

demasiado, –a too, too much; *pl.* too many

demostrativo, –a demonstrative

dentro (de) within, inside

dependiente *m.* clerk

deporte *m.* sport, amusement, recreation

derecho *m.* right; *adj.* right; **a la derecha** to the right; **derechos de matrícula** *m.* tuition fees

desastre *m.* disaster, catastrophe

descansar to rest

descolgar (ue) to take down, to unhook, to pick up; **descolgar el receptor** to pick up the receiver (*phone*)

describir to describe

descuento *m.* discount, allowance, rebate

desde since, from; **desde luego** right away, immediately, of course; **¿desde cuándo?** how long?, since when?

desear to wish, to desire, to want; **¿qué desean?** what do you wish?, what would you like?

desfile *m.* parade

despacio slowly

despedida *f.* departure, leavetaking

despedirse (i) (de) to take leave of, to say good-by to

despejar(se) to clear up (*weather*)

despertar(se) (ie) to wake up

despreciar to despise, to scorn, to disdain

después after, afterwards, then; **después de** after

destreza *f.* skill, dexterity, nimbleness

detener to stop, to detain; **deternerse** to stop

detrás (de) behind

deuda *f.* debt

devolver (ue) to return, to refund, to pay back

devoto, –a devout, pious, devoted

día *m.* day; **buenos días** good morning; **todo el día** all day; **todos los días** every day

dibujo *m.* drawing, sketch; **dibujos de muñecos** cartoons

diciembre *m*. December
dictado *m*. dictation
diecinueve nineteen
dieciocho eighteen
dieciséis sixteen
diecisiete seventeen
diente *m*. tooth; cepillo de dientes *m*.
toothbrush
diez ten
diez y nueve nineteen
diez y ocho eighteen
diez y seis sixteen
diez y siete seventeen
diferir to defer, to postpone, to put off, to differ
difícil difficult
dificultad *f*. difficulty
diga hello, say
dinero *m*. money
Dios *m*. God; vaya con Dios God be with you
dirección *f*. direction, address
directo, –a direct
director *m.;* directora *f*. director, manager
dirigir to direct, to manage; dirigirse (a) to go (toward), to address
discusión *f*. discussion
distinguir to distinguish
diversión *f*. diversion, amusement, enjoyment
divertido, –a amusing
divertir(se) (ie, i) to have a good time, to amuse oneself; divertirse un mundo to enjoy oneself immensely
divinidad *f*. divinity
doblado doubled, dubbed; doblado en español dubbed in Spanish, *with a Spanish sound track*
doblar to double, to dub (*synchronize films in another language*), to fold, to turn (*a corner*)
doce twelve
doctor *m.;* doctora *f*. doctor
dogma *m*. dogma

dólar *m*. dollar
Dolores Dolores
domingo *m*. Sunday
don Mr., don (*title used with first names only*)
donde where, in (to) which place; ¿dónde? where?
doña Mrs., Miss, doña (*title used with first names only*)
dórico, –a Doric
dormir (ue) to sleep; dormirse to fall asleep
dos two
doscientos, –as two hundred
drama *m*. drama, play
dramático, –a dramatic
dramaturgo *m*. dramatist, playwright
duda *f*. doubt; caber duda to be in doubt; no cabe duda there is no doubt
dudar to doubt
dulce sweet; *n. m.* sweet; *m. pl.* pastry, sweets, candy
durante during
durar to last
duro, –a hard

e and (*before a word beginning with an* i *or* hi)
eclesiástico, –a ecclesiastical
economía *f*. economy
económico, –a economic
economizar to economize, to save
echar to cast, to hurl, to throw; echar al correo to mail; echar ficha en la ranura to put a token in the slot; echar un vistazo a to glance at; echar una siesta to take a nap
edición *f*. edition, issue
efectivo, –a effective; hacer efectivo un cheque to cash a check
egoísmo *m*. egoism, selfishness, self-love
ejemplo *m*. example; por ejemplo for example
ejercicio *m*. exercise

él he; (*after a prep.*) him, it
elegante elegant, stylish
elegir (i) to choose, to elect
elemento *m.* element
El Greco *Spanish painter* (*born in Crete*) *of the 16th century*
ella her; (*after a prep.*) her, it
ellas they *f.*; (*after a prep.*) them *f.*
ello it (*neuter*)
ellos they *m.*; (*after a prep.*) them *m.*
embargo: sin embargo however, nevertheless
embestir to charge, to attack, to rush against
emoción *f.* emotion
emocionante touching, moving
empaquetar to pack, to wrap up
empezar (ie) to begin, to start
empleado *m.* employee
emplear to employ, to use
empujón *m.* push, violent shove; **a empujones** by pushing
en in, into, at, on
encantado, –a delighted, charmed, enchanted; gladly, with pleasure; how do you do, it's a pleasure to know you
encargo *m.* commission, errand, charge
encender to light, to inflame, to incite
encontrar (ue) to find, to meet; **encontrarse** (con) to find oneself, to meet, to be found
encuadernar to bind; **encuadernado en piel** leather-bound; **encuadernado en rústica** paper-bound; **encuadernado en tela** clothbound
endosar to endorse
enero *m.* January
enfadar to offend, to vex; **enfadarse** to be offended
enfermedad *f.* illness; **enfermedad del corazón** *f.* heart trouble
enfermo, –a ill; **estar enfermo,** –a to be ill
enfurecer to infuriate; **enfurecerse** to become furious, to become infuriated
enojar to make angry, to annoy; **enojarse** to be annoyed, to become angry
ensalada *f.* salad; **ensalada de lechuga** *f.* lettuce salad
enseñar to teach, to show
entender (ie) to understand
entonces then, at (of) that time
entrada *f.* entrance, door ticket, admission, entrée; **salón de entrada** *m.* lobby
entrar (en) to enter, to go in, to come in
entre between, among
entregar to hand over, to deliver
entremés *m.* side dish, hors d'œuvre, appetizer; comic one-act play
entretenimiento *m.* pastime. amusement, entertainment
entusiasmado, –a enthusiastic
entusiasmar to become enthusiastic
enviar to send
época *f.* period, time, age, epoch
equipaje *m.* baggage; **facturar el equipaje** to check the baggage
equivocarse to be mistaken
erudición *f.* erudition, learning, knowledge
escabechar to pickle, to souse
escaparate *m.* show window
escena *f.* scene, stage, scenery, episode
escoger to choose, to select
escolar *m. or f.* pupil, student; *adj.* scholastic, school
escoltar to escort, to convoy
escribir to write
escritor *m.* writer
escuchar to listen (to)
escuela *f.* school; **escuela elemental** *f.* elementary school; **escuela media** *f.* secondary school
ese, –a, –os, –as *dem. adj.* that; *pl.* those; **ése,** –a, –os, –as *dem. pron.* that, that one; *pl.* those

eso *pron.* that (*neuter*); **a eso de** at about; **por eso** therefore, for that reason

espada *f.* sword, blade

España *f.* Spain

español, –ola Spanish; *m.* Spaniard, Spanish

esparcir to scatter

espectáculo *m.* spectacle, show

espejo *m.* mirror

esperanza *f.* hope

esperar to hope, to wait (for), to expect

espíritu *m.* spirit

espiritual spiritual

Espronceda, José de *one of the best Spanish lyric poets of the 19th century* (*1808–1842*)

estación *f.* season, station; **estación de ferrocarriles** *f.* railroad station

estacionar to park; **estacionar el coche** to park the car

Estados Unidos *m. pl.* United States

estancia *f.* stay, small farm

estante *m.* shelf, bookcase

estar to be; **¿cómo está Ud.?** how are you?; **estar a régimen** to be on a diet; **estar al corriente de** to be informed about, to be up on; **está bien** all right; **estar lleno hasta los topes** to be jam-packed; **estar para** to be about to; **estarse** to remain, to stay

estatua *f.* statue

este, –a, –os, –as *dem. adj.* this; *pl.* these; **éste, –a, –os, –as** *dem. pron.* this (one), the latter; *pl.* these, the latter

estilo *m.* style, use, fashion

esto *pron.* this (*neuter*)

estoque *m.* sword

estrella *f.* star

estrenar(se) to show for the first time, to have its première

estreno *m.* first showing, debut, opening performance; **día de estreno** *m.*

opening day, opening night (*of a play*)

estudiante *m. or f.* student

estudiar to study

estúpido, –a stupid

Europa *f.* Europe

evitar to avoid

exactitud *f.* exactness, exactitude, accuracy

exacto, –a exact, accurate

exagerar to exaggerate

examen *m.* examination

excepto except; **excepto que** except that

exhibir to exhibit, to display, to show

existir to exist

éxito *m.* success, result; **tener éxito** to be successful, to succeed

explicar to explain

expresión *f.* expression

extranjero, –a foreign; *m.* foreigner

fábrica *f.* factory

fácil easy

fácilmente easily

facturar to check; **facturar el equipaje** to check the baggage

facultad *f.* faculty, school; **facultad de medicina** *f.* medical school; **facultad de leyes** *f.* law school; **facultad de ingeniería** *f.* school of engineering; **facultad de economía** *f.* school of economics

falta *f.* mistake, fault; **sin falta** without fail

faltar to lack, to be lacking

fallar to fail, to miss, to operate badly (*machine*)

familia *f.* family; **Familia de Carlos IV** *famous painting by Francisco Goya* (*1746–1828*); **¿qué de tu familia?** what about your family?

famoso, –a famous

farsante *m.* fraud, pretender

favor *m.* favor; **por favor** please

favorito, –a favorite

fé *f.* faith
febrero *m.* February
Felipe Philip
feliz happy
ferocidad *f.* ferocity
ferrocarril *m.* railroad
festejar to entertain, to feast, to celebrate
ficha *f.* chip, token
fiel faithful
fiesta *f.* feast, party, holiday, celebration, diversion; **celebrar una fiesta** to celebrate a feast
fila *f.* row, line, file; **hacer fila** to form a line, to get in line, to stand in line
filosofía *f.* philosophy
filósofo *m.* philosopher
fin *m.* end; **a fin de que** in order that, so that; **al fin, por fin** finally
finalmente finally, lastly
finca *f.* farm, ranch
fino, –a fine, delicate
firma *m.* firm, signature
flor *f.* flower
fondo *m.* bottom, depth, rear part; **al fondo** in the back, in the rear
forma *f.* form
fortaleza *f.* fortitude, stronghold, fortress
fotografía *f.* photograph; **sacar fotografías** to take pictures
fotográfico, –a photographic; **aparato fotográfico** *m.* camera
fracasar to fail
Francisco Francis
franqueo *m.* postage
frase *f.* phrase, sentence
fregar (ie) to rub, to scrub, to wash (*dishes*)
freír (i) to fry; *past part.* **frito;** **pescado frito** fried fish
freno *m.* brake
frente *m.* front; *f.* forehead; **en frente de** in front of, before, opposite; **frente a** in front of, facing

fresco, –a fresh, cool; **hacer fresco** to be cool
frío, –a cold; **frío** *m.* cold; **hacer frío** to be cold (*weather*); **tener frío** to be cold (*person*)
fruta *f.* fruit
fuego *m.* fire; **fuegos artificiales** *m.* fireworks
fuerza *f.* strength; **a fuerza de** by dint of, by force of, by means of; **por fuerza** by (means of) force
fumar to smoke
función *f.* performance, play, function
fútbol *m.* football, soccer
futuro *m.* future

gabán *m.* overcoat
galería *f.* gallery, lobby, balcony
gana *f.* wish, desire; **tener gana(s) de** to wish, to desire to; **tener mucha(s) gana(s) de** to wish very much to
ganar to gain, to earn, to win; **ganar la vida** to earn a living
ganga *f.* bargain
garage *m.* garage
García Lorca, Federico *Spanish contemporary poet and dramatist* (*1899–1936*)
gastar to spend (*money*)
gastrónomo *m.* gourmet, epicure, gastronome
gemir (i) to moan
general *m.* general
genero *m.* gender
gente *f.* people
gentío *m.* crowd, multitude
gerundio *m.* gerund, present participle
gobierno *m.* government
Goya, Francisco *famous Spanish painter* (*1746–1828*)
gozar (de) to enjoy
gracia *f.* grace, gracefulness
gracias *f. pl.* thanks, thank you; **mil gracias** a thousand thanks, many

thanks; **muchas gracias** thank you very much, many thanks
graduarse to graduate, to be graduated
gramatical grammatical
gran(de) large, great
gratitud *f.* gratitude
grave grave, serious
griego, –a Greek, Grecian
guante *m.* glove
guapo, –a pretty, handsome, good-looking
guerra *f.* war
guisante *m.* pea
guitarra *f.* guitar
gustar to like, to please
gusto *m.* pleasure; taste; **con mucho gusto** with pleasure, very gladly; **dar gusto** to please; **el gusto es mío** how do you do, the pleasure is mine; **me da gusto** I'm glad, it pleases me; **¡qué gusto!** what a pleasure!; **tanto gusto, mucho gusto, muchísimo gusto** how do you do, it's a pleasure to know you; **tener gusto en** to be glad to

haber to have
hábil capable, skillful
habilidad *f.* ability, skill
habitante *m.* inhabitant
hablador, –ora talkative
hablar to speak, to talk
hacer to make, to do; **hacer buen tiempo** to be good weather; **hacer calor** to be warm (hot) (*weather*); **hacer cola (fila)** to form a line, to get in line, to stand in line; **hacer fresco** to be cool; **hacer frío** to be cold (*weather*); **hacer mal tiempo** to be bad weather; **hacer sol** to be sunny; **hacer viento** to be windy; **hacerse** to become; **no hace mucho** not long ago
hacienda *f.* farm, ranch
hacha *f.* axe

hallar to find; **hallarse** to be
hambre *f.* hunger; **tener (mucha) hambre** to be (very) hungry
hasta until, to, as far as; **hasta la vista** till I see you again, see you later; **hasta las cuatro** see you at four (o'clock); **hasta luego** see you later, good-by; **hasta más tarde** till I see you later, see you later; **hasta que** until
hay there is (are); **hay que** one must, it is necessary; **no hay de que** you're welcome
helado *m.* ice cream
hermana *f.* sister
hermano *m.* brother
hermoso, –a beautiful
hija *f.* daughter
hijo *m.* son; *pl.* children
hincapié *m.* emphasis
hipocresía *f.* hypocrisy
hispanoamericano, –a Spanish American, Latin American
hola hello
holgazán, –ana lazy
hombre *m.* man; **¡hombre!** boy!, man alive!
hombro *m.* shoulder; **llevar en hombros** to carry on (one's) shoulders
hondo, –a deep, low
hongo *m.* mushroom
honor *m.* honor, fame
honorable worthy, honorable
hora *f.* hour, time; **horas y horas** hours on end
horario *m.* time schedule, timetable
horno *m.* oven, furnace; **al horno** in the oven; **cocido al horno** baked
hospedaje *m.* lodging, board
hotel *m.* hotel
hoy today
hoya *f.* hole, pit, valley
huésped *m.* guest, host, lodger; **casa de huéspedes** *f.* boarding house
huir to flee

humano, –a human
humildad f. humility, meekness

ida f. departure, outgoing; ida y vuelta round trip
idea f. idea
idioma m. language
iglesia f. church
igual equal, the same
imagen f. image, statue
impaciente impatient, anxious
impedir (i) to impede, to prevent, to hinder, to oppose, to block
imperfecto, –a imperfect
impermeable m. raincoat
importante important; es importante it's important
importar to matter, to be important; eso no importa that doesn't matter
imposible impossible; es imposible it is impossible
impresionar to impress, to film, to shoot (a film)
increíble incredible; parece increíble it is incredible
indefinido, –a indefinite
independiente independent
indicar to indicate, to point out
indicativo indicative
indirecto, –a indirect
infinitivo m. infinitive
ingeniería f. engineering
ingeniero m. engineer
inglés, –esa English; m. English
inmediatamente immediately
institución f. institution
instituto m. institute, (public) college or secondary school
inteligente intelligent
interesante interesting
interior interior, inner; ropa interior underclothing, underwear
internacional international
interpretar to interpret
interrogativo, –a interrogative
interrumpir to interrupt

invierno m. winter
invitado m. guest
invitar to invite
ir to go; ir a caballo to go on horseback, to go horseback riding; ir de compras to shop, to go shopping; ir de paseo to go for a walk; irse to go away
Irlanda f. Ireland
irregular irregular
Isabela Isabella
italiano, –a Italian; m. Italian
izquierdo, –a left; a la izquierda to the left

jefe m. chief, head, boss, leader
Jiménez, Juan Ramón Spanish poet (1881–1958), Nobel Prize, 1956
José Joseph
joven adj. young; m. young man
Juan John
Juan de la Cruz (San) great mystic poet of 16th century (1542–1591)
Juanito Johnny
juego m. sport, game, gambling; hacer juego con to match, to go well with; juegos artificiales m. fireworks
jueves m. Thursday
jugar (ue) to play; jugar al tenis to play tennis
juguete m. toy
julio m. July
junio m. June
justicia f. justice

kilo m. kilogram (2.2 lbs.)
kilómetro m. kilometer (about 0.62 mile); a unos kilómetros de aquí a few kilometers from here

la dir. obj. her, you (f.), it (f.)
lado m. side; al lado de on the side of, beside
lana f. wool
largo, –a long
las dir. obj. you (f.), them (f.)

lástima *f.* pity, shame; es lástima it's a pity, it's too bad

lastimar to hurt, to injure, to damage, to pity

lavandera *f.* laundress, washerwoman

lavar(se) to wash (oneself)

le *dir. obj.* him, you; *indir. obj.* (to) him, her, it, you

leal loyal

lección *f.* lesson

leche *f.* milk

lechuga *f.* lettuce

leer to read

lejos far, far away; a lo lejos in the distance

lengua *f.* language, tongue

lentamente slowly

lentitud *f.* slowness

León (Fray Luis de) *important mystic poet of 16th century* (1527–1591)

les *dir. obj.* you, them; *indir. obj.* (to) you, them

levantar to raise, to lift; levantarse to get up, to rise

ley *f.* law

libre free

librería *f.* bookstore

libro *m.* book

limpiar to clean

limpio, –a clean

lindo, –a pretty, neat

lírico, –a lyric, lyrical

lista *f.* list, bill of fare, menu

listo, –a smart (*with* ser); ready (*with* estar)

literatura *f.* literature

lo *dir. obj.* you, him, it; *def. art.* the

local local

loco, –a mad, crazy; loco *n. m.* madman; loca *f.* madwoman

Londres *m.* London

Lope de Vega Carpio *Spanish poet and dramatist of the Siglo de Oro* (1562–1635)

los *dir. obj.* you (*m.*), them (*m.*)

lucir to shine

luego then, next; desde luego right away, immediately, of course; hasta luego see you later, good-by; luego que as soon as

lugar *m.* place; tener lugar to take place

lúgubre sad, gloomy, dismal, lugubrious

Luis Louis

Luisito (little) Louis

lujoso, –a luxurious, de luxe

lunes *m.* Monday

luz *f.* light

llamar to call; llamar a la puerta to knock (*on the door*); llamar por teléfono to telephone; llamarse to be called (*named*)

llave *f.* key

llegar to arrive, to reach

lleno, –a full, filled

llevar to carry, to take, to bring, to wear; llevar en hombros to carry on (one's) shoulders

llover (ue) to rain; llover a cántaros to pour, to come down in buckets, to rain cats and dogs; llueve it's raining

Machado, Antonio *important representative of modern Spanish poetry* (1875–1939)

madera *f.* wood

madre *f.* mother

Madrid *m. capital of Spain*

madrileño, –a Madrilenian

madrugada *f.* dawn

maestro *m.;* maestra *f.* maestro, teacher, master

mal badly

maleta *f.* suitcase; hacer las maletas to pack the suitcases

maletín *m.* small valise, satchel

malo, –a bad, naughty, ill

mandar to command, to order, to send

mandato *m.* command, order

manejar to manage, to drive, to handle

manera *f.* manner, way; **de manera que** so as, so that; **de ninguna manera** not at all

manga *f.* sleeve

mano *f.* hand; **hecho a mano** hand made, made by hand; ¡**manos a la obra!** let's get to work!, let's go!

Manrique, Jorge *poet and author of las Coplas* (*1440?–1478*)

manta *f.* blanket

manufacturar to manufacture

manzana *f.* apple

mañana *f.* morning; *adv.* tomorrow; **de la mañana** in the morning, A.M.; **pasado mañana** the day after tomorrow; **por la mañana** in the morning; **todas las mañanas** every morning

mapa *m.* map

máquina *f.* machine, engine

maquinilla de afeitar *f.* safety razor

mar *m. or f.* sea

marcha *f.* march, journey; **ponerse en marcha** to set out, to start off (out), to start

María Mary

marido *m.* husband

martes *m.* Tuesday

marzo *m.* March

más more, most; **nada más** nothing else, nothing more, no more; **por más que** although

matador *m.* matador (*bullfighter who kills the bull*)

matar to kill

material *m.* material; *pl.* supplies

matrícula *f.* matriculation, register, list; **abonar los derechos de matrícula** to pay the tuition fees; **derechos de matrícula** *m.* tuition fees

matricular(se) to enroll, to register

mayo *m.* May

mayor major, older, oldest, bigger, biggest; **hija mayor** oldest daughter;

por la mayor parte in the main, for the most part

me me, to me, myself

mecánico *m.* mechanic

mecer to rock

medianoche *f.* midnight

medicina *f.* medicine

medicinal medicinal

medio *m.* middle, means; *adj.* half

mediodía *m.* midday, noon

mejor better, best

melón *m.* melon, cantaloupe

memoria *f.* memory; **de memoria** by heart

mencionar to mention, to point out

Menéndez y Pelayo, Marcelino *greatest literary critic of Spain* (*1856– 1912*)

menester *m.* need, want, employment; **es menester** it is necessary

menesteroso, –a needy

medio, –a half; **las diez y media** half past ten

mejor better, best

Meninas, las The Ladies in Waiting (*masterpiece of Velázquez*)

menor smaller, smallest, younger, youngest; **hija menor** younges* daughter

menos less, least, minus; **a lo (al) menos, por lo menos** at least; **a menos que** unless; **el menos** the least

mentir (ie, i) to lie, to deceive

mentira *f.* lie; **parece mentira** it doesn't seem possible, it can't be true, it is incredible

menú *m.* menu, bill of fare

menudo: **a menudo** often, frequently

mercado *m.* market

merecer to deserve, to merit

mes *m.* month

mesa *f.* table

meter to put; **meterse** to place one-self, to get in(to)

metro *m.* meter, subway

México m. Mexico
mezclar to mix, to mingle, to blend
mi, mis my
mí me
miedo m. fear; tener miedo to be afraid
mientras (que) while, meanwhile
miércoles m. Wednesday
mil a thousand
milagroso, –a miraculous
militar military
millón m. million
minuto m. minute
mío, –a my, mine; el mío, la mía mine; lo mío what is mine, what belongs to me
mirar to look (at)
Misa f. mass
misionero m. missionary
mismo, –a self, oneself, itself, same; ahora mismo just now, right now; lo mismo the same thing, the same
místico m. mystic
moda f. fashion, style; de última moda in the latest style
moderno, –a modern
modo m. manner, way, means, mood; de modo que so that, in order that; de todos modos anyway, anyhow; el modo de pensar the view, the way of thinking; modo de vivir way of life, manner of living
molestar to bother, to disturb; molestarse to put oneself out, to bother oneself
molestia f. bother, imposition, annoyance
Molina, Tirso de Spanish dramatist (1584–1648)
monarca m. monarch
monje m. monk
montaña f. mountain
moral m. mulberry tree; f. ethics, moral
morir (ue, u) to die
mostrador m. counter, stand

mostrar (ue) to show, to point out
motor m. motor, engine
mover (ue) to move
muchacha f. girl
muchacho m. boy
muchedumbre f. crowd
mucho, –a much, a lot; pl. many, a lot; adv. much, a great deal; muchas veces many times, often; no hace mucho not long ago
muerte f. death
muerto, –a dead
mujer f. woman
muleta f. small red cloth used by bullfighter
mundo m. world; todo el mundo everybody
muñeco m. puppet, doll; dibujos de muñecos m. cartoons
Murillo, Esteban Spanish painter of 17th century
museo m. museum
música f. music
musical musical; comedias musicales musical comedies
muy very; muy buenos good morning

nacer to be born
nación f. nation
nacional national
nada nothing, anything, not anything; adv. not at all; nada más nothing else, nothing more, no more; no es nada it's nothing
nadie no one, nobody, (not) anybody
natío native
natural natural; es natural it's natural
naturalidad f. naturalness
necesario, –a necessary; es necesario it's necessary
necesitar to need
negar (ie) to deny
negativo, –a negative
negocio m. business affair, deal; pl. business

ni nor, not even; **ni . . . ni** neither . . . nor

nieve *f.* snow

ningún, ninguno, –a no, not any, none; **de ninguna manera** not at all

niña *f.* child

niñita *f.* little girl

niño *m.* child

no no, not; **¿no?** isn't it so?, aren't they?, etc.

noble noble (*adj.*); *m.* nobleman

noche *f.* night, evening; **buenas noches** good evening good night; **de la noche** in the evening, P.M.; **esta noche** tonight; **por la noche** at night, in the evening; **todas las noches** every night

nombrar to name

nombre *m.* name, noun

norteamericano *m.* North American, American

nos us, to us, ourselves

nosotros we, us

nota *f.* note, grade, mark

notar to note, to notice, to mark

noticia *f.* news, piece of news; **dar noticias** to give news, to inform, to tell about

novecientos, –as nine hundred

novela *f.* novel

noveno, –a ninth

noventa ninety

noviembre *m.* November

nube *f.* cloud

nuestro, –a our, ours; **el nuestro, la nuestra** ours; **lo nuestro** what is ours

Nueva York New York

nueve nine

nuevo, –a new; **de nuevo** again

número *m.* number; size; **número treinta y ocho** size 38

numeroso, –a numerous

nunca ever, never

o or

objeto *m.* object, thing

obra *f.* work (*of art, literature*); **¡manos a la obra!** let's get to work!, let's go!; **obra maestra** *f.* master-piece

observar to observe, to notice, to remark

octavo, –a eighth

octubre *m.* October

ocupado, –a busy, occupied

ocurrir to occur, to happen

ochenta eighty

ocho eight

ochocientos, –as eight hundred

oficina *f.* office

ofrecer to offer; **¿qué se le ofrece?** what do you wish?, what would you like to order?

oír to hear, to listen; **oír hablar (de)** to hear about, to hear of

¡ojalá (que)! I wish that!; oh, would that!

¡olé! bravo!, hurrah!

olvidar(se) (de) to forget

ómnibus *m.* bus, omnibus

once eleven

ópera *f.* opera

opinión *f.* opinion

oportunidad *f.* opportunity

oración *f.* sentence

oral oral

orden *f.* order, command; *m.* order, class, category; **a sus órdenes** at your service, if you please

ordinal ordinal

original original

originalidad *f.* originality

oro *m.* gold

ortográfico, –a orthographic, spelling

os you, to you

oscuro, –a dark

otoño *m.* autumn, fall; **el otoño que viene** next fall

otro, –a other, another; **otra vez** again

Pablo Paul

padre *m.* father; *pl.* parents

paella *f. dish of rice with meat or chicken*

pagar to pay

página *f.* page

país *m.* country

palabra *f.* word

palacio *m.* palace

palco *m.* box (*in theatre*)

paloma *f.* pigeon, dove

pan *m.* bread

pañuelo *m.* handkerchief

papa *m.* Pope

papel *m.* paper, role, part; **hacer el papel** to play (act) the role

paquete *m.* pack, package; **remitir un paquete** to send a package (*by mail*)

Paquito Frankie

par *m.* couple, pair; **un par de semanas** a couple of weeks

para for, to, in order to; **para los dos** for the two (of us, of them, etc.); **para que** in order that, so that; **¿para que?** for what?, what for?

parabrisas *m.* windshield

parada *f.* stop, parade

paraguas *m.* umbrella

parar(se) to stop

parecer to appear, to seem; **al parecer** apparently; **parece mentira** it doesn't seem possible, it can't be true; **¿qué te parece?** what do you think (*of the idea*)?

pared *f.* wall

paréntesis *m.* parenthesis

parque *m.* park

parte *f.* part; **por la mayor parte** in the main, for the most part

participio participle; **participio pasivo** past participle

partido *m.* game

partir to leave, to start out

pasado, –a last, past; *m.* past

pasaje *m.* passage; **sacar el pasaje** to get the ticket

pasar to spend (*time*), to pass, to happen; **¡que lo pase bien!** good luck!

pase *m.* permit, pass; **darle pases to make passes at him** (*to maneuver the bull by means of a movement with the cape*)

pasear(se) to walk, to stroll, to take a walk

paseo *m.* walk, promenade, stroll; **dar un paseo** to take a walk; **de paseo** strolling; **ir de paseo** to go for a walk

pasillo *m.* corridor, aisle

pasivo, –a passive

paso *m.* pace, step, pass; **paso doble** *m.* two-step

pasta *f.* paste, dough, cookie; **pasta dentífrica** tooth paste

pastel *m.* pie; **pastel de manzana** *m.* apple pie

patinar to skate

patrón *m.* patron, landlord; **patrona** *f.* patroness, landlady

pavo *m.* turkey

paz *f.* peace

peculiaridad *f.* peculiarity, characteristic

pedir (i) to ask (for), to order

Pedro Peter

peine *m.* comb

película *f.* film, motion picture

peligro *m.* danger

peligroso, –a dangerous

penicilina *f.* penicillin

pensar (ie) to think, to expect

peor worse, worst

Pepe Joe

pequeño, –a small, little

perder (ie) to lose, to miss, to waste; **perder tiempo** to lose time, to waste time

perfecto, –a perfect

periódico *m.* newspaper

permanecer to remain, to stay

permitir to permit, to allow

pero but

persona *f.* person

personaje *m.* personage, character

personal personal

pertenecer (a) to belong (to)

perro *m.* dog

pesar *m.* grief; *vb.* to weigh, to be heavy; a pesar de (que) in spite of

pescado *m.* fish

pescador *m.* fisherman

peseta *f.* peseta (*monetary unit in Spain*)

peso *m.* peso (*Spanish and Spanish American monetary unit whose value varies in different countries*)

pez *m.* fish; *f.* pitch, tar

pica *f.* pike (*pole with steel point used by picador*)

picador *m.* *bullfighter on horseback who uses the pica to cut some of the neck muscles of the bull*

picar to prick, to sting, to irritate, to chap

pie *m.* foot; a pie on foot

piel *m.* leather, hide, skin; encuadernado en piel leather-bound

pieza *f.* room, piece, play

píldora *f.* pill

pimiento *m.* red pepper

pintar to paint

pintor *m.* painter

pintura *f.* painting

Pío Pius

piso *m.* floor, story

placer *m.* pleasure; ¡qué placer! what a pleasure!; tengo el placer de presentarle (les) (te) may I present, I have the pleasure to present

planeta *m.* planet

plato *m.* plate, dish, course

playa *f.* beach, shore

plaza *f.* plaza, square; plaza de toros *f.* bull ring

plural plural

pluscuamperfecto pluperfect, past perfect

pobre poor

poco, –a little, small; *pl.* a few

poder to be able, can, may; puede ser it is possible

poderoso, –a powerful

poema *m.* poem

poesía *f.* poetry

poeta *m.* poet

policía *m.* policeman; *f.* police

político, –a political

pollo *m.* chicken

poner to put, to lay, to place; ponerse to put on, to wear, to become

popular popular

poquito, –a very little, a bit

por by, during, for, over, along, per, through, because of, in exchange for, for the sake of; por más que although; por eso therefore, for that reason

¿por qué? why?

porque because

portugués, –esa Portuguese; *m.* Portuguese

posesión *f.* possession

posesivo, –a possessive

posible possible; es posible it is possible

posición *f.* position

posponer to postpone

postal postal

postre *m.* dessert

potencial *m.* (*gram.*) conditional

prado *m.* meadow; Museo del Prado *famous art museum in Madrid*

precio *m.* price

preciso, –a necessary; es preciso it is necessary

preferir (ie, i) to prefer

pregunta *f.* question

preguntón, –ona inquisitive

preocuparse (de) to worry (about)

preparar to prepare, to make ready; prepararse to prepare oneself, to get ready

preparativo *m.* preparation

preposición *f.* preposition

presentar to present, to introduce; **tengo el placer de presentarle(les) (te)** may I present, I have the pleasure to present

presente *m.* present

presidente *m.* president

prestar to lend

pretérito *m.* preterite

primavera *f.* spring

primer(o), –a first

primo *m.* cousin

príncipe *m.* prince

prisa *f.* hurry, haste; **darse prisa** to hurry; **de prisa** in a hurry, hurriedly; **tener prisa** to be in a hurry

prisionero *m.* prisoner

probable probable; **es probable** it is probable

probar (ue) to prove, to taste, to try

problema *m.* problem

procesión *f.* procession

producir to produce, to yield, to bear

producto *m.* product

profesor *m.* professor, teacher

progreso *m.* progress

prohibir to prohibit, to forbid

prometer to promise

pronombre *m.* pronoun

pronto, –a ready; *adv.* soon; **tan pronto como** as soon as

propina *f.* tip

propio, –a proper, suitable, own, himself, oneself

protagonista *m.* or *f.* protagonist, hero, heroine

próximo, –a next, nearest

pueblo *m.* town, people

puerta *f.* door; **llamar a la puerta** to knock (on the door)

pues well, since, then, why, so

pulgar *m.* thumb; **dedo pulgar** *m.* thumb

pulmonía *f.* pneumonia; **coger una pulmonía** to catch pneumonia

punto *m.* point; **en punto** exactly, sharp

puro, –a pure

que *conj.* that, than; *rel. pron.* who, whom, which, that; **el (la) que** who, the one who (which), he (she) who, which, that; **lo que** what (that which); **a que** in order that; **que no** without

¿qué? *interr. adj.* and *pron.* what?, which?; ¡qué! how! what (a)!

quedar(se) to remain, to stay, to be; **me quedo con ésta** I'll take this one; **nos quedan (unos minutos)** we have (a few minutes) left; **quedarse con** to take, to keep; **quedarse contento con** to be satisfied with

quejarse de to complain (about)

querer (ie) to wish, to want, to like, to love; **querer decir** to mean

querido, –a dear

queso *m.* cheese

quien (*pl.* quienes) *rel. pron.* who, whom, he who, the one who; **quienquiera** whoever, whomsoever; ¡**quien sabe!** who knows!

¿quién? (¿quiénes?) who?, whom?; ¿de quién? whose?

Quijote: Don Quijote (de la Mancha) *a famous novel by Cervantes published in 1605 (Part I) and 1615 (Part II)*

quince fifteen

quinientos, –as five hundred

quinto, –a fifth

radical radical

radiograma *m.* radiogram

raíz *f.* root

ranura *f.* groove, slot; **echar ficha en la ranura** to put a token in the slot

rápidamente rapidly

rápido, –a rapid

raro, –a strange; rare; ¡qué raro! how strange!

rayón *m.* rayon

razón *f.* reason; **tener razón** to be right; **no tener razón** to be wrong

real royal, real

realismo *m.* realism

rebaja *f.* rebate, reduction, discount; **tener rebaja** to have a sale

receptor *m.* receiver; **descolgar el receptor** to pick up the receiver (*phone*)

recibir to receive

reconocer to recognize, to acknowledge

recordar (**ue**) to remember, to recall

rector *m.* principal, rector, director (*of a college*)

recuerdo *m.* remembrance; *pl.* regards, best wishes

reflejar to reflect, to think

referir (**ie, i**) to refer

refrán *m.* proverb, saying

refrescar(**se**) to refresh, to cool (off)

regalo *m.* present, gift

régimen *m.* regime, rule; **estar a régimen** to be on a diet

regional regional

regla *f.* rule, policy; **en regla** in order, all right

regresar to return, to come back

regular to regulate, to adjust; *adj.* fair, regular, fairly good, so-so, all right

reír(**se**) (**i**) to laugh; **reírse de** to laugh at

relación *f.* connection, relationship

relativo, –a relative

religión *f.* religion

religioso, –a religious

reloj *m.* watch, clock

remitir to remit, to forward; **remitir un paquete** to send a package (*by mail*)

repetidamente repeatedly

repetir (**i**) to repeat

representar to represent, to present (*a play*), to perform

resfriado *m.* cold (*illness*); **coger un resfriado** to catch (a) cold

resolver (**ue**) to solve, to settle, to decide

responder to answer, to respond

restaurante *m.* restaurant

resultar to turn out, to result, to follow; **resultar aprobado** to pass (*an examination*)

retratar to portray, to depict

reunión *f.* reunion, meeting

revelar to reveal, to develop (*photo*)

revisar to revise, to review, to examine, to check; **revisar el acumulador** to check the battery

revisor *m.;* **revisora** *f.* conductor, ticket taker

revista *f.* magazine, review

revolución *f.* revolution

rey *m.* king; *pl.* king(s) and queen(s)

rezar to pray

Ribera, José *Spanish painter of 17th century*

rico, –a rich, wealthy

rincón *m.* corner, nook

Roberto Robert

rogar (**ue**) to beg, to ask, to request, to pray

rollo *m.* roll

romántico, –a romantic; *n.* romanticist

romper to break

ropa *f.* clothing; **ropa interior** *f.* underclothing, underwear; **tienda de ropa** *f.* clothing store

rosbif *m.* roast beef

Rubens, Peter Paul *Flemish painter* (*1577–1640*)

ruido *m.* noise

rústico, –a rustic, rural; **encuadernado en rústica** paper-bound

sábado *m.* Saturday

saber to know (how), to find out

sabio, –a wise, learned; *m.* wise man

sabroso, –a tasty, savory, delicious

sacar to take out, to get out, to get, to obtain; **sacar el pasaje** to get the ticket; **sacar fotografías** to take pictures

salir to go (come) out, to leave; **al salir** on (upon) leaving

salmón *m.* salmon

salón *m.* salon, large room, hall; **salón de entrada** *m.* lobby

salsa *f.* sauce, gravy, dressing

saltar to jump

salud *f.* health

saludar to salute, to greet

salvar to save

salvo, –a safe; **salvo que** save that, except

sandía *f.* watermelon

sangre *f.* blood; **sangre fría** coolness, calmness, composure

sangriento, –a bloody

Santander *city and province in northern Spain*

Santiago de Chile *capital of Chile*

santiamén *m.* instant, moment, jiffy, flash

santo, –a saintly, holy; **santo** *n. m.* saint; **santa** *f.* saint

sartén *m. or f.* frying pan

sátira *f.* satire

se himself, herself, yourself, yourselves, themselves, to him, etc.

sed *f.* thirst; **tener sed** to be thirsty

seguida: en seguida immediately, right away

seguir (i) to follow, to continue, to keep on

según according to

segundo, –a second

seguramente surely, certainly

seguro, –a sure, certain, safe; **estar seguro de** to be sure (of)

seis six

seiscientos, –as six hundred

sello *m.* (*postage*) stamp

semana *f.* week; **semana pasada** last week; **semana que viene** next week

semejante similar, like, alike, such a

sencillo, –a simple, plain; **billete sencillo** *m.* one-way ticket

sensibilidad *f.* sensibility, sensitiveness

sentado, –a seated, sitting

sentar (ie) to seat; **sentarse** to sit down

sentémonos let's sit down

sentimiento *m.* sentiment, feeling

sentir (ie, i) to feel, to regret, to be sorry; **sentirse** to feel; **¡no sabes cuánto lo siento!** you don't know how sorry I am!

señor *m.* Mr., sir, gentleman; *pl.* Mr. and Mrs.

señora *f.* lady, Mrs., madam, wife

septiembre *m.* September

séptimo, –a seventh

ser to be; **a no ser que** unless

sereno *m.* night watchman

serie *f.* series

servir (i) to serve, to be used as; **¿en qué puedo servirles?** what can I do for you?, can I be of service?

sesenta sixty

setecientos, –as seven hundred

setenta seventy

Sevilla *city in southeastern Spain*

sexto, –a sixth

si if, whether

sí yes; **creer que sí** to believe so, to think so; **esa sí que es** that certainly is; *pers. pron.* (*after a prep.*) himself, etc.

siempre always; **siempre que** provided that

siesta *f.* nap; **echar una siesta** to take a nap

siete seven

siglo *m.* century, a long long time; **esperar un siglo** to wait a very long time; **Siglo de Oro** Golden Age (*of Spanish literature, 1550–1650*)

siguiente following

sin without; *conj.* **sin que** without

sincero, –a sincere

sino but, except
síntoma *m.* symptom
sistema *m.* system
situación *f.* situation, position
sobre on, upon, above, about; **sobre todo** above all, especially
sobresaliente *adj.* outstanding; *m.* grade A
sobrina *f.* niece
social social, sociable
sol *m.* sun, sunshine; **al sol** in the sun; **billete al sol** *m.* ticket in the sun (*at a bullfight*); **hacer sol** to be sunny
solamente only
soldado *m.* soldier
solemne solemn
solo, –a alone; *adv.* only
sombra *f.* shade, shadow; **a la sombra** in the shade; **billete a la sombra** *m.* ticket in the shade (*at a bullfight*)
sombrerito *m.* (little) hat
sombrero *m.* hat
son *m.* sound, noise; **al son de** to the sound of, to the music of
sonar (ue) to sound, to ring
soñar (ue) (con) to dream (of)
sopa *f.* soup
sorprender to surprise
sorpresa *f.* surprise
su, sus his, her, its, your, their
subir to go up, to walk up, to get into, to climb
subjuntivo *m.* subjunctive
subrayado, –a underlined, underscored
substantivo, –a substantive; *m.* noun
suceso *m.* event, happening, success
sucio, –a dirty
sucursal *f.* branch
suelo *m.* ground, floor
sueño *m.* sleep; **ni por sueño** not at all, by no means
suerte *f.* luck, fortune; **¡cuanta suerte tienes!** how lucky you are!; **tener suerte** to be lucky
sufrir to suffer, to undergo, to endure

superlativo, –a superlative
supóngase que suppose
supuesto: **por supuesto** of course, naturally; **supuesto que** suppose
surtido *m.* assortment, stock, supply
suyo, suya his, her, its, your, yours, their, theirs; **el suyo, la suya** his, hers, yours, theirs, its; **lo suyo** what belongs to you (him, etc.), your (his, etc.) property

tal such (a); **con tal que** provided that; **¿qué tal?** how are you?, how are things?, what's new?; **tal vez** perhaps, maybe
también also, too
tan so, as; **tan pronto como** as soon as
tanto, –a so (as) much; *pl.* so (as) many
taquilla *f.* ticket office, ticket booth
tardar(se) en to take time (to), to be long (in), to be late, to delay in; **no te tardes** don't be late, don't delay
tarde *f.* afternoon; *adv.* late; **buenas tardes** good afternoon; **de la tarde** in the afternoon, P.M.; **hasta más tarde** till I see you again, see you later; **por la tarde** in the afternoon
tarjeta *f.* card; **tarjeta postal** *f.* postal card
tauromaquia *f.* art of bullfighting
taxi *m.* taxi, taxicab
te you (*fam.*), to you, yourself
teatral theatrical
teatro *m.* theatre
tecnicolor *m.* technicolor
tecnología *f.* technology
tela *f.* cloth, fabric; **encuadernado en tela** clothbound
telefonear to telephone
teléfono *m.* telephone; **llamar por teléfono** to telephone
telégrafo *m.* telegraph
telegrama *m.* telegram

televisión *f.* television

telón *m.* curtain; **levantar (subir) el telón** to raise the curtain; **se levanta el telón** to curtain rises

tema *m.* topic, theme, plot

temer to fear, to be afraid

temporada *f.* season, length of time, spell

temporal temporal, temporary

tempranito quite (rather) early

temprano early

tendero *m.* storekeeper

tener to have; **aquí las tiene** here they are; **no tener razón** to be wrong; **tener . . . años** to be . . . years old; **tener calor** to be hot (warm); **tener éxito** to be successful, to succeed; **tener frío** to be cold; **tener gana(s) de** to wish, to desire to; **tener lugar** to take place; **tener miedo** to be afraid; **tener mucha(s) gana(s)** to wish very much to; **tener (mucha) hambre** to be (very) hungry; **tener mucho gusto en** to be very glad to; **tener prisa** to be in a hurry; **tener que** + *inf.* to have to, must; **tener razón** to be right; **tener sed** to be thirsty

tenis *m.* tennis

teológico, –a theologic(al)

tercer(o), –a third

terminar to end, to finish

ternera *f.* veal; **costilla de ternera** veal cutlet

tertulia *f.* conversational party, gathering

ti you (*fam.*), to you

tía *f.* aunt

Ticiano: Tiziano Vecelli Titian, *greatest artist of the Venetian school of painting during the Italian Renaissance (1477–1576)*

tiempo *m.* time, weather, tense; **a tiempo** in time; **¿cuánto tiempo?** how long?; **hacer buen tiempo** to be good weather; **hacer mal tiempo** to be bad weather; **perder tiempo** to lose (to waste) time

tienda *f.* shop, store; **tienda de materiales y aparatos fotográficos** camera supply store; **tienda de ropa** clothing store

tinto, –a red (wine), dyed, tinged

Tintoretto: Jacopo Robusti *great Italian Renaissance painter (1518–1594)*

tío *m.* uncle; *pl.* uncles, uncle(s) and aunt(s)

tipo *m.* kind, type

titularse to be entitled

título *m.* title

tocar to touch, to play (*an instrument*); **me toca a mí** it's my turn; **tocar a uno** to be one's turn

todavía yet, still; **todavía no** not yet

todo, –a all, whole, every; *pron.* all, everything; **sobre todo** above all, especially; **de todos modos** anyway, anyhow; **todo el día** all day; **todos** everyone, everybody; **todos los días** every day; **todas las noches** every night

tomar to take, to drink, to eat

Tomás Thomas

tomate *m.* tomato

tomo *m.* volume, tome

tontería *f.* foolishness, nonsense

tonto, –a foolish, stupid, silly; *m.* fool; **no seas tonto** don't be silly

tope *m.* butt, end, top; **hasta los topes** up to the brim; **estar lleno hasta los topes** to be jam-packed

torero *m.* bullfighter

toril *m.* bullpen

torniquete *m.* turnstile, turnpike, tourniquet

toro *m.* bull; *pl.* bulls, bullfight, bullfighting; **plaza de toros** *f.* bull ring; **¡qué toro bravo!** what a ferocious bull!

torta *f.* cake, loaf; **torta de queso** *f.* cheesecake

trabajar to work, to act
trabajo *m.* work
tradición *f.* tradition
traducir to translate
traer to bring
tragedia *f.* tragedy
traje *m.* suit, clothes
trama *f.* plot (*of play*)
transeunte *m.* passer-by
transporte *m.* transportation
tranvía *m.* trolley (*car*)
trasporte *m.* transportation
tratar (de) to treat, to try (to); **tratarse de** to deal with, to be a question of, to be a matter of
trece thirteen
treinta thirty
treinta y uno thirty-one
tren *m.* train
tres three
trescientos, –as three hundred
trillado, –a thrashed, beaten, hackneyed
tu, tus your (*fam.*)
tú you (*fam.*)
tuyo, –a your (*fam.*), yours; **el tuyo, la tuya** yours; **lo tuyo** what is yours, what belongs to you

último, –a last, latter; **la última vez** the last time
un(o), –a a, an, one; *pl.* some, a few
universidad *f.* university
usar to use
uso *m.* use, usage
usted (Ud., Vd.); ustedes (Uds., Vds.) you
útil useful

vacaciones *f. pl.* vacation, vacation time, holiday; **estar de vacaciones** to be on vacation
vacío, –a empty
vacuo, –a empty, unoccupied, vacant, vacuous

vagón *m.* car, wagon; **vagón de primera clase** first-class car
valenciano, –a *n. or adj.* Valencian
valentía *f.* valor, courage, bravery
valer to be worth; **¿cuánto vale?** how much (is it)? how much does it cost?; **¡válgame Dios!** heaven help me!
valija *f.* valise
varios, –as various, several
vaso *m.* glass
vaya see ir; **vaya con Dios** God be with you; **vaya sí** of course
veinte twenty
veinte y nueve twenty-nine
veinte y uno twenty-one
veintinueve twenty-nine
veintiuno twenty-one
Velázquez, Diego Rodriguez de Silva *Spanish painter* (*1599–1660*)
vencer to conquer, to defeat
vender to sell
vengar to avenge
venir to come; **venirse** to come along
ventana *f.* window
ventanilla *f.* window (*of train, plane, post office*)
ventura *f.* luck, chance; **por ventura** perhaps, maybe, by chance
ver to see; **a ver** let's see
verano *m.* summer; **cursos de verano** *m.* summer courses, summer school; **verano que viene** next summer
veras: de veras truly, really
verbo *m.* verb
verdad *f.* truth; **¿no es verdad?, ¿verdad?** isn't it (so)?, aren't they?, right?, etc.
verdadero, –a true, real
verdaderamente truly, really
verde green
vermut *m.* vermouth
vestido *m.* dress, clothing
vestir (i) to dress; **vestirse** to get dressed
vez (*pl.* veces) *f.* time; **a veces** at

times; **dos veces** twice; **en vez de** instead of; **esta vez** this time; **la última vez** the last time; **muchas veces** many times, often; **otra vez** again; **tal vez** perhaps, maybe

viajar to travel

viaje *m.* trip

victoria *f.* victory, triumph

vida *f.* life, living

viejo, -a old; **el viejo** the old man; **la vieja** the old woman

viento *m.* wind; **hacer viento** to be windy

viernes *m.* Friday

vino *m.* wine; **vino blanco (tinto)** *m.* white (red) wine

virtud *f.* virtue

visita *f.* visit

visitar to visit

vista *f.* view, sight; **hasta la vista** till I see you again, see you later

vistazo *m.* glance; **echar un vistazo a** to glance at

visto (*past part.* of ver) seen

vitamina *f.* vitamin

vivir to live; **modo de vivir** way of life, manner of living

vivo, -a alive, living, bright

volante (**de dirección**) *m.* steering wheel

volar (**ue**) to fly

voluntar *f.* will, will power

volver (**ue**) to return, to go back; **volverse** to turn (around), to become

vosotros (*fam. pl.*) you

voz *f.* voice; **en voz alta** aloud

vuelta *f.* turn, return, change; **ida y vuelta** round trip

vuestro, -a your (*fam. pl.*), yours; **el vuestro, la vuestra** yours; **lo vuestro** what is yours

y and

ya already, now, by now

yo I

Zorrilla, José *romantic poet and dramatist of the 19th century* (1817-1893)

VOCABULARY: ENGLISH–SPANISH

a un, uno, una

about de, acerca de, sobre; **at about** a eso de; **be about to** estar para

accompany acompañar

account cuenta *f.;* **bank account** cuenta corriente

actor actor *m.*

actress actriz *f.*

address dirección *f.*

afraid: be afraid temer, tener miedo

after después de, al cabo de; **a quarter after eleven** las once y cuarto

afternoon tarde *f.;* **in the afternoon** por la tarde

afterwards después

again otra vez, de nuevo, volver a + *inf.*

age edad *f.;* **Golden Age** Siglo de Oro *m.*

agreed de acuerdo, convenido

air aire *m.;* **airmail** correo aéreo

all todo, –a; **all right** bueno, bastante bien; **be all right** estar en regla

allow dejar, permitir, consentir en (i)

also también

although aunque, bien que, por más que

always siempre

a.m. de la mañana

amusing divertido, –a

an un, uno, una

and y, e

announce anunciar

anything algo, cualquier cosa; (*after a negative*) nada

apparently al parecer, por lo visto

arrange arreglar

arrive llegar

art arte *m. or f.*

as como, tan; **as** (*adj. or adv.*) **as** tan . . . como; **as much . . . as** tanto (a) . . . como; **as many . . . as** tantos (as) . . . como

ask preguntar, pedir (i)

at a, en

attend asistir (a), cuidar, ocuparse (de)

back (*body*) espalda *f.;* (*room*) fondo *m.;* **come back** volver

bailiff alguacil *m.*

bank banco *m.*

be estar, ser; **be about to** estar para; **isn't it? aren't they?** ¿no es verdad?, ¿verdad?, ¿no?, ¿no es así?

because porque

bed cama *f.;* **go to bed** acostarse (ue)

beer cerveza *f.*

before *adv.* (*time*) antes (de); (*place*) delante de; *conj.* antes de que; *prep.* antes

begin empezar (ie), comenzar (ie)

behind *prep.* detrás de; *adv.* detrás

believe creer

best (el) mejor
better mejor
big grande, gran
bill cuenta *f.*
birthday cumpleaños *m. sing.*
boarding house casa de huéspedes *f.,*
pensión *f.*
book libro *m.*
bookstore librería *f.*
bound encuadernado, –a; **clothbound**
encuadernado en tela; **paper-bound**
encuadernado en rústica
boy muchacho *m.*
branch sucursal *f.*
bring llevar, traer
bull toro *m.*
bullfight corrida de toros *f.,* corrida *f.,*
toros *m. pl.*
bullpen toril *m.*
bureau cómoda *f.,* armario *m.*
burial entierro *m.;* **Burial of the Count
of Orgaz** El Entierro del Conde de
Orgaz (*masterpiece of El Greco*)
bus autobús *m.,* ómnibus *m.*
but pero, sino (que)
buy comprar
by por, de, en

café café *m.*
call llamar; **call on the phone** llamar
por teléfono, telefonear
calm calmar, tranquilizar; **calm down**
calmarse
camera aparato fotográfico *m.,* cámara
(fotográfica) *f.;* **camera shop** tienda
de aparatos fotográficos
can poder (ue)
car coche *m.,* automóvil *m.,* vagón *m.;*
dining car coche comedor *m.;* **first-
class car** vagón de primera clase *m.*
carry llevar; **carry on one's shoulders**
llevar en hombros
cartoons dibujos de muñecos *m.*
cash cobrar; **cash a check** cobrar un
cheque, hacer efectivo un cheque
celebrate celebrar, festejar

certain cierto, –a; **a certain** cierto, –a
change cambiar
charge esbestir (i)
check cheque *m.,* ficha *f.;* **check**
(*luggage*) facturar; **check** (*a motor*)
revisar; **cash a check** cobrar un
cheque, hacer efectivo un cheque
children niños *m. pl.,* hijos *m.*
church iglesia *f.*
city ciudad *f.*
clam almeja *f.*
class clase *f.*
clear aclarar, desembarazarse; **clear
up** despejarse (el cielo)
close cerrar (ie)
cloth tela *f.,* paño *m.;* **clothbound**
encuadernado en tela
clothes ropa *f.,* traje *m.*
clothing ropa *f.,* traje *m.,* vestido *m.;*
clothing store tienda de ropa *f.*
cocktail coctel *m.,* coctail *m.*
coffee café *m.*
color color *m.*
come venir; **come back** volver (ue);
come in entrar
company compañía *f.*
conduct conducir, guiar, llevar
conversation conversación *f.*
cook cocinar
cool fresco, –a; **be cool** hacer fresco
coolness sangre fría *f.,* calma, *f.,* sere-
nidad *f.,* frescura *f.*
count conde *m.*
country (*land*) país *m.;* (*in contrast
to city*) campo *m.*
courage coraje *m.,* valor *m.,* valentía *f.*
course: **of course** por supuesto, claro,
cierto, desde luego, ¡cómo no!
cream crema *f.;* **ice cream** helado *m.*
crowd muchedumbre *f.,* gentío *m.,*
multitud *f.*
curb acera *f.*
curtain telón *m.;* **raise the curtain**
levantar (subir) el telón; **the curtain rises (goes up)** se levanta el
telón

custom costumbre *f.*

customs aduana *f.;* **customs office** oficina de la aduana *f.*

cut cortar, tallar

daughter hija *f.*

dawn madrugada *f.;* **at dawn** a la madrugada

day día *m.*

dean decano *m.*

dear querido, –a

develop (*film*) revelar

die morir (ue, u)

diet dieta *f.*, régimen *m.;* **be on a diet** estar a régimen

dining car coche comedor *m.*

dint: **by dint of** a fuerza de

discuss discutir

dish plato *m.*

do hacer

door puerta *f.*

doubt *vb.* dudar; *n.* duda *f.;* **there is no doubt** no cabe duda

down bajo; **down there** por allí abajo

dramatic dramático, –a

dress vestir (i); **dress oneself** vestirse

drive conducir, manejar

eager ansioso, –a, anheloso, –a; **be very eager to** tener mucha(s) gana(s) de

early temprano

eat comer

eight ocho

elbow codo *m.*, codillo *m.;* **blow with elbow** codazo *m.*

eldest el (la) mayor

eleven once

employee empleado *m.*

end acabar, terminar

endorse endosar

enjoy gozar de; **enjoy oneself** divertirse (ie)

enroll matricular(se)

enter entrar (en)

equipment equipo *m.*, equipaje *m.*, material *m.*

err errar, equivocarse

etching aguafuerte *f.*

even aun, hasta; **even though** aun cuando

evening noche *f.;* **in the evening** por (de) la noche

ever nunca, jamás

everyone todo el mundo, todos

everything todo

everywhere en (por) todas partes

evident evidente, claro; **it is evident** es claro

exactitude exactitud *f.*

excitement animación *f.*, agitación *f.*, conmoción *f.*

exercise ejercicio *m.*

exist existir

expect esperar

fail fracasar, faltar, subir mal (en examen)

faithful fiel, leal

fall otoño *m.*

family familia *f.*

famous famoso, –a

far lejos; **far from** lejos de

father padre *m.*

fault falta *f.*, culpa *f.*, defecto *m.*

feast fiesta *f.;* **feast day** día de fiesta *m.*

feel sentir (ie), sentirse (ie); **feel like** tener gana(s) de + *inf.*

ferocity ferocidad *f.*

few pocos, –as; **a few** algunos, –as, unos pocos, unas pocas, unos, –as

fifteen quince

film película *f.;* **roll of film** rollo de películas *m.*

find hallar, encontrar (ue); **find out** aprender, saber, descubrir, averiguar

fine fino, –a; *adv.* bien

finish terminar, acabar

fire fuego *m.;* **fireworks** fuegos artificiales *m.*

firm firma *m.*, casa *f.*, compañía *f.*

first primer(o), –a

fish pez *m.*, pescado *m.*

five cinco

floor piso *m.*

fond apasionado; **be fond of** ser apasionado de, ser aficionado de

for *conj.* porque; *prep.* para, por, durante

foreign extranjero, –a

forget olvidar, olvidarse

former: **the former** aquél, aquélla

forty-third cuarenta y tres (*ordinal*)

Francis Francisco

fried frito, –a

friend amigo *m.*, amiga *f.*

front frente *f.* **in front of** delante de, en frente de

further más; **further on** más allá

general general *m.*

gentleman señor, caballero *m.*

get llegar, conseguir (i), obtener, lograr, ponerse, volverse (ue), hacerse; **get in** entrar; **get off** bajar; **get up** levantarse

gift regalo *m.*

girl muchacha *f.*

give dar; **give a lecture** dar una conferencia; **give news** dar noticias

glad alegre, contento, –a; **be glad** alegrarse (de); **I'm glad** me da gusto

glove guante *m.*

go ir; **go home** ir a casa; **go in** entrar; **go out** salir; **go shopping** ir de compras; **go to bed** acostarse (ue); **go up** subir

good bueno, –a

great grande, gran; **a great deal** mucho, –a

group grupo *m.*

half medio, –a; **half past eight** las ocho y media

hand mano *m.*

happiness felicidad *f.*

have haber, tener; **have time to** tener tiempo de; **have to** tener que + *inf.*

he él

hear oír

help ayudar

her *poss. adj.* su, sus; *dir. obj.* la; *after a prep.* ella; **hers** el suyo, la suya

here aquí, acá

herself se; *after prep.* sí; **with herself** consigo

high alto, –a

him *dir. obj.* le, lo; *indir. obj.* le, *after prep.* él; **himself** se, sí, él mismo

his *adj.* su, sus; *pron.* el suyo, la suya

holiday día de fiesta *m.*

home casa *f.;* **at home** en casa; **go home** ir a casa

hope esperar

hotel hotel *m.*

hour hora *f.;* **hours on end** horas y horas

house casa *f.;* **boarding house** casa de huéspedes *f.*, pensión *f.;* **movie house** cine *m.*

how como; *interr.* ¿cómo?; **how are you?** ¿cómo está Ud.?; ¿qué tal?; **how do you do** tanto gusto, mucho gusto, muchísimo gusto, encantado; **how long?** ¿cuánto tiempo?, ¿desde cúando?; **how much?** ¿cuánto, –a?; **how many?** ¿cuántos, –as?

hundred cien, ciento

hungry: **be hungry** tener hambre

I yo

ice hielo *m.;* **ice cream** helado *m.*

if si

immediately en seguida, pronto, inmediatamente

impossible imposible; **it is impossible** es imposible

in en, entre; *after a superlative* ·de

inhabitant habitante *m.*

interesting interesante

introduce presentar (a), introducir
it lo, la; *after prep.* él, ella, ello
its su, sus

jam-packed lleno hasta los topes; **to be jam-packed** estar lleno hasta los topes
January enero *m.*
John Juan
joy alegría *f.*
justice justicia *f.*

keep guardar; **keep (on)** + *pres. part.* seguir + *pres. part.*
key llave *f.*
kind bondadoso, –a, bueno, –a, amable
kiss *vb.* besar; *n.* beso *m.*
knock (on the door) llamar a la puerta
know saber, conocer; **you don't know how sorry I am** no sabes cuánto lo siento

lady señora *f.*; **The Ladies in Waiting** Las Meninas (*masterpiece by Velázquez*)
language idioma *m.*, lengua *f.*
large grande
last *vb.* durar; *adj.* último, –a, pasado, –a; **last week** la semana pasada
late tarde
latest último, –a; **latest news** últimas noticias *f.*
latter: **the latter** éste, ésta
lead conducir, guiar, llevar
learn aprender
least menos; **at least** al menos, a lo menos, por lo menos
leave dejar, irse, salir, partir; **leave behind** dejar; **take leave of** despedirse (i) de
lecture conferencia *f.*; **give a lecture** dar una conferencia
left izquierdo, –a; **at (to, on) the left** a la izquierda

less menos
lesson lección *f.*
letter carta *f.*
library biblioteca *f.*
like gustar, querer (ie), agradar; *adv.* como
line línea *f.*, fila *f.*, cola *f.*; **stand in line** hacer fila, hacer cola
live vivir
lodge alojar(se)
lodging hospedaje *m.*; **take up lodging** alojarse
long largo, –a; **how long?** ¿cuánto tiempo?, ¿desde cuándo?; **long time** mucho tiempo; **(to wait) a long time** (esperar) un siglo
look (at) mirar; (for) buscar; **take a look at** echar un vistazo a
low bajo, –a
luxurious lujoso, –a

maid criada *f.*
mail correo *m.*; *vb.* echar al correo; **by airmail** por correo aéreo
man hombre *m.*
many muchos, –as; **as many . . . as** tantos, –as . . . como; **many times** muchas veces; **so many** tantos, –as
March marzo *m.*
mass Misa *f.*
masterpiece obra maestra *f.*
matador matador *m.*
me me, mí; **with me** conmigo
meal comida *f.*
mechanic mecánico *m.*
meet encontrar (ue), encontrarse con; **(to gather)** reunirse; **(become acquainted with)** conocer
menu menú *m.*, lista *f.*
million millón *m.*
mine el mío, la mía; **of mine** mío, –a
minute minuto *m.*
mistaken: **be mistaken** equivocarse, engañarse
modern moderno, –a
more más; **more than** más que, más de

morning mañana *f.;* **good morning**
buenos días, muy buenos; **in the**
morning por la mañana; **tomorrow**
morning mañana por la mañana
most (el) más, la mayoría de, la
mayor parte de
mother madre *f.*
movie(s) cine *m.;* **movie house** cine
m.
moving emocionante, conmovedor
Mr. señor *m.;* **Mr. and Mrs.** señores
Mrs. señora *f.*
much mucho, –a; **how much?** ¿cuánto,
–a?; **very much** muchísimo
museum museo *m.*
mushroom hongo *m.*
must deber de + *inf.,* tener que +
inf.
my mi, mis

nap siesta *f.;* **take a nap** echar una
siesta
naturalness naturalidad *f.*
need necesitar
never nunca, jamás
new nuevo, –a
New York Nueva York
news noticia *f.;* **give news** dar noticias; **latest news** últimas noticias *f.*
newspaper periódico *m.*
next próximo, –a, siguiente
nine nueve
no *adv.* no; *adj.* ninguno, –a, ningún;
no one nadie
not no
novel novela *f.*
now ahora

occupied ocupado, –a
o'clock (*omitted in translation*): **it is**
five o'clock son las cinco
October octubre *m.*
of de
offer ofrecer
office oficina *f.,* despacho *m.*
often a menudo, muchas veces

old viejo
older mayor
oldest el (la) mayor
on en, a, sobre, acerca de
one un, uno, una; **no one** nadie; **the**
one who (**that**) el (la) que; **the**
ones who (**that**) los (las) que
onion cebolla *f.*
only sólo, solamente
open abrir
or o, u
order orden *m. or f.;* **in order to** para
originality originalidad *f.*
other otro, –a
our nuestro, –a; **ours** el nuestro, la
nuestra
out fuera

pack empaquetar, empacar
package paquete *m.,* bulto *m.*
paint pintar
painter pintor *m.*
paper papel *m.;* **paper-bound** encuadernado en rústica
Paris París
park parque *m.; vb.* estacionar
pay pagar; **pay the tuition fees** abonar
los derechos de matrícula
people gente *f.,* pueblo *m.*
per cent por ciento
perhaps quizá(s), acaso, tal vez, por
ventura
permit permitir
philosopher filósofo *m.*
phone *vb.* llamar por teléfono, telefonear; *n.* teléfono *m.*
photographic fotográfico, –a
pity lástima *f.;* **it's a pity** es lástima
place lugar *m.;* **take place** tener lugar,
celebrarse
plane avión *m.,* aeroplano *m.;* **by**
plane en avión
platform andén *m.*
play comedia *f.,* drama *m.,* pieza *f.*
playwright dramaturgo *m.*
pleasant agradable

please por favor, tenga Ud. la bondad de + *inf.*, haga Ud. el favor de + *inf.*
poet poeta *m.*
poetry poesía *f.*
politics política *f.*
poor pobre
pope papa *m.*
postage franqueo *m.*
post office correo *m.*, oficina de correos *f.*
present presentar; may I present tengo el placer de presentarle (les), (te)
president presidente *m.*
pretty bonito, –a, lindo, –a
price precio *m.*
probably probablemente; (*also fut. or cond. of verb*) he is probably there estará allí
problem problema *m.*
procession procesión *f.*, desfile *m.*
professor profesor *m.*
promise *vb.* prometer; *n.* promesa *f.*
provided (that) con tal que, siempre que, a condición que
punish castigar
put poner, colocar; put on ponerse

quarter cuarto *m.*

railroad ferrocarril *m.*; railroad station estación de ferrocarriles *f.*
rain llover (ue); it's raining llueve
read leer
realism realismo *m.*
reassure asegurar
register (*in school*) matricularse; (*letter*) certificar una carta
religious religioso, –a
remember acordar (ue), acordarse de; recordar (ue), recordarse de
restaurant restaurante *m.*
return volver (ue), regresar
rich rico, –a; very rich muy rico, riquísimo

right derecho, –a; all right bueno, bastante bien; at (on, to) the right a la derecha; right away en seguida
road camino *m.*, carretera *f.*
role papel *m.*
roll rollo *m.*
romantic romántico, –a
Rome Roma
room cuarto *m.*
royal real
run correr; (*of machines*) andar

saint san, santo, santa
Saturday sábado *m.*
say decir; you don't say! ¡no me digas!
seat asiento *m.*
seated sentado, –a
second segundo, –a
see ver
sell vender
send enviar, mandar; send a package (*by mail*) remitir un paquete; send a telegram enviar (mandar) un telegrama
sharp *adv.* en punto
shave afeitar(se)
she ella
shirt camisa *f.*
shop tienda *f.*; camera shop tienda de aparatos fotográficos
shopping de compras; go shopping ir de compras; make purchases, shop hacer compras
shoulder hombro *m.*; carry on one's shoulders llevar en hombros
shove empujón *m.*
show mostrar (ue), enseñar; *n.* espectáculo *m.*, fiesta *f.*, sección *f.*, función *f.*
sign cartel *m.*, letrero *m.*, muestra *f.*, seña *f.*
sit sentarse (ie); sit down sentarse
slowly despacio, lentamente
smoke fumar
snow nieve *f.*
so tan, así, tanto; so much tanto, –a;

so many tantos, –as; **think so** creer
que sí

sock calcetín *m.*

some alguno (algún), –a; unos, –as,
algunos, –as

son hijo *m.*

soon pronto; **as soon as** apenas, en
cuanto, luego que, tan pronto como

sorry: be sorry sentir (ie, i); **you
don't know how sorry I am** no sabes
cuánto lo siento

soul alma *f.*

sound sonar, tocar

soup sopa *f.*

Spain España

Spanish español, –a; *n.* español *m.*

spark plug bujía *f.*

speak hablar

spectacle espectáculo *m.*

spite: in spite of a pesar de

stamp sello *m.*

stand estar de pie; **stand in line** hacer
cola, hacer fila

star estrella *f.*

station (**railroad**) estación, estación
de ferrocarriles

statue estatua *f.*, imagen *f.*

stay *vb.* quedarse, permanecer; *n.*
estancia *f.*

steak bisté *m.*, biftec *m.*, bistec *m.*

stop *vb.* parar, pararse, detenerse; *n.*
parada *f.*

store tienda *f.;* **clothing store** tienda
de ropa *f.*

storekeeper tendero *m.*

strange extraño, –a, raro, –a

stroll paseo *m.;* **take a stroll** dar un
paseo, ir de paseo

student estudiante *m. or f.*

study estudiar

subway metro *m.*

successful: be successful tener éxito

such tal, tanto

suitcase maleta *f.*

Sunday domingo *m.*

sunny: be sunny hacer sol

sure seguro, –a, cierto, –a; **a sure**
cierto, –a

table mesa *f.*

take tomar, llevar; **take a look at**
echar un vistazo a; **take a nap** echar
una siesta; **take** (**go for**) **a stroll** dar
un paseo, ir de paseo; **take leave of**
despedirse (i) de; **take place** tener
lugar; **take up lodgings** alojarse

talk hablar

tasty sabroso, –a, gustoso, –a

taxi taxi(metro) *m.*

teach enseñar

telegram telegrama *m.;* **send a telegram** enviar (mandar) un telegrama

telephone *vb.* telefonear, llamar por
teléfono; *n.* teléfono

tell decir, contar (ue)

ten diez

tenth décimo, –a

than que; (*before a numeral*) de

thank you gracias

that *conj.* que; *dem. adj.* ese, esa;
aquel, aquella; *dem. pron.* ése, ésa;
eso; aquél, aquélla; **that of** el de,
la de

the el, la, los, las; (*neuter*) lo

theatre teatro *m.*

their su, sus; **theirs** el suyo, la suya

them *dir. obj.* los, las; *indir. obj.* les;
(*after a prep.*) ellos, ellas

theme tema *m.*

theological teológico, –a

there allí, allá; **there is** (**are**) hay

these *dem. adj.* estos, –as; *dem. pron.*
éstos, –as

they ellos, ellas

thing cosa *f.*

think pensar (ie), creer; **think about**
pensar en; **think so** creer que sí

third tercer(o), –a

thirsty: be thirsty tener sed *f.*

thirteenth trece (*ordinal*)

thirty treinta

this *dem. adj.* este, esta; *dem. pron.*
éste, ésta, esto; **this one** éste, ésta
those *dem. adj.* esos, –as; aquellos, –as;
dem. pron. ésos, –as; aquéllos, –as
three tres
ticket billete *m.*, entrada *f.*
tie corbata *f.*
time tiempo *m.*, hora *f.*, vez *f.;* **a long
long time** un siglo; **have time to**
tener tiempo de; **long time** mucho
tiempo; **many times** muchas veces;
on time a tiempo
tip propina *f.*
to a, hasta
today hoy
tomorrow mañana; **tomorrow morning**
mañana por la mañana
tonight esta noche
too (*also*) también; (*much*) demasiado
toothbrush cepillo de dientes *m.*
toy juguete *m.*
travel viajar
treat tratar (de)
trolley tranvía *m.*
trumpet clarín *m.*, trompeta *f.*
Tuesday martes *m.*
tuition fees derechos de matrícula *m.*
twenty veinte
twenty-third veinte y tres (*ordinal*)
two dos

umbrella paraguas *m.*
uncle tío *m.*
understand comprender, entender (ie)
university universidad *f.*
until *prep.* hasta; *conj.* hasta que
up arriba; **go up** subir
upon sobre, en
us nos, nosotros
usher acomodador *m.*

vacation vacaciones *f. pl.*
very muy; mismo, –a
visit visitar
volume tomo *m.*, volumen *m.*

wait esperar; **wait a very long time**
esperar un siglo
waiter camarero *m.*
want querer (ie), desear
we nosotros, –as
weather tiempo *m.;* **how is the
weather?** ¿qué tiempo hace?
week semana *f.*, ocho días; **last week**
la semana pasada; **two weeks** quince
días
well bien
what *interr. pron.* ¿qué?, ¿cuál?; *rel.
pron.* lo que, cuanto; **what a!**
¡qué!
when cuando; *interr.* ¿cuándo?; **since
when?** ¿desde cuándo?
where donde, adonde, de donde;
interr. ¿dónde?, ¿adónde?
which que, el que, el cual, lo que,
lo cual; **those which** los (las)
que; **which?** ¿qué?, ¿cuál?; **which
(one)?** ¿cuál?; **which (ones)?**
¿cuáles?
while *conj.* mientras, mientras que
white blanco, –a
who *rel. pron.* que, quien, quienes;
he who el que, quien; **she who** la
que, quien; **the one who** el (la)
que, quien; **the ones (those) who**
los (las) que, quienes; **who?**
¿quién?; **whoever** quienquiera
whom que, el (la) que, el (la) cual;
after a prep. quien, quienes; **whom?**
¿quién?, ¿quiénes?
whose cuyo, –a; **whose?** ¿de quién?,
¿de quiénes?
why ¿por qué?
window ventana *f.*, ventanilla *f.*
wish querer (ie), desear; **what do you
wish?** ¿qué desean Uds.?
with con; **with me** conmigo; **with
you** contigo
without sin, sin que, que no
work *vb.* trabajar; *n.* trabajo *m.*, obra
f.
world mundo *m.*

worry apurarse, inquietarse, tener cuidado, dar cuidado; **don't worry** pierda Ud. cuidado

worse peor

would that! ¡ojalá que! (*takes subj.*)

write escribir

wrong: be wrong no tener razón

year año *m.*

yes sí

yesterday ayer

yet todavía; **not yet** todavía no

you tú, Ud., Uds., vosotros; le, lo la, los, las, ti, os; **with you** contigo

young joven

younger menor

youngest el (la) menor

your tu, su, vuestro, –a; **yours** el tuyo, la tuya; el suyo, la suya; el vuestro, la vuestra

INDEX

(Numbers refer to pages)